CREATIVITY IN EDUCATION

Also available:

Duncan Grey: *The Internet in School*
Richard Hickman (ed.): *Art Education 11–18*
Helen Nicholson (ed.): *Teaching Drama 11–18*
Catherine Matheson and David Matheson: *Educational Issues in the
    Learning Age*
Angela Thody, Barbara Gray and Derek Bowden: *Teacher's Survival Guide*
John Wilson: *Key Issues in Education and Teaching*

Creativity in Education

Edited by
Anna Craft, Bob Jeffrey and Mike Leibling

CONTINUUM
London and New York

Continuum
The Tower Building
11 York Road
London SE1 7NX

370 Lexington Avenue
New York
NY 10017–6503

First published 2001

British Library Cataloguing-in-Publication Data
A catalogue record for this book is available from the British Library.

ISBN   0–8264–4863–1 (paperback)
       0–8264–4846–X (hardback)

Typeset by Kenneth Burnley, Wirral, Cheshire.
Printed and bound in Great Britain by Biddles Ltd, *www.biddles.co.uk*

Contents

Acknowledgements

As editors we want to express our gratitude and admiration first and foremost to the contributors themselves. From our initial soundings and from contacts made during the process of collecting articles each author has responded with enthusiasm and a concern to assure the success of this publication. Each has professionally considered our critiques and squeezed more time from their very busy schedules to review and amend their contributions, many times in some cases. Their perseverance and commitment to this project has been even more laudable given the willingness with which they freely contributed their time, energy, experience and insights. We are heartily thankful to them and trust that our efforts live up to their expectations.

Our thanks are also due to the Open University Creativity in Education Community, which we founded and co-ordinate. It was this disparate but focused group of people, meeting both face to face and electronically for discussions about creativity and education, which drew us together in the first place. The community has strongly supported the conception of this book.

We would also like to thank the Open University for enabling some of our time, and for providing electronic support which has speeded up the process and, we hope, has contributed to the quality of this collection. In fact, due to the birth of Anna's second child, Ella, in the middle of this project, it probably would have been put back in time without the electronic environment enabling us to engage in almost synchronous debate at a variety of times of the day and night! Thanks are also due to Mike's organizations 'Strategy Strategy' and 'Trainset' for generous amounts of time which enabled him to work on this project.

We would like to acknowledge the role of Anthony Haynes, the commissioning editor at Continuum, whose enthusiasm for the project determined its gestation, and for the supportive relationship he quickly established with us, taking a strong interest in the shaping of this collection – his timely inputs to our editing process were immensely helpful.

Finally, a word of thanks to those close to us who have helped us to create a space to nurture and develop this project through to completion.

We hope that the book will provide a valuable and thought-provoking resource to readers.

Preface

Throughout the world, national governments are reorganizing their education systems to meet the challenges of the twenty-first century. One of the priorities is promoting creativity and innovation. In the new global economies, the capacity to generate and implement new ideas is vital to economic competitiveness. But education has more than economic purposes: it must enable people to adapt positively to rapid social change and to have lives with meaning and purpose at a time when established cultural values are being challenged on many fronts.

But what is creativity? Is everybody creative, or just a select few; and can creativity be taught? This collection of essays sets out to explore the nature and purposes of educating for creativity.

In 1997, the UK government asked me to establish and chair the National Advisory Committee on Creative and Cultural Education (NACCCE) Our report, *All Our Futures: Creativity, Culture and Education*, was published in the summer of 1999. Many of the papers in this collection respond to the themes of that report. Like the NACCCE, they argue that educating for creativity is a rigorous process based on knowledge and skill; that creativity is not confined to particular activities or people; that creativity flourishes under certain conditions and, in this sense, it can be taught.

Like *All Our Futures*, these essays aim to give a textured understanding of what creativity is, why promoting it is a necessity not an option, and how it can be done in a sure-footed, professional and reasoned way. This is an important and timely contribution to a debate that lies at the heart of what it is to be educated in the twenty-first century.

KEN ROBINSON
Professor of Education, University of Warwick
Chair, National Advisory Committee on Creative and Cultural Education

About the Contributors

Margaret A. Boden is Professor of Philosophy and Psychology at the University of Sussex, in the School of Cognitive and Computing Sciences. She is a Fellow of the British Academy and a member of the Academia Europaea, and a past Chairman of the Royal Institution of Great Britain. She is also a Fellow of the American Association of Artificial Intelligence, and of its European and British equivalents. Her research is highly interdisciplinary. Much of it is of interest to practising artists and students of the humanities, as well as to scientists of various kinds. She holds degrees in the medical sciences, in philosophy, and in psychology (including an ScD from Cambridge and a PhD from Harvard). She has published widely on creativity, artificial intelligence, artificial life, and the philosophy of mind. Her work has been translated into 16 foreign languages.

Ken Gale is a Senior Lecturer in the Faculty of Arts and Education at the University of Plymouth, teaching on a range of post-compulsory education programmes from Certificate to Masters level. His particular interest lies within the philosophy of education and the study of post-structural theory as it applies to teacher education. He is married to Helen, has three children, Katy, Reuben and Phoebe and lives in Cornwall.

Laura Haringman, BEd Hons, MEd, has spent a number of years teaching within the state, voluntary aided, denominational and private sectors in primary schools. Her career has been interrupted briefly to accommodate and foster the arrival of three sons, now aged 12, 7 and 5. A two-year family secondment to Switzerland allowed her the opportunity to observe the international school system alongside that of the canton of Zurich. She is presently teaching part-time as an EMTAG specialist, specifically addressing raising the achievement of minority ethnic children in a community primary school. During her MEd she also participated in a research project on creativity jointly led by the Open University and Gallaudet University of Washington, USA.

Susan Humphries is the Headteacher of the Coombes Infant and Nursery School which she opened in 1971. Her initial vision was to provide a true 'kindergarten' for the children in the school, many of whom were the witnesses of extreme violence in Northern Ireland. Over the years, the Coombes School environment has been developed and improved so that it now is a true learning and teaching resource for the whole school family. The educational ethic is flexibility with outward multisensory approaches to children's learning. Susan is a regular lecturer in the USA, Sweden and other parts of Northern Europe. She is a regular contributor to the media in the UK and abroad.

Dame Tamsyn Imison, MA, BSc Hons, FRSA, DBE, was, until July 2000, Headteacher at Hampstead School, London. She has contributed to many government advisory groups (most recently being a member of the National Advisory Committee on Creative and Cultural Education) and has taken a lead role in many initiatives in the sciences, arts, equal opportunities and management in education. From September 2000 she is focusing on her own doctoral study as well as a number of new national policy initiatives.

Mathilda Marie Joubert trained as a musician before teaching in primary, secondary, further and higher education. She worked in policy development in the fields of arts, education, creativity and arts education and was Research Officer to the National Advisory Committee on Creative and Cultural Education. She is currently an independent consultant on arts education and creativity to the Royal Society for the Encouragement of Arts, Manufactures and Commerce (RSA) in London. Her interests (and degrees) range from music, the arts, education, and creativity to cognitive neuropsychology.

Jenny Leach works in the Centre for Research and Development in Teacher Education at the Open University, where she is currently an Associate Director of the Learning Schools Programme, which focuses on the role of ICT (information and communication technology) in teaching and learning. Her interest in creativity and culture began with her work as a teacher of English in schools in rural Kenya, inner-city London and a Scottish new town. She is co-author of the experimental web site Moving Words and co-editor of a new international journal focusing on ICT and education, *ECI* (Education, Communication and Information).

Bill Lucas is Chief Executive of the Campaign for Learning. Under his leadership the Campaign has launched Family Learning Day, created the National Learning Forum and developed a range of activities to promote learning at work. Bill advises government, business and voluntary sector organizations on a range of learning issues. Before his appointment to the Campaign for Learning he was Chief Executive of 'Learning through Landscapes'. Bill has also been Deputy Headteacher of a large secondary community school, a Commissioning Editor, and the Head of a Creative Arts faculty. Bill is a prolific writer and speaker. His next book, to be published by Nicholas Brealey in 2001, is *Your Mind: A User's Guide*.

Bethan Marshall taught English in London comprehensives for several years, before taking up her current post as lecturer in education at King's College, London. For five years she combined this work with that of a local education authority advisory teacher. She is a frequent commentator on educational policy, writing regularly for the broadsheets as well as the *Times Educational Supplement*. Her first book, *English Teachers – The Unofficial Guide*, has recently been published.

Kevin McCarthy is a teacher, researcher and consultant with Re:membering Education (www.remember.mcmail.com). Since 1975 he has worked in a range of contexts, from early years to higher education. He is currently lecturing part-time at University College, Chichester. His current passion, beside creativity, is the chance to create learning communities through the new Personal and Social Education/Citizenship orders.

Susan Rowe has worked at the Coombes School for the last 22 years as an involved helping mother, as secretary, as a classroom teacher and now as Deputy Headteacher. She shares Susan Humphries' pedagogical philosophy and educational vision, and is committed to active, experiential learning. Like Susan Humphries, she is keyed in to a child-centred approach to teaching and learning. She contributes to teaching and learning issues across the world, but most particularly in Sweden and West Africa. She also contributes to the media in Europe and West Africa.

Leslie Safran founded The Otherwise Club nearly eight years ago as a community centre for families choosing to teach their children out of school. She has a BA Hons from King's College, London, an MA from the University of Alberta, and an MA from The Tavistock Centre, London. She is currently working for a PhD at the Open University on the effects of long-term home-based education on the adults involved. She has two children, neither of whom has been to school.

Peter Woods is a Research Professor in Education at the Open University, where formerly he was Director of the Centre for Sociology and Social Research. He has been researching 'creative teaching in primary schools' since the 1980s. His latest books, *Critical Events in Teaching and Learning* (Falmer Press), *Creative Teachers in Primary Schools*; *Teachable Moments* (with Bob Jeffrey) (both Open University Press), and (with Mari Boyle and Nick Hubbard) *Multicultural Children in the Early Years* (Multilingual Matters, 1999) are products of this research. He has also published work recently on qualitative methodology, namely *Researching the Art of Teaching* (Routledge, 1996); and *Successful Writing for Qualitative Researchers* (Routledge, 1999).

About the Editors

Anna Craft is a Senior Lecturer in the Faculty of Education and Language Studies at the Open University, having taught as a primary teacher in inner London, and as a teacher fellow in a London university, before moving on to curriculum development at the National Curriculum Council just as the National Curriculum was introduced. At the Open University she teaches a range of postgraduate courses from Masters' through to doctoral level; her specialisms are primary education and teacher development. She founded and co-convenes the Creativity in Education Community at the Open University and writes about and researches creativity in learning, drawing particularly on philosophy and psychology. She lives in London with her partner Simon and two small children, Hugo and Ella.

Bob Jeffrey is a Research Fellow at the Open University and prior to this was a primary teacher for over twenty years in London. He has worked predominantly with Professor Peter Woods researching primary teacher creativity and the intensification of primary teachers' work. The former research resulted in the publication of *Teachable Moments* and the latter in the publication of *Testing Teachers* – an account of primary experiences of OFSTED inspections and, together with Geoff Troman and Mari Boyle, *Restructuring Schools and Restructured Teachers*. He also takes a keen interest in metholodology and has published articles in this area. He is currently researching the perspectives of primary school children in relation to their creative learning.

Mike Leibling is director of Strategy Strategy™ and Trainset® having spent the previous 20 years as a strategist in the 'creative' realms of advertising. His experience spans government, industry, commerce, education and the not-for-profit sectors, working with organizations and with individuals. He trains, coaches and mentors – and has been actively teaching (or, to be more accurate, helping people and organizations to learn) in one form or the other, since he was 10 years old. He has always been fascinated by the question 'How can we be the best we can be?' and is currently building Trainset® as an organization that 'can help absolutely anyone handle any situation they might find themselves in'.

Abbreviations

BCC	'big C creativity'
CAME	Cognitive Accelerated Learning for Mathematics Education
CASE	Cognitive Accelerated Learning for Science Education
CATS	credit accumulation and transfer
CD	compact disc
CEAC	Central Advisory Committee on Education
CPD	continuing professional development
CSILE	Computer Supported Intentional Learning Environment
DCMS	Department for Culture, Media and Sport
DES	Department of Education and Science
DFEE	Department for Education and Employment
ELG	early learning goal
FEFC	Further Education Funding Council
FENTO	Further Education National Training Organization
GCSE	General Certificate of Secondary Education
GTC	General Teaching Council
HEFC	Higher Education Funding Council
HMI	Her Majesty's Inspectorate
ICT	information and communication technology
ILT	Institute for Learning and Teaching
LCC	'little c creativity'
NACCCE	National Advisory Committee on Creative and Cultural Education
NCC	National Curriculum Council
NLS	National Literacy Strategy
OFSTED	Office for Standards in Education
PE	physical education
PSE	personal and social education
QCA	Qualifications and Curriculum Authority

RE	religious education
RSA	Royal Society for the Encouragement of Arts, Manufactures and Commerce
SACRE	Standing Advisory Conferences on Religious Education
SAT	Standard Assessment Task
SMSC	spiritual, moral, social and cultural
TEC	Training and Enterprise Council
TTA	Teacher Training Agency
UCET	University Council for the Education of Teachers

For learners and teachers in all our lives,

particularly

Simon Stanley,
Hugo and Ella Craft-Stanley
and Helene and Isadore Leibling
for their patience, support, love, guidance
and good common sense
and for unfailing colleagues, especially Peter.

Introduction

The Universalization of Creativity

Bob Jeffrey and Anna Craft

The framing and evolution of this book reflects changing thinking about the elusive concept of creativity and its relevance to the current contemporary world of education and we suggest that there has been a universalization of the conception of creativity. We see the current creativity discourse:

- operating in the economic and political field;
- acting as a possible vehicle for individual empowerment in institutions and organizations; and
- being used to develop effective learning.

The contributions to this edited collection reflect that universalization both in the breadth of contexts examined and in the variety of creativity issues addressed by the authors. The universalization of creativity in education has been influenced by developments in creativity research and by the political contemporary scene, and it is to these two arenas that we briefly turn to contextualize how the issue of creativity has been brought to the forefront of educational policy and practice.

BACKGROUND

Researching creativity

Research into creativity in the 1980s and 1990s became rooted in a social psychological framework in which it is recognized that social structures affect individual creativity (Rhyammar and Brolin, 1999). The previous stage of creativity of research, from the 1950s focused on psychological determinants of the individual on genius and giftedness. One of the major developments in this phase was that the emphasis shifted away from measurable outcomes-based and product-linked approaches such as, for example, those developed by Torrance in the 1960s and 1970s, including tests of creative ability (Torrance, 1974), to investigations which focused on understanding the creative mind in terms of intelligence (Gardner, 1993a). (There are, of course, some overlaps between these periods.)

According to Rhyammar and Brolin (1999) there were three major lines of development from the 1950s focusing on personality, cognition and how to stimulate creativity. This was supported by the philosophical debate from the 1970s which saw creativity as moving away from product outcomes and being connected with imaginativeness (Elliott, 1971). During the 1980s a new line was developed, that of social psychology and systems theory, where environmental conditions were taken into account. Within these four lines of development (i.e. personality, cognition, stimulating creativity and social theories) there were specific foci: the person who creates; the creative process; environmental factors and the outcome. During the 1990s, due to the development of the fourth line – social psychology – research into creativity became more comprehensive, integrating these specific foci, and began to focus more on the creativity of ordinary people within the education system. At the same time the methodology for investigating creativity in education has also shifted from positivist, large-scale studies aiming to measure creativity, towards ethnographic, qualitative approaches to research focusing on the actual site of operations and practice. In education, for example, Fryer (1996) explored teachers' conceptions of creativity; Beetlestone (1998a) focused on creativity in the early years' classroom; Woods (1990; 1995) and Woods and Jeffrey (1996) explored teacher creativity; and Craft (1996) how to nourish the creative teacher.

The writers in this volume (all referenced without a date, to distinguish them from other published references) are all concerned with the ordinary, rather than the extraordinary, with a range of domains of application, not simply with the arts, and none involve the quantitative measurement of creativity. Indeed several are written from first-hand experience (see Safran, Haringman, Imison, and Rowe and Humphries in particular). Reflecting a major line of debate in creativity research, some contributors argue that creativity is a general characteristic (see Lucas and Imison) and others that, following Feldman *et al.* (1994), it is domain specific (see Craft). Attempts to capture the elusiveness of creativity are exemplified in the book by the identification of differing but relevant characteristics for conceptualizing it: control, ownership, relevance and innovation (Woods); imaginative activity to produce outcomes both of originality and of value (Joubert); possibility thinking and problem-posing (Craft); seeing, thinking, inventing and questioning (Lucas); mindful learning (Safran); knowledge from society, self-confidence from social situations and time to play (Boden); risk-taking (Joubert). According to Beetlestone (1998a) there are relevant criteria for creativity but no definitive ones.

Political and economic influences on the potency and pedagogy of creativity
The globalization of economic activity has meant greater competitiveness for markets and calls for nation-states to raise the educational standards of their

potential labour force. In the UK this notionally began in 1976, with the now famous Ruskin College, Oxford, speech of the then Prime Minister James Callaghan when he and others challenged the influential creativity discourse that emanated from the Plowden Report (1967). The report linked creativity to specific sorts of pedagogies, which it espoused, namely those that were 'child centred' and where creativity was interpreted as meaning 'self-expression'. This pedagogic approach was subject to critiques that suggested that creativity involved more than self-expression and that children could not be expected to 'discover' for themselves without significant knowledge input (Cox and Dyson, 1971).

Since the late 1980s, educational programmes, structures, organizations, curriculum, pedagogies, accountabilities, conditions of teachers' work and their professional status have all been reconstructed (Woods *et al.*, 1997) and education in general became a top priority for the incoming New Labour government in 1997. The reconstruction of education became of paramount importance throughout the Western world, although the direction of the reconstructions varied and in some cases went in opposite directions, e.g. France loosened its central control whereas it increased in England. One of the common objectives was to make education systems more effective in assisting the nation-state to secure higher employment, and maintain economic performance.

At the same time as manufacturing began to disperse globally, space was created for new forms of wealth production through increased marketing, the growth of service industries, electronic communications and e-commerce markets, the 'weightless economy' (Seltzer and Bentley, 1999, p. 14). These organizations began to maximize the intellectual and creative capabilities, as well as the physical energy and general intelligence, of the labour force. As Seltzer and Bentley put it:

> While qualifications are still integral to personal success, it is no longer enough for students to show that they are capable of passing public examinations. To thrive in our economy defined by the innovative application of knowledge, we must be able to do more than absorb and feed back information. Learners and workers must draw on their entire spectrum of learning experiences and apply what they have learned in new and creative ways. A central challenge for the education system is therefore to find ways of embedding learning in a range of meaning for contexts, where students can use their knowledge and skills creatively to make an impact on the world around them. (1999, pp. 9–10)

The fundamental shift from focusing on individual traits and abilities to organizations, climates and cultures has had the effect of universalizing creativity. First, it is easier to alter environments than it is to affect personalities, and second it has encouraged perspectives that suggest that everybody is capable of being creative given the right environment (see Safran, Lucas, Haringman, Rowe and Humphries).

The universalization of creativity created new manifestations. In the 'genius, giftedness' period of creativity research it was noted that the small number of people so endowed would challenge existing paradigms and resist conventional forms (Gardner, 1993a). The current competitive discourse has resulted in many institutions and organizations encouraging everybody to be creative in terms of improving the institution's performance and the creation of ways in which the organization can diversify in order to expand.

Encouraging a climate of creative purpose and challenge appears also to act to disperse a culture of blame and 'whinging'. Encouraging creativity in organizations may well not only enhance market share, but also serve to ensure higher levels of commitment from employees. Modern organizations now have good reason to develop democratic cultures that encourage creativity (see Lucas). Education is seen to have a role in this policy area as well as in the economic one. The promotion of collaborative practices and 'teamwork' prepares pupils and students for work in organizations that need to be creative and single minded if they are to be effective in their highly competitive markets or in service industries that are underpinned by high levels of accountability (Ball, 1994; Hargreaves, 1994).

The economic imperative has led the British government to prioritize learning achievements but the technical and bureaucratic processes which have been employed – subject-centred level grading of achievement of both teachers and pupils – has, it is argued, (Woods and Jeffrey, 1996; Woods *et al.*, 1997) led to the diminution of creativity in education. Ironically, the business world is now advocating that learning should take place through creative practices, those involving projects, problem-solving and different perspectives (Seltzer and Bentley, 1999). These were precisely the pedagogic approaches that were being advocated by educationalists in the 1960s (Blyth, 1988), albeit that some thought many schools were implementing these ideas incompetently (Alexander, 1995)

'TEACHING FOR CREATIVITY' OR 'CREATIVE TEACHING'?

The economic and political developments outlined above have ensured the maintenance of a creativity discourse, albeit one that now has new champions. The universalization of creativity has legitimated the value of general creativity in our society for economic purposes, but what of its role in education? One recent and significant initiative in this regard was the commissioning by the government of 'All Our Futures: Creativity, Culture and Education', from the specially constituted National Advisory Committee on Creativity, Culture and Education (NACCCE), chaired by Professor Ken Robinson (the NACCCE Report). It could be argued that the commissioning of the report was an attempt by the government to publicize its support for creativity at a time when it was, in fact, furthering the instigation and implementation of a technical (i.e. non-creative) approach to teaching and learning in schools. Nevertheless, the report highlighted the importance of creativity, not only for education, but as an essential vehicle for economic, social and individual development. It encapsulated three contemporary discourses concerning creativity and education: the role of creativity in the Western world at the turn of the millennium; reconceptualizations of the nature of creativity; and the reconstruction of appropriate pedagogies to meet a reprioritization of educational aims and objectives.

The NACCCE Report faced up to the issues of creativity in education by highlighting what the authors saw as the difference between 'teaching for creativity' and 'creative teaching'. The contributions in this volume also appear to reflect these two foci thus substantiating the NACCCE Report's identification of these two themes as central to the debate about creativity in education. We suggest that where contributors are developing the idea of 'teaching for creativity', the major consequence for teachers and learners is a 'creativity for empowerment'. Where they focus on 'creative teaching' they appear to be suggesting that it is an 'effective pedagogy'. In spite of our division of the contributions into two similar categories, the perspectives presented in this book reflect some of the experiences, observations, dilemmas, tensions and constraints within and between these perspectives.

Creativity for empowerment

As organizations have moved their production to areas of the world with lower labour costs or trimmed their workforces to maintain competitiveness by reducing commodity or service prices, Western labour career patterns have been reconstructed increasingly as 'portfolio careers' (see Lucas), a situation in which people are encouraged to acquire many different jobs throughout their working lives. People need to be more creative in maintaining income and standards of living (see Craft, Lucas). The relationship between creativity and work has become more symbiotic as we enter the twenty-first century (see Craft, Imison, Joubert, Lucas, Leach).

The argument that people need to be creative to survive in the twenty-first century has been further influenced within educational studies, by both the social psychology focus and the prioritization of personal 'agency' emanating from the 'interactionist' branch of sociology which highlights coping strategies (Hargreaves, 1978) as the creative management of situations. Individual coping strategies and 'interests at hand' (Pollard, 1990) are governed by the situation and, it is argued, individuals are constantly being creative in balancing the interests of the personal self and their social identity (Craft, 1997; Shagoury-Hubbard, 1996; Woods, 1990; Woods and Jeffrey, 1996) (see Craft, Safran, McCarthy, Woods). From this perspective it is accepted that innovatory behaviour can be considered creative if innovations are new to the person, new to the person's previous way of thinking and if new in a historical sense (see

Boden). These perspectives see creative teaching as often empowering the individual who exhibits 'self-determination' (Craft, 2000; Woods, 1995) (see Safran, Woods, McCarthy, Craft, Leach).

In positive cultures it has been documented that individuals not only feel commitment to the organization due to the contributions they make towards its core values and their implementation, but that they can also feel more control over the employment of their creative energy as well as personal ownership (see Woods, Rowe and Humphries); not so much a disposition but a personal contribution. Nevertheless there are tensions, dilemmas and constraints (Woods *et al.*, 1997) for workers, including teachers, who find themselves interested in developing an institution's progress and empowered by their involvement but constrained by the limited goals and objectives of the institution resulting in ambivalence in terms of their own self-identity (Casey, 1995). There is both personal 'extensification' – where people enhance their status and skills – and 'intensification of work' – where people have more work and they have to work faster (Woods *et al.*, 1997).

A further major issue of the current creativity discourse that has generated an 'empowerment' culture is that it switches the responsibility for social change from governments and large global forces back to the individual in whom the dilemmas and conflicts of power within society are realized (Mills, 1959). The individual is then challenged to overcome these dilemmas, tensions and constraints (Craft, 2000; NACCCE, 1999) (see Craft, McCarthy, Imison). Empowerment is seen as essential to survival and the locus of creativity is once again seen as lying within the individual, but universalized, and at the same time organizations and institutions seek to use this individual creativity in a competitive environment. In this case the individual's creativity, although now universalized, is tied to the main arena of life – the organization (Morgan, 1986) (see Safran, for alternative perspectives). The debate concerning the relationship between the individual and the environment in terms of creativity permeates the current creativity discourse and is evidenced in the contributions to the first part of this volume, to which we now turn.

Joubert opens the book with this debate and a summary of the NACCCE Report on which she worked as research officer. She describes five key concepts for classroom pedagogy: using imagination; fashioning processes; pursuing processes; being original; and judging value. She focuses particularly on 'teaching for creativity' which she sees as: encouraging beliefs and attitudes, motivation and risk-taking; persistence; identifying across subjects; and fostering the experiential and experimental. She then outlines some of the responses to the report and the barriers to implementation. She sees the implementation of the report over ten years incorporating a continuing debate about teaching, learning and creativity. Interestingly she advocates teachers becoming 'facilitators', exactly the opposite recommendation reached by the Alexander *et al.* report (1992) commissioned by the Conservative government in 1992 (sometimes referred to as the 'Three Wise Men' report). They advocated more direct teaching.

Bill Lucas, Chief Executive of the Campaign for Learning, argues that schools need to be more creative for the twenty-first century. He conceives of creativity as 'seeing, thinking, inventing unquestioning' and challenges Gardner's perspective of 'specific domain' creativity, suggesting that creativity is a 'state of mind'. He outlines pedagogic principles and draws upon pupil perspectives to enhance his case for more creativity, more student participation and a more collaborative pedagogy.

Craft highlights the contemporary necessity for people to be self-directed and the need for the application of universal creativity. She focuses on problem-solving and coping strategies and argues that people need to be innovative in their daily lives. For her, resistance to constraints, and surviving, are creative and she exemplifies this with three case studies, after which she draws out a list of characteristics that assist creativity and therefore the management of life.

Woods focuses on the relationship between creativity and literacy. He provides examples of personal development through creative reading – 'finding your identity' and how it is used in 'child development'. Second, he focuses on reading as empowerment – of finding a voice, using critical literacy and reading as therapy. Finally he shows how reading and rewriting can be enriching. He suggests these are creative approaches to literacy and justifies them by exemplifying their power, processes and outcomes.

Safran comes from alternative education – home education – and she shows how the employment of 'mindful teaching and learning' empowered her children and herself as a parent-teacher. Creativity arising from collaborative practices is exemplified as well as the empowerment gained from allowing students to control the pace and composition of their learning experiences. She highlights the importance of the emotional relationship and the social context for creative teaching and learning.

The NACCCE Report emphasizes that 'teaching for creativity' should be the priority whereas 'creative teaching', which they imply is the use of creativity to manage the constraints of imposed policies and ensure a successful implementation of the latter, should be supported but not be the main focus. However, the contributors in the next section value creative teaching and learning as an end in itself *and* as a vehicle for creative empowerment.

EFFECTIVE PEDAGOGIES FOR FOSTERING CREATIVITY IN EDUCATION

There appear to us to be seven major issues raised by the contributors in the second section of the book which concern pedagogy and creativity.

First, the 'school effectiveness movement' has focused on importing often over-technicized educational practices from international and contrasting situations and contexts into education institutions in order to improve achievement levels (Creemers, 1997; Gray *et al.* 1996; Sammons, 1999; Sammons *et al.*, 1995; Stoll and Fink, 1996). However, the 'effectiveness' of these approaches has been challenged as inconsistent and often inappropriate to the specific context to which they were imported (Slee *et al.*, 1998). Our contributors argue that creative teaching and learning can be effective and take into account local contexts (see Rowe and Humphries, Imison, Safran, Gale, Leach). Taking into account the importance of the emotions and self-identity is seen as part of an effective and socially responsible creative pedagogy (see McCarthy, Safran, Woods). Teaching, it is argued, is an art rather than a technical exercise. The nature of people within the situation and the situation itself need to be interpreted and redefined to ensure effective learning (Woods and Jeffrey, 1996).

Second, the NACCCE Report wrestled with the problem of developing a conceptualization of creativity across the curriculum and not just limited to the arts subjects (see Marshall, Woods). The acquisition of arts subject knowledge appears to have been seen by the government (Blunkett and Smith, 2000) and OFSTED in particular (NACCCE, 1999) as a separate activity from developing the creative self. Creativity in this conceptualization is seen as a specific attribute of the 'arts' curriculum and it is argued that those involved in the NACCCE Report have been unable to persuade the government otherwise (see Joubert). Creativity as only an arts-based phenomenon is rejected as unnecessarily narrow by many of the contributors to this volume (see Woods, McCarthy, Imison, Safran, Lucas, Coombes, Marshall, Rowe and Humphries, Leach) who argue that creativity crosses all subjects and domains. However, creativity is also conceived of by some authors in this volume as relating to particular domains, and the concept of an archetypal creative person is challenged by the argument that it is the boundaries, epistemologies and knowledge already contained within specific learning communities that stimulate and fertilize creativity (see Boden, McCarthy, Craft, Marshall, Leach).

A third issue is how far teachers should focus upon engaging the individual's interest and commitment to the subject matter in hand. The intensive use of grading systems and achievement levels may well ensure a captive audience bent on improving their personal status. The issue of teaching creatively to achieve better results is one that so concerned the members of the NACCCE Report that they indicated their preference for 'teaching for creativity' over 'creative teaching' and it also concerned some of our contributors (see Safran, Haringman, Lucas, Gale). The centralization of the curriculum, the introduction of prescriptive practices and the prioritization of testing has been justified in terms of raising standards of achievement. However, we would argue that it is the central values of education that need broadening. Achievement levels do need to be improved, but we also need to see our society continuously develop its ideals, not narrowing or reversing them. The Norwegian National Curriculum has the following core value: 'Education must demonstrate how creative energy and inventiveness have constantly improved the context, content and quality of human life' (Beetlestone, 1998a, p. 1). The contributions in this volume by Lucas, Joubert, Woods, Marshall and Leach all explore, in different ways, the issue of values in education.

Fourth, some of the characteristics of creative teaching and learning are also acknowledged as being potentially dangerous by some authors in this volume, (see Marshall, Safran, Lucas, Gale). Whilst it is fairly easy to show the relevance of creative practices for engaging learners and generating a commitment to learning (see McCarthy, Imison, Safran, Rowe and Humphries), it is less easy to convince politicians and policy-makers that creative teaching and learning, which might also involve questioning current perspectives and practices, is beneficial to society, in spite of an economic discourse that, to some considerable extent, demands it (see Lucas, Joubert and Marshall). There are examples of creative practices in the UK pointing in the direction of values that we, as editors, feel should be supported. The development of learning communities (Woods, 1998) – as described by Coombes, McCarthy, Imison, Safran and Leach – is a significant development in shifting the way in which learning is conceived. Similarly significant are recent reconceptualizations of progressive education (Sugrue, 1997; Woods, 1999). The engagement of pupils in evaluating the learning process (Pollard *et al.*, 1997 Jeffrey, 2000) is another huge step also acknowledged in this volume by Lucas, Imison and Safran, as is the promotion of alternative perspectives for every learning context, a theme developed by Gale, McCarthy and Safran.

Fifth, the significance of 'play/playing' has not been totally overcome by a discourse of derision (Ball, 1994). Craft (2000) argues that the early opportunities to play and playing are essential for developing creative adults. This does not mean leaving learners alone, but stimulating them in terms of engagement and environmental investigations. On the other hand, neither does it mean guided 'discovery' along narrow predetermined lines (Beetlestone, 1998b). Playing with information, materials and ideas is a central feature of creative practices for people of all ages (see McCarthy, Gale, Haringman, Rowe and Humphries, Safran, Boden). According to Beetlestone (1998a), to learn creatively means tearing down and building up . The current emphasis of our schools curriculum promotes basic skills learning first, and government ministers suggest that creativity comes later. However, 'play/playing' is now considered a highly valued strategy used in some organizations to encourage creative endeavour and social cohesion (see, for example, de Bono's [1992] 'six hats' strategy for effective team thinking, or Handy's [1990] discussion of the way we see ourselves and how we operate in organizations).

The sixth issue is whether we can teach creativity. Writing in the 1970s, Smith (1976) suggested that it was not possible and that one could only set the conditions, to allow the natural creativity of young children to be less constrained (see Rowe and Humphries). However, currently, connections are being made with creativity and 'thinking skills' as discussed by Boden. As Seltzer and Bentley put it, 'The key challenge is to shift the focus away from what people *should* know and on to what they should be able *to do* with their knowledge. This is essential to developing creative ability' (Seltzer and Bentley, 1999, p. 25, original italics). The government is now promoting thinking skills in the early years of the secondary school.

Finally, the role of ICT in stimulating and supporting creativity is an issue which needs to be addressed. How far is new technology a tool for creativity, and how far does it determine both the output of creativity and a definition of it (see Leach, Boden)?

We turn, now, to the second part of the book, which focuses on pedagogy, to outline in brief the content of each chapter.

Boden opens this part and argues that we *can* teach creativity. For her, knowledge and creativity are not opposed but bound together; the latter cannot exist without the former. Creativity, from her perspective, is a result of 'playing' and working with the rules and epistemologies of specific areas, even though the learner may not, at first, be conscious of having this knowledge. She outlines three types of creativity: combinational, exploratory and transformational. The first combines old ideas in new ways, the second and third arise out of the culturally determined domain. The exploratory type permits creativity within the rules, whereas transformational creativity also permits changes to the rules of the conceptual space. She proposes alerting children to the fact that there are systematic styles of thinking and that teachers can only be creative if they have some knowledge of the subject matter with which they are engaged.

Gale's context is teacher education and he suggests that teaching through alternative perspectives is a creative process for both lecturer and student. He outlines a model of teacher education that would use four specific perspectives to interrogate any learning situation: a humanist one; a reflective practitioner approach; the use of critical theory; and a post-modern perspective.

Marshall, using more of a conflict model, argues that a polemical approach (controversial argument) to the teaching of English, for example, is a creative act. English, for her, is art and one cannot reduce it to science, as the élitists Leavis and Elliot did, or as the political left attempted to do in opposition to the aforementioned. She follows Hazlitt's approach, recently promoted by Tom Paulin in his book on this eighteenth-century writer, of 'engaged disinterestedness'. All writing, she argues, is polemical and, therefore, so is critique. Creative teaching and learning, she argues, therefore involves the promotion of assertions incorporating an expectation of critique and questioning – not a scientific assertion of fact. So, creativity is taken further from the psychological and nearer to the social.

McCarthy also makes connections between creativity and a curriculum area – religious education. He argues that the characteristics of creative pedagogies he has observed in classrooms, by teachers engaged in the subject, are similar to some of the characteristics of spirituality. This is achieved through focusing on education as personal development. He shows how early OFSTED programmes attempted to encourage creativity and then focuses on two case studies of teachers who use creative practices to great effect in their work and at the same time develop their pupils as people.

Imison offers three case studies of how she acted creative in a leadership role. She shows the importance of being innovative in the face of constraints and barriers for both the institution – a secondary school – and the individuals involved. This is one of those chapters that attends both to an effective pedagogy and according to her resulting empowerment.

Haringman focuses on the relationship between being a parent and a teacher and how they impact on one another in the home and in the workplace. Being creative in both contexts is what makes both roles productive and rewarding. She also shows how creative approaches prevent her being overwhelmed by the time constraints of being both a teacher and parent.

Rowe and Humphries describe in some detail the values and nature of the creative school they have constructed over the last 25 years. They outline the importance of the school environment, the local community and experiential learning. They explain how they have incorporated the National Curriculum, the literacy and numeracy hours, design and technology and ITC (Information Technology Communication) into a creative learning experience. According to Lucas (this volume) Coombes School is the vision of the future.

Leach suggests that creativity belongs in 'communities' rather than residing entirely in the individual. She goes back into history to suggest that Milton was influenced by Galileo and that Haydn's creation was connected with scientist, William Herschel. She also argues that technology influenced these creative developments as it does today. She proposes that creativity should be rooted in a democratic practice of sharing and developing learning, and that it is less a result of genius. Mental life, she argues, is lived with others. Learning communities, she suggests, are stimulated by the pursuit of knowledge and they encourage the individual to develop this shared knowledge creatively. She exemplifies this thesis with three case studies and concludes by suggesting that the sorts of learning communities exemplified by her case studies encourage the development of the creative individual.

SUMMING UP

And so we come full circle. Creativity is good for the economy, good for the individual, good for society and good for education. This discourse is gaining ground but, like all concepts, it is continually evolving (Beetlestone, 1998a).

It was important to us in conceptualizing the book, that we included a range of perspectives, as well as themes in order to explore the terrain. Thus, the volume includes the voices of the parent, the academic /researcher, the teacher, the policy-maker, the theorist, the teacher educator, the campaigner, the lecturer and the headteacher. The chapters represent a range of experience and concerns on creativity in education and include pieces which are polemical in style, as well as those which are analytical. We see this range as a strength and as representing an inclusive approach to the fostering of creativity, while at the same time recognizing that there may be other voices which are not present and which could have been included.

In dividing the contributions according to the issue of teaching for creativity and creative teaching we are not siding with one or the other. We would argue that both empowerment and the development of creative skills are not only relevant to both individuals and institutions but that they should be intertwined together.

REFERENCES

Alexander, R. (1995) *Versions of Primary Education*. London: Routledge.

Alexander, R., Rose, J. and Woodhead, C. (1992) *Curriculum Organization and Classroom Practice in Primary Schools: A Discussion Paper*. London: HMSO.

Ball, S. (1994) *Education Reform: A Critical and Post Structural Approach*. Buckingham: Open University Press.

Beetlestone, F. (1998a) *Creative Children, Imaginative Teaching*. Buckingham: Open University Press.

Beetlestone, F. (1998b) *Learning in the Early Years: Creative Development*. Leamington Spa: Scholastic.

Blunkett, D. and Smith, C. (2000) 'Government response to all our futures: creativity, culture and education'. Letter to the Chair of the Report, C99/11548. London: DFEE.

Blyth, W. A. L. (ed.) (1988) *Informal Primary Education Today: Essays and Studies*. Lewes: Falmer Press.

de Bono, E. (1992) *Serious Creativity: Using the Power of Lateral Thinking to Create New Ideas*. London: HarperCollins.

Casey, C. (1995) *Work, Self and Society: After Industrialism*. London: Routledge.

Cox, C. B. and Dyson, A. E. (1971) *The Black Papers on Education*. London: Temple Smith.

Craft, A. (1996) 'Nourishing educator creativity: A holistic approach to CPD', *British Journal of In-Service Education*, **22**(3), Autumn, 309–22.

Craft, A. (1997) 'Identity and creativity: education for post-modernism?', *Teacher Development: International Journal of Teachers' Professional Development*, **1**(1), 83–96.

Craft, A. (2000) *Creativity across the Primary Curriculum: Framing and Developing Practice*. London: Routledge.

Creemers, B. (1997) *Effective Schools and Effective Teachers: An International Perspective*. Warwick: Centre for Research in Elementary and Primary Education.

Elliott, R. K. (1971) 'Versions of creativity', *Proceedings of the Philosophy of Education Society of Great Britain*, **5**(2).

Feldman, D. H., Czikszentmihalyi, M. and Gardner, H. (1994) *Changing the World, A Framework for the Study of Creativity*. Westport, CT and London: Praeger.

Fryer. M. (1996) *Creative Teaching and Learning*. London: Paul Chapman.

Gardner, H. (1993a) *Creating Minds: An Anatomy of Creativity Seen through the Lives of Freud, Einstein, Picasso, Stravinsky, Eliot, Graham and Gandhi*. New York: Harper-Collins.

Gardner, H. (1993b) *Multiple Intelligencies: The Theory in Practice*. New York: Harper-Collins.

Gray, J., Reynolds, D., Fitz-Gibbon, C. and Jesson, D. (eds) (1996) *Merging Traditions: The Future of Research on School Effectiveness and School Improvement*. London: Cassell.

Handy, C. (1990) *Inside Organizations*. London: BBC Books.

Hargreaves, A. (1978) 'Towards a theory of classroom coping strategies'. In L. Barton and R. Meighan (eds) *Sociological Interpretations of Schooling and Classrooms*. Driffield: Nafferton Books.

Hargreaves, A. (1994) *Changing Teachers, Changing Times – Teacher's Work and Culture in the Post-Modern Age*. London: Cassell.

Jeffrey, B. (2000) 'Primary pupils perspectives and creative learning'. Paper presented at the BERA Conference. Cardiff.

Mills, C. W. (1959) *The Sociological Imagination.* New York and Oxford: Oxford University Press.

Morgan, G. (1986) *Images of Organizations.* London: Sage.

National Advisory Committee on Creative and Cultural Education (NACCCE) (1999) *All our Futures: Creativity, Culture and Education.* London: DFEE.

Plowden Report (1967) *Children and their Primary Schools.* Report of the Central Advisory Council for Education in England. London: HMSO.

Pollard, A. (1990) 'Towards a sociology of learning in primary schools', *British Journal of Sociology of Education,* **11**(3), 241–56.

Pollard, A., Thiessen, D. and Filer, A. (eds) (1997) *Children and their Curriculum: The Perspectives of Primary and Elementary School Children.* London: Falmer.

Ryhammar, L. and Brolin, C. (1999) 'Creativity research: historical considerations and main lines of development', *Scandinavian Journal of Educational Research,* **43**(3), 259–73.

Sammons, P. (1999) *School Effectiveness: Coming of Age in the Twenty-First Century.* Lisse, The Netherlands: Swets and Zeitlinger.

Sammons, P., Hillman, J. and Mortimore, P. (1995) *Key Characteristics of Effective Schools: A Review of School Effectiveness Research: A Report by the Institute of Education for the Office for Standards in Education.* London: OFSTED.

Seltzer, K. and Bentley, T. (1999) *The Creative Age: Knowledge and Skills for the New Economy.* London: Demos.

Shagoury-Hubbard, R. (1996) *Workshop of the Possible: Nurturing Children's Creative Development.* York, Maine: Stenhouse.

Slee, R., Weiner, G. with Tomlinson, S. (eds) (1998) *School Effectiveness for Whom: Challenges to the School Effectiveness and School Improvement Movements.* London: Falmer.

Smith, J. A. (1975) *Creative Teaching of Reading in the Elementary School.* Boston: Allyn and Bacon.

Stoll, L. and Fink, D. (1996) *Changing our Schools: Linking School Effectiveness and School Improvement.* Buckingham: Open University Press.

Sugrue, K. (1997) *Complexities of Teaching: Child Centred Perspectives.* London: Falmer.

Torrance, E. P. (1974) *Torrance Tests of Creative Thinking.* Lexington, MA: Ginn and Company (Xerox Corporation).

Woods, P. (1990) *Teacher Skills and Strategies.* Lewes: Falmer Press.

Woods, P. (1995) *Creative Teachers in Primary Schools.* Buckingham: Open University Press.

Woods, P. (1998) 'Talking about Coombes: features of a learning community'. In J. Retallic, B. Cocklin and K. Coombe (eds) *Learning Communities in Education.* London: Routledge.

Woods, P. (1999) 'Reconstructing progressivism'. Paper prepared for ISATT conference, Dublin, July.

Woods, P. and Jeffrey, B. (1996) *Teachable Moments: The Art of Teaching in Primary Schools.* Buckingham: Open University Press.

Woods, P., Jeffrey, B., Troman, G. and Boyle, M. (1997) *Restructuring Schools, Reconstructing Teachers: Responding to Change in the Primary School.* Buckingham: Open University Press.

Part One
CREATIVITY AND INDIVIDUAL EMPOWERMENT

Chapter 1

The Art of Creative Teaching: NACCCE and Beyond

Mathilda Marie Joubert

ALL OUR FUTURES

In the 1920s Bertrand Russell said: 'We are faced with the paradoxical fact that education has become one of the chief obstacles to intelligence and freedom of thought' (Hunt, 1979, p. 127). Towards the end of the twentieth century some members of the educational establishment felt that this statement was true again, because of a lack of creativity in the education system. Three future NACCCE members approached the government with a proposal to investigate the opportunities for the promotion of creativity in the current education system, and in February 1998 the National Advisory Committee on Creative and Cultural Education (NACCCE) was officially established. The NACCCE was set up jointly by the Secretary of State for Education and Employment, David Blunkett, and the Secretary of State for Culture, Media and Sport, Chris Smith, with the following terms of reference: 'To make recommendations to the Secretaries of State on the creative and cultural development of young people through formal and informal education: to take stock of current provision and to make proposals for principles, policies and practice' (NACCCE, 1999, p. 4*)*.

In practical terms the eighteen NACCCE members set out to identify the obstacles that were preventing the flourishing of creativity in education and to propose action to the government to remedy the situation. In June 1999 the committee published its report to government entitled *All our Futures: Creativity, Culture and Education* (NACCCE, 1999). Although fully funded by government, the NACCCE was set up as an independent advisory body, not a government think tank. This had the distinct advantage that the committee could give advice without any political interference, but also the disadvantage that the report would remain an advisory document with no guarantee of becoming official government policy.

All our Futures addresses a range of educational issues, including the school curriculum, assessment, pedagogy and teacher training as well as discussion on the need for and nature of creativity in education. This chapter focuses predominantly on creative teaching and learning in the classroom and aims to address a number of key questions. How did the NACCCE define creativity? What did the NACCCE report say about the nurturing of creativity through teaching and learning? How can these principles be practically applied in the creative classroom? How has the report been received, both by government and other agencies? What obstacles stand in the way of implementing the recommendations of the report? How can we ensure the future of creative pedagogies in our classrooms? I believe that creativity in education is imperative to the future survival of the education system. But this chapter is not about the 'Why'; it is about the 'How' of creative education.

DEFINING CREATIVITY

The NACCCE defined creativity as 'imaginative activity fashioned so as to produce outcomes that are both original and of value' (NACCCE, 1999, p. 29). What does this mean in terms of classroom pedagogy? There are five key concepts embedded in the NACCCE definition, which we have to unravel in order to fully understand it: using imagination, a fashioning process, pursuing purposes, being original and judging value.

Using imagination

Young children have a natural ability for using their imagination. They play imaginary games with imaginary friends and take flights of the imagination to far-off places, like fairyland. One might think that these games and fantasy flights do not bear any resemblance to serious creative activity, but they are, in fact, the seeds that grow into superb creative abilities, provided the right fertilizer is added: applied imagination (see below). To imagine something is to create a mental image, picture, sound or even a feeling in your mind; it can be imaginary, i.e. not real, or realistic, but it is a thought process that establishes a new idea or image that was not there before.

Imagination can mean a range of things including imaging, supposing and being imaginative. The NACCCE was particularly concerned with the latter; it may involve imaging and supposing, but not necessarily. Imagination, as defined and used by the NACCCE, is principally to do with seeing new or other possibilities. It is this power that enables creative people to offer novel perspectives to ordinary situations. Many children lose this natural power of imagination once they are faced with the formal structures of schooling; most never regain this ability.

A fashioning process

Creativity is an active process of fashioning, shaping, moulding, refining and managing the creative idea or activity (NACCCE, 1999, p. 31). You must apply yourself to the creative process and you must want to find a solution or a new perspective to a problem or situation. Sometimes problem solutions or novel ideas may dawn upon you unexpectedly or casually, but work must then be made of them to turn thoughts or ideas into creative action. There are certain conditions which may foster one's creativity, such as effective leadership by others, motivation or delegation, but if you merely sit about and wait for someone else to solve a problem or to come up with novel interpretations, creativity will not flourish. Although creative insights can sometimes come about accidentally, Nolan (1987, p. 91) asserts that accidental creativity is a poor substitute for deliberate use of our creative abilities. Children should be given opportunities to actively develop and practise their creative potential.

Pursuing purposes

Free thinking and imaginary flights develop children's mental dexterity, but the pursuit of purposes is the fertilizer that can change ideas into reality. The NACCCE (p. 29) describes creativity as 'applied imagination'. Creative activity aims to produce tangible outcomes. These outcomes can range from a creative thought, to a new theory, a scientific formula or a new work of art. The purpose may change during the pursuit of it, but the creative activity is still directed towards a goal.

A practical example of a change of purpose during the pursuit is the invention of Post-it Notes. A worker at 3M was preparing an adhesive solution, but made it too weak. The glue was a failure; it could not even keep the pages of a writing pad together. The worker then distributed these failure notepads to his colleagues, since they could not be sold. His colleagues soon discovered how useful these individual pages with weakened glue were and Post-its were born. An adhesive was pursued as purpose; Post-its were the outcome. The goal changed, but there was a goal in mind all along.

Being original

Many people do not see themselves as creative, because they compare their abilities to those of the few creative geniuses throughout history. Children may also compare their own performance with that of their teacher, a parent, or someone who is exceptionally skilled at one specific thing, which may lead them to think that they are not particularly creative. But there are different levels of creative achievement, each of which has its time, place and value. The NACCCE (p. 30) distinguishes three categories of originality: historic, relative and individual.

Historic

The Beethovens and Einsteins of this world were uniquely creative in relation to other people in their field; they displayed historic originality. When Einstein developed his relativity theory and when Beethoven introduced a choir into a symphonic work (the Ninth Symphony), these ideas were completely new and original to mankind.

Relative

When one's work is original in relation to that of a particular peer group, relative originality is displayed. In other words, one child's essay or invention may be original in comparison to that of other children of his or her age group, because he or she took a different approach and came up with something novel to the particular group.

Individual

Individual originality can be seen when a person's work is original in relation to his or her own previous work. For example, when a child does a science experiment and 'discovers' the laws of gravity, it is not new knowledge to humankind, but it is new and original to that individual child. If a child repeatedly uses exactly the same instrumentation, musical elements and sequences when composing pieces of music, the output may be deemed repetitive or even boring. But if the same child then starts experimenting and using different musical elements, the new composition may be deemed original, because it differs from the individual child's previous attempts.

All three forms of originality are valid and should be encouraged at school, particularly individual originality. Children should be encouraged to improve on their own previous performance and to come up with new, original ideas. Expectations which are too low will bore children, since they will present no challenge, whilst expectations that are too high will be overwhelming and destructive to their self-esteem. Progress in original thinking will be made when the optimum level of challenge is found, which will be different for each child. The NACCCE (p. 30) suggests that exceptional, historic talent will flourish when individual and relative originality is nurtured.

Judging value

Nobody ever grew taller by being measured. So why is it necessary that we should judge the value of our creative output? The NACCCE (p. 31) opinion is that it is important to evaluate our creative ideas or outcomes against the intended purposes since some outcomes may be highly original, but completely inappropriate for the situation at hand. This evaluative judgement can be applied both throughout and at the end of the creative activity, depending on the activity and the context. Creative thinking involves some critical thinking to evaluate which ideas work and which do not (p. 31). For example, in brainstorming or idea-generating situations, it is important to learn how to judge which ideas might work and which not. Judging value through self-evaluation can also serve as formative feedback, which could improve our future or current creative endeavours.

Judging the value of creative outcomes can be very difficult. It is often the case that creative accomplishments are only valued over the course of time: there was a riot at the première of Stravinsky's *The Rite of Spring*, and Galileo Galilei was brought before the Inquisition and sentenced for postulating that the earth was moving around the sun. Today *The Rite of Spring* is universally accepted as one of the landmark pieces of twentieth-century music, and the sentence passed on Galilei was formally retracted by the Pope, although only in 1992! (Parry, 1997, p. 704). Sometimes judgement should also be deferred, since critical judgement at the wrong time can kill creativity.

How, then, should teachers evaluate the creative work of their pupils, since they cannot wait 100 years to see if little Susan's painting will stand the test of time? It is important always to use a variety of evaluative methods and to allow failure and learn from it. If failure is not allowed, children will tend to play it safe and never take creative risks. Reward experimentation and new approaches. Teachers should determine clear criteria for excellence for the task at hand, but be flexible and be prepared to be surprised. It may be possible to identify age-specific goals or standards for creativity, as proposed by Romanink (in Lubart and Sternberg, 1998, p. 65), and there may be differences between the evaluation of the creator and others (NACCCE, 1999, p. 31). There may also be cultural differences regarding creativity and its evaluative judgement (Lubart and Sternberg, 1998, p. 66). It is thus important to also make use of peer review and self-evaluation by pupils, as this may produce a variety of value judgements, contributing to an evaluation profile.

CREATIVE TEACHING AND LEARNING

Creative teaching is an art. One cannot teach teachers didactically how to be creative; there are no fail-safe recipes or routines. Some strategies can help to promote creative thinking, but teachers need to develop a full repertoire of skills, which they can adapt and apply to different situations. Explicit knowledge, which is conveyed as information, should be internalized before it can be brought back to life as personal knowledge (Leadbeater, 1999, p. 29). This involves training, practice and reflection. Creative habits can be very useful, but I feel compelled to add a warning note. Sometimes people are unable to adapt learnt strategies to differing circumstances and to make them their own. They become entrenched in a mental rut of a specific way of doing things, which is inherently uncreative. The only difference between a groove and a grave is the depth. As with so many other things, balance is the key; it is not merely a choice between one or the other.

The NACCCE report distinguishes between teaching creatively and teaching for creativity. Teaching creatively is defined as 'teachers using imaginative approaches to make learning more interesting, exciting and effective' and teaching for creativity as 'forms of teaching that are intended to develop young people's own creative thinking or behaviour' (NACCCE, 1999, p. 89). The former is regarded as a key component of all good teaching, but it does not guarantee that the children are learning or developing their own creative potential. Teaching for creativity cannot be achieved without creative teaching, but it goes one step further by also developing the creative abilities of all children. This is what is needed in an education system for the twenty-first century.

Lawrence Stenhouse (NACCCE, 1999, p. 95) said: 'Teaching is not to be regarded as a static accomplishment like riding a bicycle or keeping a ledger: it is, like all arts of high ambition, a strategy in the face of an impossible task.' In teaching, there are always new challenges; creative teachers manage them with great aplomb. Experience has shown that creative teachers constantly reinvent themselves and adapt their teaching styles and strategies to different situations as required. Without a firm core identity, flexible behaviour can be deeply risky, but if teachers remain firmly rooted in terms of their identity and core principles, it allows them to feel free to use flexibility in terms of what they do. This is a difficult but exciting and rewarding process, which could prevent stagnation and mental starvation.

Creative teaching involves risk-taking for teachers who may have to leave the security of the structured lesson behind. They may be asked to demonstrate their own creative processes, and expose all the uncertainties and false starts involved in it (Ireson *et al.*, 1999, p. 222). Creative teachers should be prepared to learn from their pupils and not be afraid of looking foolish. They need to explore their own creative talents – both in teaching and other areas of interest – in order to promote creativity in their pupils. The NACCCE (1999, p. 90) suggests that teachers cannot develop the creative abilities of their pupils if their own creative abilities are suppressed. It is, however, important to bear in mind that teacher creativity should not stifle pupil creativity.

Teaching for creativity

The NACCCE (p. 90) proposed that teaching for creativity involves three key tasks or principles: encouraging, identifying and fostering.

Encouraging

In teaching for creativity, teachers should encourage certain beliefs and attributes in their pupils. The NACCCE report (p. 90) points out that 'the first task in teaching for creativity in any field is to encourage young people to believe in their creative potential, to engage their sense of possibility and to give them the confidence to try'. Success breeds success. If children are encouraged to use their creative talents, self-esteem and confidence will be built, leading children to hunger for more success.

There is a range of attributes needed for creativity, which are also developed by creativity. Although some children may already have developed or discovered some of these attributes, it may be latent in others. They should therefore be encouraged to come out if they are latent or dormant, and once these attributes are there, they should be fostered. The encouragement of attributes like risk-taking, independent judgement, commitment, resilience in the face of adversity and motivation will contribute to the development of children's creative potential (NACCCE, 1999, p. 90).

Teachers can provide extrinsic forms of motivation, e.g. incentives or rewards, but it is also important that children are encouraged to develop intrinsic forms of motivation, e.g. curiosity. The former will aid the immediate acquisition of knowledge or skills at school, but the latter will sustain a person's interest in a field and encourage an individual to become a lifelong learner. Once children have developed or found their individual forms of intrinsic motivation, extrinsic motivation should be applied cautiously, as it might stifle creativity.

Risk-taking carries with it the potential for gain or loss, but it is often only through creative risks that huge successes are achieved. Young adolescents are under a lot of peer pressure and depend on group security. If the foundations for a risk-taking attitude are not laid while children are young, they may be afraid of risking uncertain outcomes during this period. Older adolescents have a strong desire to assert their independence (Pitts *et al.*, 1999, p. 29). This desire can be channelled into creative activity, but only if they have achieved creative successes before.

Persistence is another key attribute that should be encouraged in teaching for creativity. Children should learn that there is more than one way to solve a problem or interpret a situation. They should not give up after one attempt, failed or successful; they should always be encouraged to try a range of different approaches and to persevere. Flexibility is a creative attribute, which is often better in young people, since older people can get entrenched in a standard 'correct' way of doing things (Lubart and Sternberg, 1998, pp. 62–3). Teachers should therefore encourage their pupils to retain this youthful flexibility and they should aim to regain it themselves. Willingness to grow, openness to new experiences (Lubart and Sternberg, 1998, p. 64), the capacity to think for oneself (NACCCE, 1999, p. 92) and the appropriate use of humour are further creative attributes that should be encouraged and developed while at school.

Identifying
Creative activity is possible in all subjects at school and in all areas of life. The arts are often termed 'the creative arts'. This is a serious misnomer, since the arts can sometimes be taught or practised in very uncreative ways, and mathematics, history or literacy can be taught in highly creative ways. But each individual will have their creative strengths in different areas and it is the role of teachers to help children identify these strengths.

Sometimes a person's creative strengths may fall outside the norm and are therefore discredited. At least two of the NACCCE members had personal experience of this. At school Lenny Henry was constantly told to stop being funny and to get serious – today he is one of Britain's leading comedians. Harry Kroto was a good academic student, but also liked drawing pictures and presenting things schematically. He was told to stop doodling and to concentrate on serious things like mathematics and science. Luckily Harry ignored the advice, because it was his drawing ability that helped him to discover the third allotrope of carbon through visual representation of the atom structure, for which he was awarded the Nobel Prize for chemistry in 1996. We have to widen our concept of achievement to identify the creative strengths of all young people (NACCCE, 1999, p. 59). Some people are only creative once they recover from their school education, because their talents were unrecognized at that time. Many never recover, and those are the people that the education system is currently failing.

Creativity is to a certain extent domain specific: a creative artist is not necessarily going to be a creative mathematician and a creative pianist is very seldom a creative cellist too (NACCCE, 1999, pp. 37–8). But some creative skills, e.g. problem-solving strategies, self-organization or divergent thinking skills, are generic and can be transferred to other areas once they have been learnt in a specific domain. Once children have identified their creative strengths, they should be encouraged to analyse their creative strategies and approaches through meta-cognitive thinking. This knowledge could then be applied to other areas or domains, but two caveats should be added to this condition. Ireson *et al.* (1999, p. 223) point out that you need a knowledge base in order to transfer skills learnt in one domain to another domain, i.e. you cannot be creative on the violin if you have never seen or played one before. Second, Sternberg (1996, pp. 382–3) emphasizes that previous experience with similar problems or situations can either help (positive transfer) or hinder (negative transfer) solving a particular problem. If strategies learnt in one domain are not applied flexibly to other domains they could be more hindrance than help. The whole literature on transfer is, however, still contentious, so even the transfer of core skills is not universally agreed upon by researchers.

Fostering
Teachers should foster the creative potential of all children and the best way to enhance creativity is through the process of being creative (NACCCE, 1999, p. 91). It is not healthy to only watch sport; in order to get fit you must physically do it. It is the same with creativity; practice does make better. Children enjoy being creative and 'learning by doing' (p. 91). What a child has created, invented or discovered himself, he will remember and value. Learning is, after all, a process of discovery. Even though our education system is based on acquiring existing knowledge, it is new knowledge for the learner (Nolan, 1987, p. 14). Creative activity can also serve as evaluation of learnt material; children really understand a concept if they are able to apply it creatively.

Fostering creativity also involves allowing and encouraging experimental activity. The American engineer Buckminster Fuller said: 'there is no such thing as a failed experiment, only experiments with unexpected outcomes' (Parry, 1997, p. 696). Children and teachers should be allowed time to experiment, to develop personal teaching and learning styles and to reflect on creative activities and achievements. But too often curricular constraints do not allow teachers the flexibility or the time to do this. No teacher ever chose a career in teaching because of their love of the National Curriculum, but with all the curricular, assessment and inspection constraints imposed on teachers today, they often end up teaching the curriculum instead of teaching children – the real reason for choosing a career in education.

A lot of flexibility can, however, be brought into the classroom in spite of policy constraints. Teachers should respect unusual questions and give credit to original ideas. Try to encourage the contribution of each child and use both open and closed questions. Children should also be allowed and encouraged to question the validity of assumptions or established theorems, for this is how new concepts are developed (NACCCE, 1999, p. 95). Encourage them to innovate, not merely to imitate. There are some instances where modelling can be very beneficial to the development of children's creative abilities, e.g. modelling curiosity. Teachers must use their judgement about when to apply it and when to encourage independent thinking.

Creativity can also be fostered through actual and mental play. There is a range of pedagogical benefits of play in early childhood:

- it motivates children and enhances learning;
- it provides a context for exploration and experiment;
- it is the child's 'work'; and
- it is developmentally appropriate (Siraj-Blatchford, 1999, p. 24).

Most of these benefits are also applicable to actual and mental play for children of all ages. Of course, not all play is creative, e.g. snakes and ladders is a game based purely on luck and routine with no particular skill or creative thinking involved. But other games do encourage creative thinking, e.g. in hide and seek a child has to think of a new hiding place every time and this involves creative thinking. Creativity is also fostered and developed through mental play or thoughtful playfulness, which involves conjuring up, exploring and developing ideas or possibilities and then critically evaluating and testing them (NACCCE, 1999, p. 92).

The school and classroom environment is also crucial to the fostering of creative abilities. Creativity can be stimulated by an environment full of ideas, experiences, interesting materials and resources, and in a relaxing atmosphere where unique ideas are encouraged (NACCCE, 1999, p. 102). A creative environment takes the child's fear of failure into consideration. Mistakes are acceptable and part of the creative process, and children are motivated to try again and to learn from their mistakes. Creative leadership can engender an ethos of valuing creativity in school which could lead to a school culture characterized by an emphasis on mobility of ideas and flexibility of perspective, and a constant raising of new possibilities (NACCCE, 1999, p. 102). Creativity will flourish in such an environment.

CURRICULUM, ASSESSMENT, INSPECTION AND TEACHER TRAINING REFORM

Although this chapter focuses mainly on creative teaching and learning, I will briefly allude to the NACCCE report's recommendations for curriculum, assessment, inspection and teacher training reform. All the committee's recommendations are aimed at raising the profile of creative education in schools.

The report's curriculum recommendations address three key concerns: the need for balance, prescription and the basic assumptions of education (pp. 86–7).

- *The need for balance.* The current hierarchy of subjects is unhelpful to the promotion of creative education. The NACCCE suggests that the existing distinction between core and foundation subjects should be removed. Literacy and numeracy are regarded as important skills, not subjects, but the remainder of subjects should all be on the same level. Instead of benefiting the subject, science has in fact suffered because of its position in the core curriculum. Much of the creativity and experimentation in science has been lost because of the curriculum, assessment and inspection constraints on core subjects.
- *Prescription.* The National Curriculum is too full, despite the reductions of the 2000 review. There is not enough time or space in the curriculum to give teachers the freedom to be creative, to experiment and to allow children to experiment. The NACCCE therefore recommends that the content of the curriculum should be reduced.
- *Basic assumptions of education.* Successive curriculum reviews have just tinkered at the edges, but the NACCCE advocates the need for a fundamental and structural review of some of the basic assumptions of education which are currently imbedded in the National Curriculum. We inherited a nineteenth-century education model, but is it still relevant in the twenty-first century? We believe that there are only ten subjects in the world, and when another one comes along, e.g. drama, we must squash it in somewhere, because we are married to the current structure. We believe children grow up in four instalments, i.e. the current four key stages, without ever considering whether they are developmentally the right groupings. And we accept the structure of the school day and year as a given, even though it was designed to cope with children having to bring in the harvest in the nineteenth century. The NACCCE report does not say that everything

should necessarily change, but the committee believed that some real debate should be held over this inherited curriculum structure and its relevance today.

In terms of assessment, the NACCCE (p. 116) suggests that greater emphasis should be put on formative assessment in schools, i.e. assessment that is intended to improve the day-to-day quality of teaching and learning. At present some subjects are assessed through formative assessment, performed by teachers, and others are tested through objective and external summative assessment on which league tables are based. Only the latter is used in judging school effectiveness. This gives the message that teacher assessment is not important or valued. Formative assessment can promote creative teaching and learning, summative assessment can detract from it. The NACCCE also proposed that the recording burden imposed by the assessment system should be reduced and that the Qualifications and Curriculum Authority (QCA) should undertake research on assessing children's creative development.

The NACCCE (pp. 114, 117) recognizes the need for inspection teams to be accountable, but also warns that without flexibility, inspection teams can become insensitive to the qualities and nuances of work in individual schools. The committee therefore advised that the Office for Standards in Education (OFSTED) framework for school inspection should be further developed to take fuller account of creative education and of the processes of teaching, learning and assessment it involves. The Office for Standards in Education has significant influence on national education policies, yet the current inspection framework is focused on very narrow and specific targets. The NACCCE (1999, pp. 115, 117) therefore suggests that OFSTED should provide the government with the wide-ranging inspection-based information and professional advice it needs to develop and carry out its policies for education, e.g. to measure the effect that the current focus on core subjects has on the foundation subjects. This will inform government of how those policies are working out in practice and ensure a constructive link between school and policy-related inspections.

The NACCCE's main recommendation for teacher training is that the importance of creative teaching, learning and thinking should be promoted in all disciplines throughout initial teacher training, in continuing professional development (CPD) and during training for the National Professional Qualification for Head Teachers (pp. 163–5). It is also suggested that providers of initial teacher training should be enabled to bid to become centres of excellence in different specialisms, supported by additional funding and facilities and that a new category of Accredited Teaching Assistant with particular expertise in the field of creative education should be instated.

RESPONSE TO THE NACCCE REPORT

All our Futures has had a very positive reception from all sectors, including education, business, science, the arts and trade unions. Everyone felt that this was a long overdue report, which conveyed the collective feelings of many people concerned with the education of the nation's young people. Our education system has to adapt and become more creative in order to prepare young people adequately for the twenty-first century. The NACCCE (1999, pp. 18–25) describes the unprecedented economic, technological, social and personal challenges that face our pupils and us today and tomorrow. The only future thing that we can be certain of is uncertainty. Manual tasks will increasingly be performed by computers, but machines can never replace humans in jobs where creativity is required. It is therefore imperative that the education system encourages children to develop their creative potential. The report made 59 wide-ranging recommendations of how this can be achieved. Des Dearlove, business correspondent to *The Times*, even described it as 'a report that should have every chief executive and human resources manager thumping the table and demanding action' (Dearlove, 1999). But, most importantly, how did the government respond?

The government funded the whole NACCCE inquiry, including the production and distribution of the committee's report, but not much was done to publicly promote the report. Many people in education do not even know of the existence of the report and it seems that the government would like to keep it that way. Although copies of the report are available free of charge on request, the government was not prepared to send copies of the report, or even an executive summary, to all schools, not even if sponsorship was provided. A privately funded executive summary was eventually sent to all schools in October 2000 without government sanction.

A joint response to the report was issued by the Department for Education and Employment (DFEE) and the Department for Culture, Media and Sport (DCMS) in January 2000, more than six months after its publication. The response contains some encouraging messages: the government has asked the QCA to do further work on the role of creativity and the arts in the curriculum, 'creative development' has been included as one of the curriculum areas in the new Early Learning Goals (ELGs) foundation stage curriculum and the government is piloting a professional development programme for secondary teachers on higher-order thinking skills, although not creativity *per se*. But the response falls short of a full commitment to the promotion of creativity across the whole of education.

Of the 40 NACCCE recommendations addressed to the government, only sixteen are dealt with in the government response and some of these only partially. No commitment is made to implement any of the assessment, inspection or teacher training recommendations, e.g. although the forthcoming review of initial teacher training is mentioned, no promise is made that it will take account of creative education. No commitment is made for a future fundamental review of the National Curriculum to address the NACCCE curriculum recommendations as outlined above. And no reason is given for the omission of the other 24 recommendations.

There are also some fundamental flaws in the thinking about creativity throughout the response. Although the government agrees at the outset that creativity is not only about the arts, they keep on reverting back to this assumption by using the two terms as synonyms or in conjunction with each other, e.g. referring to all the current government initiatives in the area of arts education or asking the QCA to do further work on the role of creativity and the arts in the curriculum. The focus on creativity and the arts was originally meant as one thing, but the QCA has agreed to treat them as two separate issues in their research. The use of the term 'creative development' as one of the curriculum areas of the ELGs also indicates that creativity is still seen as a discreet subject area, usually equated to the arts, and not as a pervasive approach to the whole education system. Welcome though the focus on higher-order thinking skills may be, it is not the same as creativity. Not all higher-order thinking activities require creative or original thinking – some require logical or routine thinking patterns – and not all creative activity is achieved through thinking skills – some may involve original practical or physical skills and abilities (NACCCE, 1999, p. 34).

The current Labour government is sending some very confusing messages regarding this report and it is difficult to determine why. Why did they commission the whole inquiry and spend taxpayers' money to fund it if they did not intend taking the advice to heart? In the next section some of the possible barriers to influencing policy are discussed.

BARRIERS TO IMPLEMENTATION

Machiavelli said, 'There is nothing more difficult to carry out, nor more doubtful of success, nor more dangerous to handle, than to initiate a new order of things' (Nolan, 1987, p. 1). The politics of creativity consists of an intricate network of dynamic forces, all impacting on the implementation of a new order of creativity in education.

Language lessons

Creativity is a very elusive concept to define, and even when defined, it is interpreted in a variety of different ways, e.g. is creativity in education the same as creativity in business? We have clear language for understanding achievement in mathematics, where everyone understands and means the same things, but not with creativity. We still lack a common conceptual language, understood by all, to enable us to discuss creativity in education and across other sectors. It seems that even scholars of creativity do not have a shared language for creativity.

Political problems

The agenda for the promotion of creativity set out in the NACCCE report is not an easy one. The recommended changes cannot be achieved overnight; they are long-term, visionary transformations. This is at odds with the whole political system, which is geared towards quick-fix targets, which can be achieved within a few years before the start of a new election campaign. There are also immense political pressures on the education system to be shown to raise standards of achievement. Creativity in education is a very evasive concept; you cannot merely tick a box to indicate higher standards of creative achievement. Creativity may be too difficult to measure for a government that wants to prove it is tough on targets.

Ideological impediments

The current Labour government has to live with the legacy of the progressive education policies of Old Labour in the 1960s. Many people blame those policies for most of the problems in the education system and they associate progressivism with creativity. We have to reclaim the meaning of the word 'creativity'. Creativity should be rigorous, it is grounded in knowledge and skills and there should be a balance between freedom and control in all creative activities. In the 1990s the pendulum swung too far back to the other side and we had only control and accountability. It is time for the pendulum to swing back again and reach equilibrium in the middle. The NACCCE (p. 89) emphasizes that it should not be an either/or situation; we need elements of both progressive and traditional teaching methods in our education system today.

Bureaucratic burdens

Most people in the Civil Service are career Civil Servants: they move from one government department to the other. This enables them to bring a diverse set of experiences to each new job, but it does not guarantee that they have any real knowledge of, experience in, or passion for the area they work in, e.g. education. They may be very effective at briefing politicians, but they may not be equally effective at prescribing educational or pedagogical policy. Because Civil Servants are trained to maintain political neutrality, they are often opposed to big changes. Lubart and Sternberg (1998, p. 64) confirm this idea when they say, 'creative ideas often threaten those who have a stake in the existing order'. Implementing the recommendations of the NACCCE report also requires cross-divisional and cross-departmental working. The Civil Service works in very hierarchical ways and its ability for real 'joined-up' thinking and working is highly questionable.

Creative constraints

Creativity is not an easy option; it involves risk-taking, innovative thinking and requires visionary leadership. The really creative leader will devise creative ways to overcome the politics of creativity. Spiel and Von Korff (1998) studied the implicit theories of creativity held by people in four different professions: politicians, scientists, artists and schoolteachers. The politicians showed the lowest participation rate and the lowest number of associations for the concept of creativity. The key question is why? Is it due to lack of time, lack of interest in the topic, lack of commitment to creativity or, perhaps, due to lack of creativity itself? Leadbeater (1999, p. 51) also questions the creativity of the Civil Service: 'The public sector suffers not just from poor productivity compared with much of the private sector, but from an innovation deficit as well . . . entrepreneurship and risk-taking are discouraged.'

THE WAY FORWARD

In an ideal world we would want the government to commit to the promotion of creativity in education and to implement all the recommendations of the NACCCE report, ranging from a new curriculum structure to new assessment, inspection and teacher training arrangements. This will not be easy and the government will need all strength to its elbow in order to achieve this. The government may be waiting to see if there is enough support from the teaching profession before committing to a creative education agenda. If this is the case, I would urge the profession to provide this support.

Once the commitment from government is there to actively promote creativity in education, the changes suggested by the NACCCE could still not be achieved overnight. An action plan would be necessary to get from where we are now to where we want to be and I suggest that a ten-year transitional timetable for change should be drawn up. A good example is the timetable developed by the Royal Society for the Encouragement of Arts, Manufactures and Commerce (RSA) for the implementation of their competence-led curriculum model (Bayliss, 1999). Change on the scale advocated by the NACCCE or the RSA would impact on every facet of the education system: teacher training, assessment and qualifications, and curriculum management in addition to the production of new teaching and learning materials. A consultation and marketing policy would also be needed. The RSA believed that the scale of change should not be a sufficient reason for not proceeding and therefore developed a long-term strategy to achieve the transformation from the current system to a new competence-led framework. The RSA has now started implementing a pilot of the project.

There are two ways of bringing about change: a top-down or bottom-up approach. The NACCCE was given the opportunity to advise government on the implementation of a top-down approach to the promotion of creativity in education. Unfortunately, until now, the present Labour government has chosen not to implement this strategy. For the time being we are, thus, left with the bottom-up approach. It will be down to the teaching profession itself to promote creativity in schools and hopefully the policy will eventually catch up with the practice (Joubert, 1999). This method is no disadvantage; it could, in fact, be a distinct advantage. A top-down approach can evoke feelings of hostility and teachers can feel underestimated and undervalued, whereas a bottom-up approach can ensure a feeling of ownership towards the initiative.

A good example of this principle is the government's literacy and numeracy strategies and it can be compared to ideas of 'Taylorism'. Leadbeater (1999, p. 55) tells of Frederick Winslow Taylor who greatly influenced thinking of companies and organizations at the start of the twentieth century by suggesting that higher productivity was possible if managers could standardize and simplify work into a series of easily imitated steps. This turned organizations into 'well-oiled machines, operated by brainless drones'. This is exactly what the present government is doing to teachers with the literacy and numeracy strategies and hours. Taylor's approach might have been relevant at the start of the twentieth century, but certainly not in the twenty-first century. As Leadbeater (1999, p. 55) points out, 'the strengths of Taylor's de-humanized organizations – their regimentation and repetition – became their weakness: they eliminated initiative and individual responsibility'.

Teachers should be the ones to change pedagogy, not politicians or bureaucrats. The onus rests on teachers, individually and collectively, to promote opportunities for creative teaching and learning in their classrooms and schools. There is a need for a wide-ranging debate on issues concerning creative teaching and learning, involving a range of organizations and individuals. The new General Teaching Council (GTC) can play a key role in co-ordinating the debate by gathering teachers' views and experience in the field. (Hopefully it will not become merely another bureaucratic institution.) The University Council for the Education of Teachers (UCET), the Teacher Training Agency (TTA) and individual teacher training institutions can all help inform the debate, and OFSTED's role in influencing pedagogy should not be underestimated. But this pedagogical debate must be owned and led by teachers, informed by research. If such a debate was politically led, it could cause even higher levels of prescription in education, deskilling of teachers and encouragement of conformity – exactly the opposite of creativity.

There are examples of good creative teaching practice in spite of current policies, not because of them (Joubert, 1999). This is possible when teachers apply the same creative attributes that they are aiming to encourage and foster in their pupils: persistence, perseverance, resilience in the face of adversity and the belief that there is more than one possible way of doing things. Teachers should develop ways of promoting creativity in education within the current legal requirements and constraints of the curriculum, assessment and inspection. Valerie Bayliss (1998) puts it aptly: 'We cannot afford poverty of vision, let alone poverty of aspiration. There are always risks in changing, but the risk of failing to change is much greater.'

There is a range of exciting challenges and opportunities ahead for teachers in order to foster creativity in education. Criteria for excellence in creativity are not clearly defined, which means that teachers have to try to define them according to their circumstances. The development or definition of a common conceptual language and framework for creativity is another challenge facing not only the teaching profession, but also everybody interested in the promotion and fostering of creativity. This will involve the encouragement of real collaboration between different sectors – education, business, arts, sciences, etc. – at all levels.

Although much can be done to change pedagogy through a bottom-up approach, the debate on policy issues must be kept alive. I predict that lobbying the DFEE will not have that much effect – not even an official inquiry persuaded them – but directly lobbying the TTA, OFSTED and the QCA may have more effect. We should also encourage individual teacher training institutions to develop initial training and CPD courses in creative teaching and learning.

One of the biggest challenges ahead for teachers is to be able to adapt to the ever-increasing pace of change. It is estimated that 75 per cent of the scientific knowledge that we will need in 40 years' time is still not invented (Barnes, 1998). The traditional role of teachers as transmitters of knowledge is changing to one of facilitators of learning. Although there are political pressures on teachers 'to teach' in the traditional sense of the word, it is essential that the knowledge revolution should be made open to pupils, and teachers must facilitate this process. The future of schools as geographical locations is also under threat. We need to be able to adapt to these changing circumstances and help shape the future of our nation. Mastering the art of creative teaching will help us do this. We ignore it at our own peril.

But, most importantly, there is a range of recommendations in the NACCCE report directly addressed to headteachers, teachers and schools. The challenge, the opportunity and the incentive are there for teachers to make creativity in their own schools a reality. It may be time for teachers to act in spite of the policy, not because of it. It will be a net gain to the education system if only one teacher develops the creative potential of young people in his or her classroom. Think of the benefit if all teachers did it. Creativity is not a new burden to be opposed upon teachers: it is an enabling device, which will help raise standards of achievement by allowing children to develop their potential. There is nothing to lose in trying. To make a mistake is nothing, but to do nothing is definitely a mistake.

REFERENCES

Barnes, A. (1998) 'English in the National Curriculum'. In *Take Care, Mr Blunkett*. London: ATL.

Bayliss, V. (1998) *Redefining Schooling: A Challenge to a Closed Society*. London: RSA.

Bayliss, V. (1999) *Opening Minds: Education for the 21st Century*. London: RSA.

Dearlove, D. (1999) '"Get creative" or perish'. *The Times (Management-Plus* insert), 5 August, 1.

Hunt, J. (ed.) (1979) *The Hamlyn Pocket Dictionary of Quotations*. London: Hamlyn.

Ireson, J., Mortimore, P. and Hallam, S. (1999) 'The common strands of pedagogy and their implications'. In P. Mortimore (ed.) *Understanding Pedagogy and its Impact on Learning*. London: Paul Chapman.

Joubert, M. M. (1999) 'Creativity: from practice to policy, *Modus*, **17**(8), 246–8.

Leadbeater, C. (1999) *Living on Thin Air: The New Economy*. London: Viking.

Lubart, T. I. and Sternberg, R. J. (1998) 'Creativity across time and place: lifespan and cross-cultural perspectives'. *High Ability Studies*, **9**(1), 59–74.

National Advisory Committee on Creative and Cultural Education (NACCCE) (1999) *All our Futures: Creativity, Culture and Education*. London: DFEE.

Nolan, V. (1987) *The Innovator's Handbook: The Skills of Innovative Management: Problem Solving, Communication and Teamwork*. London: Sphere Books.

Parry, M. (ed.) (1997) *Chambers Biographical Dictionary*. Edinburgh: Larousse.

Pitts, S., Harland, J. and Selwood, S. (1999) 'A review of the literature'. In J. Harland and K. Kinder (eds) *Crossing the Line: Extending Young People's Access to Cultural Venues*. London: Calouste Gulbenkian Foundation.

Siraj-Blatchford, I. (1999) 'Early childhood pedagogy: practice, principles and research'. In P. Mortimore (ed.) *Understanding Pedagogy and its Impact on Learning*. London: Paul Chapman.

Spiel, C. and Von Korff, C. (1998) 'Implicit theories of creativity: the conception of politicians, scientists, artists and school teachers', *High Ability Studies*, **9**(1), 43–58.

Sternberg, R. J. (1996) *Cognitive Psychology*. Fort Worth: Harcourt Brace College.

Chapter 2

Creative Teaching, Teaching Creativity and Creative Learning

Bill Lucas

INTRODUCTION

Everyone is talking about creativity. The Prime Minister [Tony Blair] speaks of creating a nation of creative talents where we compete on brains not brawn. The Secretary of State for Education and Employment [David Blunkett] has articulated a vision of a Learning Age in which the creativity, enterprise and scholarship of everyone are harnessed for the common good. The National Advisory Committee on Creative and Cultural Education has proposed a national strategy to ensure that creative and cultural education is explicitly recognized and provided for in schools. The rhetoric sounds good and Ken Robinson's impressive report, *All our Futures: Creativity, Culture and Education* (NACCCE, 1999), makes many sensible structural recommendations.

But, encouraging as these initiatives are, they still miss the point. For despite the existence of some extraordinarily creative headteachers and teachers, most schools retain too many features which are fundamentally uncreative. While it is a commonplace of creativity that it can excel in the most inhospitable of environments, it is not good enough to rely on the exceptional or the accidental. All schools need to be able to create and maintain the conditions in which creativity can thrive. Before we initiate this we need to reassess what we know about how people learn most effectively and whether the impact of current reward systems contributes to creative classroom activity. While there are obvious implications for schools in establishing the role of creativity in effective learning, there are some equally clear messages for parents and other professional educators. The context for creativity is as much the home, the local museum or the learning centre as it is the classroom. The backdrop for this chapter is the wide canvas called lifelong learning.

CREATIVITY AND THE EDUCATIONAL CONTEXT

Two recent influences on schools

Since 1990 there have been two key strands of policy affecting schools. The first of these has been the standardization of provision. The curriculum has been standardized into ten or so subjects. The outputs of schools have been marshalled into a format where they can be regularly inspected and, at the same time, league tables ensure that the main criteria by which a school is judged are examinations or tests. Needless to say there have been measurable improvements in the ability of pupils to do well under test conditions and OFSTED is therefore praising more schools now. But as Alfred Einstein observed that our theories determine what we measure, the way we measure what we teach also indicates our attitude towards creativity. The current trend in assessment procedures to marginalize coursework, especially where it constitutes all of the examined work, is disappointing. High standards of moderation in examinations like the 100 per cent coursework Creative Arts course I helped to create in the early 1980s not only fostered creative learning but also led to excellent opportunities for teachers' professional development.

The other major influences on schools during the past decade – local management of schools and greater financial autonomy – have encouraged individuality of provision. This is evidenced by the plurality of models of state education currently available, for example, beacon schools, training schools, specialist schools and education action zones. But the mechanisms which have brought about these changes have been largely financial. Schools naturally adapt creatively when they are really in charge of their economic destiny. When schools first became financially autonomous, I remember experiencing an enormous sense of exhilaration and creative freedom. Where once we were taking decisions about which books to buy, we were able to think about the relative benefits of employing more staff, carpeting the classrooms or developing the landscape of the site. Financial devolution had the potential for fostering creativity in schools. But in my experience of running two educational charities, Learning through Landscapes and the Campaign for Learning, the truth is that the majority of schools have become less, not more, creative places.

The wider picture

In the world beyond school, the pace of change has been extraordinary. This is most obvious in the area of technology. In February 2000, Bill Gates came to London and talked of an e-learning revolution that would transform education. The combination of all pupils gaining access to laptops, the web and the development of voice-activated computer devices of all kinds does indeed offer creative opportunities. It is wonderful to think of all children connected to the most amazing electronic library and museum in the world. Equally it is appalling simply to equate 'access to information' with 'learning'. Digital television also promises a brave new world, offering as wide a range of opportunity as did that based on the microchip.

While advances in technology have brought creative opportunities, they have also brought a certain tyranny. In particular they have done something very strange to our concept of time. When faxes were first invented we rushed frantically to read them while their hard copy 'brothers and sisters' languished in our in-trays. With e-mail it is worse still. The ease with which people now 'copy' messages means that we all have a tenfold amount of reading to do. We can do virtually anything anywhere at anytime. Consequently our days have become more crowded. For many people the unbounded nature of our work eats into home time. We arrive home later and, as parents, have less energy and less time to spend with our children. We are generally busier, noisier and more stressed. Changes at work include more portfolio working, and an increase in self-employment. More of us are working in knowledge companies, the creative industries and the e-service sector. While some people are just working longer hours, others are reorganizing their patterns of working life. This is powerfully described by Valerie Bayliss (1999). However, schools seem more resistant to change. Their architecture, their terms, their hours of attendance stubbornly remain as they were a century ago, in spite of some, who propose alternative options, like John Abbott and Sir Christopher Ball.

Change in this area appears to be constrained by the power of the current orthodoxy that seems to emphasize teaching not learning. According to Chris Woodhead, formerly Her Majesty's Chief Inspector of Schools, who attacked me in his 2000 annual lecture (Woodhead, 2000), I am wrong to suggest, as I do again here, that by 'learning to learn' you can become a 'more effective learner'. The skills of 'learning to learn' can be developed and improved just as you can become a better reader or a more confident speaker by understanding the process.

The dead weight of IQ

Much of what is uncreative in schools can be traced back to what happened in 1904 in Paris. The French Minister of Public Instruction of that period created a commission to distinguish which children were not succeeding in school due to 'mental defectiveness'. As a result of this commission Albert Binet and his colleague Theodore Simon designed IQ tests to meet this need out of a desire to help and protect these children. However, the resulting IQ test has exerted a pernicious influence on the education systems the world over. The existence of IQ tests as the benchmark for intelligence has led to an unhelpful distinction between academic and creative arts subjects due to the difficulty of assessing the latter. Art is apparently only academic if studied for its history rather than its science, and craft and drama and personal development defy the straitjacket of any IQ test. For two decades, Howard Gardner's work (1983) has made it clear that we all have a number of intelligences. Whether there are eight, as he currently suggests, or more as some others have argued, the point is that there is more than one kind of intelligence. Understanding multiple intelligence theory is, I believe, a fundamental principle of creativity. And a number of UK schools are now waking up to this fact.

Defining creativity

Creativity itself is notoriously difficult to define. The definition contained in Ken Robinson's report seems to me to be constrained: 'Imaginative activity fashioned so as to produce outcomes that are both original and of value' (NACCCE, 1999, p. 29). My own attempt is somewhat freer: 'Creativity is a state of mind in which all of our intelligences are working together. It involves seeing, thinking and innovating. Although it is often found in the creative arts, creativity can be demonstrated in any subject at school or in any aspect of life.' Creative people question the assumptions they are given. They see the world differently, are happy to experiment, to take risks and to make mistakes. They make unique connections often unseen by others.

In schools, creativity is often mistaken for disobedience or rudeness in young people. Pupils are expected to act passively and receive instruction as their forebears did 100 years ago. A recent MORI poll undertaken by the Campaign for Learning, and quoted in *Learning to Learn* (Lucas and Greany, 2000) asked pupils which activities took place most frequently in their classroom. The three activities mentioned most frequently were:

* Copying from the board or a book: 56 per cent.
* Listening to a teacher speak for a long time: 37 per cent.
* Have a class discussion: 37 per cent.

While we must be cautious about interpreting surveys, which are based exclusively on pupil perceptions, I think it would be fair to say that if these activities represent the reality of most classrooms then creativity does not appear to be dominant. Knowing what we know about how we learn, it is difficult to accept that such a heavy reliance on passive activities, as indicated by the first two in the list, can be harnessing the full range of emerging adolescent intelligences.

CREATIVE POSSIBILITIES

Can creativity be learned?

Many teachers undoubtedly feel uncomfortable about the idea of teaching creatively, for, like leadership, they argue it cannot be learnt. You are either born with it or not. They may go on to suggest that you can teach art or management but not creativity or leadership. Whilst there is a grain of truth in this, it is only a single seed. It would help the cause of 'creativity teaching' if we conceptualize it as a particular 'state of mind' rather than as an 'imaginative activity'. Teachers could then create an environment in which creativity can thrive, instead of worrying so much about whether they are being 'imaginative' enough to pass on their talents to their pupils. Lenny Henry, the comedian, makes this case very compellingly:

> There are people in the world who have to create to live – it's just something they have to do. There are others who live to create. And then there are people (most of us I think) who are creative, but don't know what to do with it – how to use it. I think these people could be nudged in the right direction by teachers. (Lenny Henry, quoted in NACCCE, 1999, p. 58)

Teachers can help merge the objectives of creative survival with the desire and satisfaction of being creative.

There are four key conditions for creative learning which are particularly relevant in the school context.

1. *The need to be challenged* both by having goals set for us and by being helped to set our own. We need this to be done in a supportive but demanding atmosphere where, if we fail, we learn from that failure.
2. *The elimination of negative stress.* If the brain is over-stressed, it ceases to operate at higher levels. Our most primitive survival instincts take over and dominate. Sometimes it is clear that stress has become so endemic in a school that neither pupils nor teachers can give expression to their full selves.
3. *Feedback.* Without skilled feedback, we will not learn to distinguish what was quite good from what was stunningly brilliant. We will not learn which approach works better and, most importantly, we will not acquire the habit of internal feedback reflection. With effective high-quality feedback we acquire self-knowledge, deepen our self-esteem and continue to be motivated to learn.
4. *The capacity to live with uncertainty.* Teachers who are seeking to encourage creativity cannot expect to have all the answers. However, they can offer robust and workable alternative structures and processes to their pupils which can be developed and personalized. Creative teachers are interested in knowledge, but they are more interested in skills and even more interested in attitudes and values. They are hungry to learn themselves and keen to pass on their 'appetite' for their chosen interest.

Some people argue that creativity is domain specific, that the same individual can be creative in science but not in geography, for example. I disagree. Too often creativity is confused with confidence. While I agree with much of what Howard Gardner argues about intelligences, he is wrong when he says that:

> Creativity differs from intelligence in two additional respects. First the creative person is always operating in a domain or discipline or craft. One is not creative in general; even Leonardo da Vinci, perhaps the world's ultimate Renaissance man . . . was creative in certain domains, like painting and invention, and not nearly as creative in other. (Gardner, 1999, p. 117)

I would argue that it is a matter of complete conjecture as to whether Leonardo da Vinci was or was not creative in a range of areas not known to Howard Gardner! It also seems to me that when you read further into *Intelligences Reframed*, it does not limit creativity to domains. It appears to me that Gardner is positioning creativity as an overarching intelligence itself. As I argued earlier, I believe that creativity is a 'state of mind' and not another intelligence.

Learner-centred creativity

At the heart of the relationship between a creative teacher and their pupils is a respect for the individual learner. The following list gives an indication of some of the ways in which respect for an individual's creativity can be encouraged:

* Being respectful rather than dismissive.
* Encouraging active not passive learning.
* Supporting individual interests rather than standardized curriculums.
* Engaging many learning styles not one.
* Encouraging and exploring emotional responses.
* Posing questions not statements.
* Offering ambiguity rather than certainties.
* Being open-ended rather than closing-down.
* Being known as surprising rather than predictable.
* Offering many patterns rather than a standardized model.
* Moving the 'classroom' to varied environments.
* Recognizing multiple intelligences.
* Including visual representations as well as auditory ones.
* Including tactile and experience-based activity.
* Stimulating social as well as private learning.

It is most important to be clear that this is not a charter for a 'liberal' classroom with little structure or assessment of achievement. In fact it is the reverse. As Professor Susan Greenfield (quoted in NACCCE, 1999, p. 62) has put it: 'Original thought, and respect for originality of others, must surely lie at the heart not just of creativity, but also individuality – our only chance of twenty-first century escape from zombie-ness.'

The Campaign for Learning MORI poll, cited earlier, also reveals pupil preferences for learning. The top five choices were:

1. Work in small groups to solve a problem: 33 per cent.
2. Work on a computer: 33 per cent.
3. Have a class discussion: 28 per cent.
4. Talk about my work with a teacher: 22 per cent.
5. Take notes while my teacher talks to me: 22 per cent.

Pupils think that they should spend less time listening to teachers and more on problem-solving with computers. They would like a more varied diet of activities than they currently receive. It seems entirely worthwhile to ask learners for their views. After all, it is their levels of self-esteem, confidence and motivation which will determine whether the environment is likely to be one in which they can engage their intelligences creatively.

CREATIVITY IN PRACTICE

I can think of no better example of creativity in practice than Coombes County Infant School in Arborfield, near Reading. The school's headteacher [co-author of Chapter 12, page 159], Sue Humphries, and her staff, demonstrate how it is possible to provide an environment in which creativity can thrive. Everything about the site challenges conventional expectations. The grounds of the school are the most powerful statement of the power of interest in individuality and care that I know. Once a barren, featureless space, it is now a haven for both wildlife and the young imagination of children. It contains ponds, trees, sculptures and flowers, sheep graze on the sports field and mini-beasts of all kinds scuttle around in a range of conducive habitats. An amphitheatre provides an outdoor theatrical and musical space. Huge stones replicating Stonehenge are set in the ground. Everywhere there are seats and interesting objects to be sat under or played on. You can find almost every species of willow on the site. There are linguistic and mathematical puzzles to be solved and there are curious biological experiments under way. The external environment shouts creativity at any visitor.

Indoors is the same. On a Friday in October 1999, the school played host to the launch of Family Learning Weekend. The place was alive with parents and visitors, but to me, as someone who had visited the school on many occasions, the interesting thing was that there was not much that was different from a typical Coombes day. In one class there was a museum with chairs from down the years brought in by staff, parents and borrowed from collections. A world of history lay beneath your bottom in a most imaginative and intriguing way. In another class there was an artist painting the scene from the window with her young apprentices sketching away at her feet. Outside, birds of prey were on show so that anyone could fathom the difference between a kestrel and a sparrow hawk. Opportunities for textiles work, study in the grounds and computer learning were abundant, and to illustrate all this the school has developed an excellent intranet site.

But it is the social environment which interests me even more. No one shouts at Coombes. Everyone is respectful and each child is treated as an individual. You can see this from the quality of the exchanges between staff and pupils, for the staff are deeply skilled in questioning skills. They know when to leave space for thought and when to supply the structure which will help a child to grow and learn. It was no surprise to me to read the school's stunning OFSTED report. And herein lies a conundrum. If Coombes can be truly creative and raise standards in a mixed catchment area with a shifting population of army services children, why cannot all schools? If Coombes can do what it wants within the National Curriculum and meet the attainment targets of Her Majesty's Inspectorate, why cannot all schools? The answer, of course, is leadership. Coombes is the result of an extraordinary talent and visionary, Sue Humphries. Sue is a headteacher in a million and has consequently gathered around her an extraordinary staff and network of innovative educators. Having said that, creativity is too important to be left to the happenstance of a spectacularly creative headteacher. On every one of the indicators listed on page 40, Coombes scores as the kind of place where a young Leonardo da Vinci would be able to discover that his creativity could come alive in many domains beyond painting and invention.

UNDERPINNING CREATIVITY

Learning to learn

I started by saying that we need to reassess what we know about how we learn most effectively. And this is exactly what 24 schools are currently exploring in a Campaign for Learning action research project, Learning to Learn. It is the intention of the project that, by engaging 'the heart' of what it is to be an effective learner, we will make significant progress in understanding more about the conditions which are likely to foster creativity. The map in Figure 2.1 (opposite) gives the clearest indication of our core concerns.

As I said at the beginning of this chapter, I believe creativity is a 'state of mind'. It requires the capacity to live with complexity and uncertainty. It will be difficult to nurture it in communities where only certainty is rewarded.

Living creatively

By way of an end-piece, I thought I should share an example from my own life. In the list of things that may foster creativity, I included the idea of 'supporting individual interests'. I appreciate that this is a difficult aspiration to fulfil in the school environment. It is easier at home. Essentially it involves making space in your life for what is most important to you. My wife, Henrietta, and I believe this is the heart of our own creative development. In the world of faxes, e-mails and noise I described earlier, finding space for yourselves and for your family, for the interests you wish to pursue and for the friends to whom you wish to be more deeply attached is very important.

We take time out every summer to spend a couple of days reviewing what our priorities are to be for the coming year, life-planning for the time ahead. We walk, think, talk, dream and actively search for our next steps together. If we do not actively develop our own creativity, time passes us by and we can only regret the missed opportunities. There were three results from last year's review. Henrietta decided to find out more about becoming a professional wildlife pho-

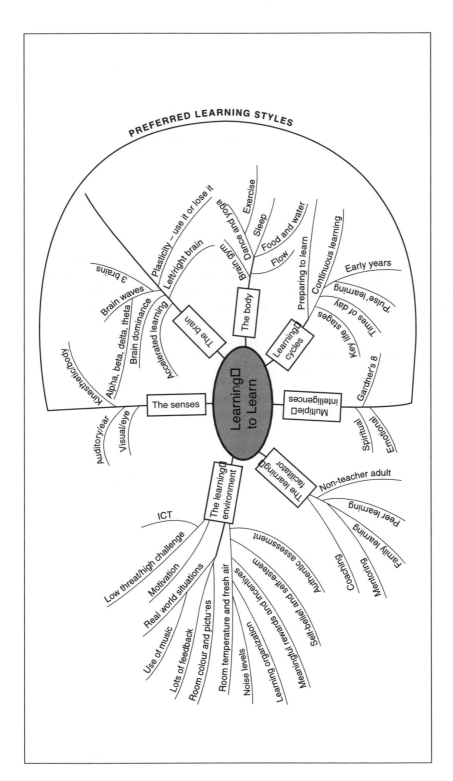

Figure 2.1: What is learning to learn?

tographer, I determined to write a book about the mind. And both of us promised to create a large wildlife pond in our garden with our son, Thomas. These are small steps in the great scheme of things, but the fact that each has happened or is happening now reinforces our belief that we can determine our own creative opportunities. In an ever-changing world we need to carry on learning throughout our lives, and how we do so is critically important. My strong hunch is that those who do so successfully, while actively seeking to develop their own creativity, will become more fulfilled and happy: as well as making lots of mistakes along the way, of course.

In order to actualize creativity in schools I would like to see greater co-ordinated thought in two areas. First, far more attention needs to be given to the kernel of the teacher's pedagogy – an understanding of how we learn to learn. This will be the key skill of the twenty-first century, the means of unlocking the creative potential within us all. As Guy Claxton puts it: 'Learning to learn is the lifelong shadow of learning itself' (Claxton, 1999, p. 9). Second, I am convinced that more structured interventions by creative mentors and coaches in school environments will be essential, binding the real worlds of families into the formal educational structure. To achieve this every school needs to have a member of staff identified and resourced as a 'family learning co-ordinator'. The wealth of talent in our schools is a deep one. Let us hope that, in this century, every teacher and every pupil will leave their school feeling that they have experienced a place where their creativity has been nurtured.

REFERENCES

Bayliss, V. (1999) *Redefining Work*. London: RSA.

Claxton, G. (1999) *Wise Up: The Challenge of Lifelong Learning*. London: Bloomsbury.

Gardner, H. (1983) *Frames of Mind: The Theory of Multiple Intelligences*. New York: Basic Books.

Gardner, H. (1999) *Intelligences Reframed: Multiple Intelligences for the 21st Century*. New York: Basic Books.

Lucas, B. and Greany, T. (2000) *Learning to Learn: Setting the Agenda for Schools in the 21st Century*. London: Campaign for Learning.

National Advisory Committee on Creative and Cultural Education (NACCCE) (1999) *All our Futures: Creativity, Culture and Education*. London: DFEE.

Woodhead, C. (2000) Annual lecture by Her Majesty's Chief Inspector of Schools, RSA, London, February.

Chapter 3

'Little c Creativity'

Anna Craft

ROUTE-FINDING THROUGH UNCERTAINTY

In previous writing, (Craft, 1996a, 1997a; 1997b; Craft and Lyons, 1996; Craft *et al.*, 1997), I have developed a concept of 'little c creativity' (LCC). It is a concept which I postulated as one which may be helpful in looking at the education of young children at the start of the twenty-first century. As the uncertainties of life in industrialized societies at the start of the twenty-first century seem to increase, patterns of life which may have been more predictable in earlier times are now much less so. This is the case in a variety of ways, for example:

- *Social structures*, where families, communities and individuals mesh much less predictably than in earlier times.
- *The economy*, both local and global. Here a range of factors including the pace of change, reduced market certainties, the mixing of previously state-run enterprises with the private sector, the interconnectedness of individual countries with the global economy and changing demographics across different countries, means that the face and shape of the marketplace is changing rapidly. It is certainly the case that some aspects of economic change have involved a uniformity in the marketplace, where national and multinational business conglomerates operate both production and retail parts of the economy, thus going beyond local culture and custom. However, alongside the apparent uniformities, where one now expects to see the same chain stores evident in the high street of all small towns, nevertheless the pace of change is such that individuals working within the economy cannot expect jobs for life or even to be able to use specific skills for life. And as consumers, individuals find themselves faced by a plethora of short shelf-life choices.
- *Technology,* and the spiral of change associated with it, is another element

which brings uncertainty to individuals' lives at the start of the twenty-first century. Information and communication technology in particular pervades all aspects of life including buying a bar of chocolate, travelling on a bus and getting money out of a bank account. Computers help to run almost all aspects of life, and are thus in the background for us all. An increasing percentage of the population have their own personal computer which gives them, potentially, access to a rapidly shifting information system which is worldwide and instantaneous.

One of the effects of the intensification of change in each of these elements of society – social relations, the economy and technology – is that individuals are required to be increasingly self-directed, for it would appear that during the twenty-first century, these qualities will be even more in demand. One way of describing the quality of self-direction might be 'little c creativity', or LCC, which involves the quality of personal agency. For, I have suggested, it is LCC which enables individuals to find routes and paths to 'travel' in many aspects of their lives.

LCC AS DISTINCT FROM HIGH CREATIVITY

'Little c creativity' is distinct from 'high creativity', which I take to mean the extraordinary creativity of the genius, in any particular field such as science, art, dance, mathematics, etc. High creativity I take to have certain characteristics, such as innovation/novelty, excellence, recognition by the field within which it takes place and a break with past understandings or perspectives. Many studies of creativity have focused on this extraordinary, paradigm-shifting sort, which many call 'high creativity'. Feldman *et al.* (1994) have suggested that such high creativity is emergent from three nodes of a triangle: the individual, and their talents and interests; the domain in which they operate; and, finally, the field (of judges – of existing, culturally accepted experts). The model works dynamically. The admission of new creative minds into a domain by the field is the recognition of the potential of 'big C creativity'; in other words, of the kind of creativity which actually changes the domain, they refashion it. The people who are high creators are those who change domains of knowledge, or create new ones.

The psychological literature on high creativity focuses on a range of aspects of the concept, including persons, processes, products and, in the case of some writers, places. In order to demonstrate the difference in order between LCC and high creativity, I shall focus on persons, and on the work of Gardner. Thus what follows is illustrative rather than a complete study.

Creative persons

Gardner (1993) has studied personality and biographical factors which may be associated with 'high creativity', by looking at the work and lives of seven great creators (Freud, Einstein, Picasso, Stravinsky, Eliot, Graham and Gandhi), selected for their representation of the seven intelligences. There are, of course, problems with Gardner's selection as he himself admits: the study includes only one woman, it is time-bound and to an extent geographically/culturally bound (to, mainly, early twentieth-century Europe). As each represents work in a specific domain at a specific point in time, it is temporally and content-wise narrow and thus the work of each individual might be challenged from different cultural or temporal contexts.

Similarities between the seven creators included 'rapid growth, once they had committed themselves to a domain' (p. 364). Another common feature was a level of self-absorption and self-promotion, in the interests of the work itself. Another similarity was 'the amalgamation of the childlike and the adult like' (p. 365). Gardner noted that each experienced a feeling of being under siege during their 'greatest creative tension' (p. 367).

He also noted social-psychological similarities, for example that love, within the homes in which they each grew up, 'seems to have been conditioned on achievement' (p. 367), that each household was quite strict, so that 'ultimately, each of the creators rebelled against control' (p. 367), that each creator had a personal sense of social marginality, which they used 'as a leverage in work' (p. 368) to the extent that 'whenever they risked becoming members of "the establishment" they would again shift course to attain at least intellectual marginality' (p. 368). He also described the ten-year cycle of creativity experienced by each of these individuals, consisting of initial break-through followed by consolidation, succeeded ten years later by a subsequent breakthrough which was more integrative, and so on and so on. He indicates that each of these creators was 'productive each day' (p. 372), and that in the nature of their creativity, each demonstrated the capacity to identify and then explore 'asynchrony' or dissonance with others within their field of endeavour. For Gardner, asynchrony refers to 'a lack of fit, an unusual pattern' (p. 41). Breaking away from an established wisdom is in his view an essential aspect of the creative process as demonstrated by these seven individuals.

In his more recent study of the extraordinary mind Gardner (1997) develops a new taxonomy of creativity, distinguishing four types of extraordinary creator: masters, makers, introspectors and influencers. This taxonomy comes out of the different foci which human beings have. Influencers and introspectors are people who are particularly involved in the world of human beings: introspectors, in their own world, and influencers, in trying to influence other people. Makers and masters can be interested in anything, including people. But they tend to approach it not through direct contact but more through ideas, and through symbolic representation in domains. They tend to be writers and scientists. Makers and masters, then, are oriented towards domains. Influencers and introspectors are oriented towards people. From an early age, people seem to be drawn either towards people or towards objects.

Gardner (1997) also identifies three characteristics of extraordinary or high creators, whatever part of the taxonomy they represent:

- *Reflection*: making time to reflect, in a variety of ways.
- *Leveraging*: picking out what they are good at and really pushing that.
- *Framing*: the spin put on things which do not work out. Creative people neither ignore nor are put off by failure but instead ask 'What can I learn from this?' – the ability to look defeat in the eye and say 'What can I learn from this?' Great creators have learned this lesson well.

These three qualities (Gardner, 1997) may also be appropriate and relevant to the creativity of ordinary people. Certainly some of the characteristics of high creators (childlike qualities, feeling under siege, being on the edge, high energy and productivity) which Gardner identifies in *Creating Minds* (1993), also emerged as a characteristic of 'ordinary' educators in one of my research projects (Craft, 1996a; Craft and Lyons, 1996). So, we might expect to see some of the qualities described above, in ordinary individuals: the childlike playfulness, the feeling of being under siege whilst being creative, the connection between love and achievement, the wish to be 'on the edge', high energy and productivity, and so on. And, of course, it could be that each kind of creativity involves different personal responses. For parents and teachers, the feeling of being under siege, for example, is very common!

One further position posited by Gardner is that creativity is not a single entity (Craft, 1996b). He suggests it is not therefore psychometrically ascertainable, for example, as 'thinking diversely, or divergently', around which tests can be constructed. His argument is that such tests, although reliable (i.e. they can be replicated), are not particularly valid for creative thinking. It is not the case, for example, that people who are good at thinking up many uses for a rubber band, or a brick, are particularly creative. It is conversely not the case that creative people are able to come up with many uses for a rubber band or a brick. Nevertheless, many psychologists continue to use this singular, narrow definition of creativity, which is also closely associated with an approach to measuring psychological phenomena through norm-distributed, product-defined, psychological tests.

Gardner suggests that creativity is the ability to solve problems or fashion products, and to raise new questions (an important issue to confront in education). He suggests that creative individuals do this regularly. It is their mode of existence. Something that is creative has to be both novel and has to be accepted (though of course the acceptance is cultural, and values related, and thus we have to pay attention to the domain in which people are creative). He emphasizes, with his colleagues Feldman and Czikszentmihalyi (Feldman *et al.*, 1994), the individuality of each person's creativity, and the mix of skills and domains which it may draw upon and be expressed within. Together they emphasize as valid demonstrations of creativity, performance in real-life scenarios rather than in dry, theoretical ones.

The point of this trawl through some of Gardner's recent studies of high creativity has been to form a starting point for distinguishing between high and ordinary creativity, or BCC ('big C creativity') and LCC ('little c creativity'). 'Little c creativity', by contrast, focuses on the resourcefulness and agency of ordinary people, rather than the extraordinary contributions and insights of the few. It has to do with a 'can-do' attitude to 'real life' as may become clear from the discussion of examples and counter-examples, which I examine next.

Examples and counter-examples

What follows are examples of behaviour that might be described as LCC, and an example of behaviour which might not be.

Inventing a meal

Working out how to cook something with a very limited range of ingredients, would be an example of possibility thinking, the process that I see as being at the heart of LCC. For it seems to me that this is a situation in which habitual or familiar options are closed down, due to the limitation in the range of ingredients. Thus, considering other possibilities becomes necessary if something is to be cooked at all. The person concerned must generate and implement possibilities – or at least, one possibility. This example involves taking some action in the world to overcome a potential blockage.

But, what makes this *creative* as opposed to a basic coping strategy? One response to this might be that LCC is indeed a concept invented to describe engagement with the everyday challenges of life, particularly in the context of intensification and change as described above.

So, is 'little c creativity' then to mean the same as 'coping with life'? To this I would want to respond that they are not necessarily synonymous terms. For, 'coping with life' must cover an enormous spectrum of responses, from those involving active engagement with the challenges life produces, to those involving complete disengagement with these. Both ends of the spectrum might be described as coping with life. But in the concept of LCC, I highlight the kind of response that involves active engagement.

This is not to say that a response will necessarily be 'thought through' as opposed to intuitive. For one person making new food combinations through limited ingredients may do so through 'feel' and intuition, where another might do so through 'thinking it through' in a more step-by-step fashion. What they both have in common however, I would suggest, is the use of prior knowledge about the ingredients and what could be done with them.

So, we might now ask, would an 'accidental' food combination count as an example of 'little c creativity'? In other words, if two of the ingredients accidentally got mixed together and formed an edible dish, would this count as creative? Here I would want to draw a line, and to suggest that for an outcome to be judged as creative there must have been some conscious intention involved in its creation. This distinguishes fantasies and dreams from acts of creativity. But, our questioner might persist, what if the accidental combination was indeed a workable meal? Surely it could, ultimately, be regarded as a creative outcome? For, perhaps just as significant as intention, is 'recognition' that something useful has been created.

So far then, we are getting a picture from this example, of LCC as involving the active and intentional taking of action in the world, as a way of coping with everyday challenges, which may involve knowledge-based intuition just as much as step-by-step thought.

But, we might ask, surely something that is creative must be in some way or other innovative? Does the example of inventing a meal involve innovation? Here the question is raised of the context of innovation. I want to propose that there may be a spectrum of innovation, at one end of which is something which is novel to the agent but not necessarily to the wider world, and at the other end of which is novelty to the wider world. Given this spectrum, the example of inventing a meal *may* involve innovation at either end of the spectrum. On the other hand, this example may not *necessarily* involve innovation, for a person may be faced with the same limited range of ingredients on more than one occasion and may thus learn a repertoire of coping responses in terms of successfully producing meals from these.

So far then, we are getting a picture from this example, of LCC:

- as involving the active, conscious and intentional taking of action in the world;
- as a way of coping with everyday challenges, which may involve knowledge-based intuition just as much as step-by-step thought;
- as involving innovation (which the particular example given may or may not include).

Let us take a look at a second instance of LCC, in order to draw out some further generalizations about it. The following two examples are based on people known to the author, and are used with their permission. Real names have not been used. I acknowledge that the examples beg questions about the context of actions taken by the individuals and about culturally based (and potentially biased) interpretations of these actions. However, I hold to the examples as useful illustrations of what LCC might or might not include.

Norah

Now in her mid-thirties, Norah came to England in her early twenties from rural Kenya, hoping to study as an undergraduate here, and then to work. Having discovered both difficult to attain, she adjusted her goals and registered instead with an employment agency providing cleaners. She also began evening classes in dressmaking. Within months she had negotiated with her employers for direct work which meant she no longer paid a cut to the agency. She made such good progress in the dressmaking course and enjoyed it so much that she persuaded one employer to loan her their sewing machine, and progressed on to a more advanced course on soft furnishings. Three years later she had set up a small business, making curtains and other soft furnishings alongside her cleaning work. In her late twenties Norah married and a year later began a family. She was able to continue her soft furnishing business in the early years and later returned to cleaning for many of her former employers, having a loyalty towards them. She has plans, as her children grow older, to develop her sewing skills further, venturing into the fashion industry. She currently studies fashion at evening classes in order to help achieve this goal.

She seems to me to demonstrate LCC in her readiness and ability to find her way around blockages to her initial expectations and to make the most of her situation by generating possibilities and believing in her own ability to see ideas through.

The Norah example also involves a development – a 'moving on' in her occupation and self-image. This is a feature that I suggest is implicit in LCC. For if a person is open to possibilities and willing to try options which may lead towards a goal, whether or not this is a goal previously identified, a modified goal (as in the case of Norah) or (as in the case of the inventing a meal example) a goal created through the particular challenge which life has presented, then necessarily what will result is some sort of change, or development.

The Norah example raises another question though. To what extent is LCC about solving problems, to the exclusion of identifying them in the first place? For Norah was faced with an initial set of aims which could not be achieved; these she then modified. Thus, initially, Norah solved a given problem. However, what Norah's story also illustrates is that problem identification is also an aspect of LCC – for at this later stage in her life Norah is now identifying a new set of objectives for herself and her young family, which she is following through in a way which may lead her into a new set of working and parenting arrangements.

What the Norah example seems to illustrate then about LCC is that it involves a development, a 'moving on' and also that it may involve problem identification as well as problem-solving. I want to go on now to look at a counter-example to try and shed some light on what does *not* count as LCC behaviour.

Jimmy

Jimmy is an upholsterer by training. In his early thirties now, he worked from his late teens until his late twenties as an upholsterer for a local small business. When the owner retired however, Jimmy lost his job and has since then worked only sporadically. Initially, with strong encouragement from his partner, John worked as a painter and decorator for one of his friends. That came to an end when Jimmy took a short-notice holiday for three weeks at a busy time of the year, leaving his friend with jobs to fill and nobody to do them. By the time he returned, someone else had filled his spot. Since that time, he has not worked in paid employment. He has found it difficult to seek out any other paid job and has sunk progressively into a despondent pattern of television-watching, beer-drinking, late nights and late mornings. He now takes on some childcare responsibilities in that he collects his two primary-aged children from school, but does this unwillingly, as he does not see this as his role. He feels this despite the fact that the reason his partner is not there for the children in the after-school slot is that she has now taken the initiative and gone back to work as a nanny, to earn the family some income at least.

Jimmy believes that the world is unfair, that he has been punished in some way and that he is unfit for employment. Although he exhibits very macho behaviour when with his male friends, he does not feel at all confident as far as employment is concerned. His attitude and behaviour is a source of conflict between him and his partner and he feels there is no way out.

It seems to me that Jimmy has not exhibited LCC, for, faced with equivalent challenges in his life to those that faced Norah, he is unable to initiate any response to these. He seems to find it impossible to generate possible alternatives and to follow these through to gain a better life for himself. This much seems indisputable.

A question we might ask flowing from Jimmy, is whether LCC is an all-or-nothing attribute, i.e. is it conceivable that Jimmy might have manifested LCC at another stage in his life, for example when leaving school and deciding to become an upholsterer's apprentice, and that indeed he might at a later stage in his life again manifest more LCC? For people are not necessarily consistent across the span of their lives, in their responses to similar instances. Indeed, it might be argued, might we not expect individuals over time and with experience, to get more accomplished at LCC rather than less so? In response to this question I would want to adopt a developmentalist model of LCC, and to suggest that, the more successful experience of LCC an individual has, the more likely they are to continue to operate in this way in other contexts. In addition, as I have argued elsewhere (Craft *et al.*, 1997), the concept of LCC may be a culturally saturated one too, so that in Western culture where the individual and the marketplace are held in high esteem, LCC is a prized virtue. In a more conformist or repressive culture, LCC might be perceived as an inappropriate process, not to be encouraged. Clearly, the cultural context is likely to affect a person's experiences of LCC and their ability to operate it. Of course this may not a necessarily predictable relationship. For example, in a national context where choice and personal autonomy are severely reduced, the culture of finding alternatives may be very strong indeed.

As a counter-example of LCC then, Jimmy's example hopefully demonstrates so far:

- that lacking an ability to operationalize LCC may affect a person's ability to cope with basic challenges which life throws at them, through an inability to

pose questions which may lead to possible ways around blockages or problems;
- that a person's ability to operationalize LCC may vary at times through their life and that the cultural context may have an interaction with this.

This last point is crucial, for my proposal is that LCC can be shaped and encouraged, and thus that schools and our wider education provision have a role to play in fostering it.

So far, what I hope the instances and counter-instance will have helped to clarify is that LCC describes an approach to life which is driven to find solutions and ways through all situations, an approach to life which assumes 'can do'. It contrasts with an attitude of being stuck when faced with uncertainty or blockages. Specific criteria, which I have suggested as separating those behaviours that would count as LCC from those which would not, are that LCC:

- involves the active and intentional taking of action in the world;
- is a way of coping with everyday challenges, which may involve knowledge-based intuition just as much as step-by-step thought;
- involves innovation (which these examples may or may not include);
- involves a 'moving on';
- may involve problem identification as well as problem-solving.

By contrast I have suggested that lacking an ability to operationalize LCC may affect a person's ability to cope with challenges which life throws at them and that a person's ability to operationalize LCC may vary at times through their life. The cultural context may have an interaction with this.

LCC IN ITS POLITICAL CONTEXT

Some might ask, what is LCC for? It might be argued that LCC appears to offer a response to a political context of technical rationality in that it posits an individualist stance of 'resistance' to such an approach to existence. To take an example from within primary education in England in 1999, the current political context can be seen as one in which the artistry of teaching is being undermined by a technicist view of pedagogy. Hence the introduction of a range of centrally drawn-up, compulsory programmes of content to be taught within literacy and numeracy in particular, together with recommended appropriate strategies to achieve the successful 'delivery' of these. For some schools, the implementation of the literacy strategy is compulsory; for others it is not, although other factors have contributed to a majority of primary schools taking up both. The major assumptions about pedagogy which underpin the national strategies for literacy and numeracy appear to be:

- that successful teaching is a 'technical' activity which can be prescribed by policy-makers; and
- that if teachers are 'told' what to do they will be able to carry out instructions in a way which produces high results in learner achievement.

In this context, a teacher who achieves an LCC response to the literacy and numeracy hours (by, for example, working holistically with the curriculum while meeting both pedagogical and curriculum demands of the strategies) may be seen to be offering a form of resistance to such a technicist approach. For he or she is adopting an approach which is driven by an assumption that it is both desirable and possible to have a personal response as a professional which keeps open the possibility that even tightly drawn up instructions may be carried out in a variety of ways. Such a response may be considered by some to be 'resistance' in that it seems to assume that teaching is artistry rather than a technicist activity.

In response to the sort of argument embedded in that kind of example, I want to suggest that certainly LCC is a concept which emphasizes individual agency. On the other hand, LCC is not framed with reference to 'resistance' within a political context; it is not attached to these kinds of extrinsic goals, rather it is posited as a skill which is necessary for individual survival in a rapidly changing and chaotic world. To that extent it is framed as having an extrinsic purpose. I would argue that although LCC may appear to offer a counter-position to what some might call a currently dominant form of political existence, this is not a broader intention embedded within the concept itself. Thus, although LCC may have that effect, it is not a 'political' concept in intention.

A three-way framework for LCC

What follows is an outline of the qualities of LCC, which I have proposed elsewhere in more detail (Craft, 1996a, 1997a, 1997b, 1998a, 1998b; Craft and Lyons, 1996; Craft *et al.*, 1997). I go on to refine and simplify this framework in the final part of the chapter.

At the core of adaptability and flexibility, which the start of the twenty-first century is demanding of people both young and old is, I have suggested, the notion of 'possibility'. Thus LCC involves at its heart, the notion of 'possibility thinking', or asking, in a variety of ways, 'What if?'. So, what are the components of possibility thinking?

I have suggested that possibility thinking involves three necessary perspectives, each offering a different set of dominating issues and values in the exploration of creativity. Each of the three parts of the framework – *agents*, *processes* and *domains* – offers a 'frame' or a perspective through which to both observe and also foster creativity. All are necessary parts of the whole.

Agents
The term 'agent' implies activity undertaken by the person concerned. I want to propose that each individual plays out their LCC in a unique way, according to their talents, skills and aspirations. The ways in which an individual path-finds through their life will reflect choices which they make both consciously and non-consciously. Choices will be played out in the styles of operating in the world with which the individual is familiar and comfortable; these may be influenced by the surrounding culture as well as features of the individual. Choices will reflect knowledge available to them, as well as their strengths and weaknesses in making use of certain kinds of knowledge. There may be 'essentialist' or general characteristics which are displayed by individuals who display highly developed LCC. 'Essentialist' implies that these characteristics somehow capture the 'essence' of LCC. For example, a person with high LCC enters life situations with the attitude of 'What if?' – which implies a positive, open approach to possibilities which could develop. And the notion of 'development' is important, for it seems to me that implicit in it is change. Ultimately then, agency involves change.

Acts of LCC necessarily involve being 'in relationship' with someone or something, or both – one cannot be creative with respect to nothing.

Processes
The processes that LCC draws upon may include intuitive and non-conscious ones as well as others that are rational and/or conscious. It has been suggested that even Aristotle's own rationalist work on the virtues acknowledges the less rationalist, less cognitive and perhaps less predictable roles of the intuitive, affective and conative (Tobin, 1989). 'Little c creativity' also involves using one's imagination; not being satisfied with what already exists, but considering other possibilities, which may include ones we do not yet know about. It may therefore involve both problem-solving and problem-finding. It may involve both divergent and convergent thinking.

In addition, processes may also be external to the individual. From my empirical work, artists in particular report feeling that they are being directed by 'universal' forces which are external to themselves (Craft and Lyons, 1996). Such findings echo the notions put forward by Abraham *et al.* (1992), who suggest a powerful relationship between chaos, creativity and imagination, and the soul of the world. It is also close to the perspective argued for by some scientists (for example, Bohm and Peat, 1989) who suggest that underneath the 'explicate' world (i.e. what we experience as the reality of our lives) is an 'implicate' one, external to individuals, but 'in connection' with them, which involves generative potential. As scientists, they suggest that we need to foster our access to the implicate orders which underpin our explicate understandings, for they are the source of our creativity.

Domains

Just as Dearden (1968) argues that 'creativity . . . is not confined to the arts' (p. 147), I have proposed that LCC is a notion which applies to any domain. It is not purely about the creative arts. The importance of acknowledging the role of domain was first highlighted by Feldman *et al*. (1994). 'Little c creativity' is, I would argue, about *all* knowledge, not simply the academic domains but all of life. Considering the many domains of creativity also reminds us that the personal agency and process aspects of creativity are only a part of the picture, and not the whole of it.

The dimensions of creativity which I have introduced as forming the three-way framework are, I have suggested, the components of a 'way of life' – possibility thinking.

NECESSARY QUALITIES OF POSSIBILITY THINKING

I want to propose a number of qualities, or features, in possibility thinking, which are all necessary for LCC.

Self-determination and direction

These, it seems to me, are fundamentally necessary to enable personal route-finding in life, at a variety of levels from the mundane to the significant. A person could not be said to be manifesting LCC if they were not also exhibiting these qualities.

Innovation

For something to be considered creative at all it must involve a degree of innovation (i.e. 'doing it differently'). It seems to me innovation is therefore necessary even if the outcome is not yet observable. A creative outcome may be an idea and not yet in the public domain for scrutiny. Certainly, I would argue, a person could not be said to be showing LCC behaviour if this did *not* involve innovation. I have suggested (Craft, 1999) as has the National Advisory Committee for Creative and Cultural Education (1999) that there is a spectrum of novelty or innovation. Thus at one end is something which is novel to the child, but not necessarily to the wider world. At the other are ideas or actions which are novel in the eyes of a wider field. 'Little c creativity' may often involve novelty or innovation for the agent, but not in a wider field. As discussed earlier, formulations of high creativity such as that of Feldman *et al*. (1994) put more emphasis on originality in a field.

Action

It seems to me that action must also be necessary to LCC. For without some sort of action, even if this is an idea and is not yet operationalized, it is not creative.

Thus a person could not be said to be exhibiting LCC if there were no action (even an idea) which was an outcome of their deliberation or processing.

Development

Innovation and action will lead inevitably to development, and LCC is about continual development on to a new 'place'. This can be observed empirically, as shown in the example of Norah earlier in the chapter. My proposal is that development is another necessary element to LCC, for without some sort of development, LCC cannot be said to have occurred.

Depth

I have argued (Craft, 1988; 1999) that unless one recognizes what it is that one has done either in ideas or in action, the result cannot be said to be truly creative as opposed to serendipitous chance. Here I want to raise a question about the use of the term 'depth' however. It may not be the most appropriate term to describe what is meant here. 'Awareness of convention' might be more appropriate since what is meant is knowing that one has been creative with reference to previous convention (either one's own or that of a wider field). In this, what I am suggesting is in accord with Warnock's (1977) discussion of learning – hers is set in the context of the scope of the school curriculum. She suggests that deep concentration on one area through specialization is far more likely to lead to an imaginative response than is a superficial trawl through a lot of different subjects.

Risk

Risk as defined in my earlier writings means 'not knowing how one's ideas may land', or 'turn out'. My emphasis is on the possibility that the intended result may not occur (e.g. finding a new route to drive home may not yield the result, trying out a new combination of food for a meal may or may not work, a musician trying a new career path may hit on something which works for them, but may not – and so on).

To establish whether risk is necessary to LCC, we need to focus on the meaning of risk. It seems to me that there is a spectrum of what could be meant. At one end of the spectrum, risk may be taken to mean 'the possibility that the intended result may not occur'. On this interpretation, it seems to me that *any* act or thought may involve risk in this sense, but that does not of itself make any act or thought creative. In other words, risk in this sense is not sufficient as a condition for LCC to occur. On the other hand, at the other end of the spectrum is a definition of risk, which involves much more personal investment in the possibility that the intended result may occur, or may not occur. In other words, the agent's weighing of possible benefits and losses as outcomes, are part of what entices them to take the risk or avoid it. It is this end of the spectrum, which I want to suggest, is necessary for acts of LCC. For unless the outcome matters, and unless there is a motivation and intention by the agent to achieve a certain kind of outcome, it seems to me that an act cannot be called an act of LCC.[1] It is this movement towards intention then, which lies at the root of proposing risk as necessary to LCC. I am suggesting that an act cannot be called one of LCC if a risk, which matters to the agent, has *not* been taken.

It rather looks as though risk and development/change may be interconnected, too; a general point, which also applies to other necessary features.

Being imaginative

I would argue that coming up with a possibility which is novel and unexpected, by seeing more than is evident initially, must be necessary for LCC. For an outcome that is *not* novel or unexpected could not be considered to be a product of LCC.

Posing questions

In my earlier writing I have defined the posing of questions as being at root about openness to possibility. Here it seems to me that logically, LCC must involve openness to possibility, for otherwise new possibilities cannot be conceived of. Thus I want to suggest that the posing of questions is a necessary feature of LCC. For LCC could not be achieved without openness to possibility in the posing of questions.

Play

I argue in my previous writing that play, as in being open to playing with ideas and new possibilities/combinations, is logically necessary to LCC. I would hold to this in that, without toying with possibilities, new ones cannot be opened up.

Overall then, it seems to me that all the features are necessary. In discussing risk, I also noted that some might be interconnected with others.

The interconnections might go something like this. The first cluster of concepts could be seen as concerned with activity and with outcomes, or 'ends'. Some of the cluster appears to be logically interrelated also. To take development: it is difficult to see how development could take place without change also taking place. Similarly innovation must logically involve change. In turn, development and change must logically lead to an outcome even if this is an idea. If we are talking of activities involving self-determination, it is hard to see how a person could exhibit this in their life without change and development occurring. Although a person may be operating self-determination and choose to remain unchanged in some way – an idea which has been put forward by Glover

(1988) in his discussion of self-creation. Risk, in the strong sense defined above (i.e. of something mattering enough to the agent for there to be some risk of failing in undertaking an idea or action), also is surely logically connected to outcomes, for risk in LCC is defined in relationship to outcomes.

The second cluster of concepts, being imaginative, posing questions and play, may also be seen as interconnected. The posing of questions within 'possibility thinking' on the one hand and play on the other, are at times connected, in that play may sometimes (although not always) involve possibility thinking. Both imaginativeness and creativity involve a questioning core of 'possibility thinking'. The overarching reason for suggesting that these three concepts might be clustered together is that by contrast with the first cluster these may all be described as being to do with the generative processes of creativity itself.

Two concepts, however, which cut across the two cluster groupings which I am suggesting, are 'innovation' and 'imaginativeness', for imaginativeness involves having new ideas.

The interconnections discussed above have not been acknowledged in my earlier work and would lead to a simpler, cluster structure for LCC, one to do with self-determination, action, innovation, risk and development, and the other to do with being imaginative, posing questions and play. This cluster structure will need further examination in future work.

SUMMARY

Summing up, then, I have suggested:

- that life in the twenty-first century demands of ordinary people that they develop 'little c creativity' as a life skill, and that this is the business of learners and teachers alike;
- that LCC is distinct from 'high creativity';
- that what counts as LCC is determined by the extent to which the agent is intentionally open to exploring possibilities and is taking action in the world. It may include problem-finding as well as problem-solving and is a way of coping with everyday challenges which may involve knowledge-based intuition just as much as step-by-step thought. 'Little c creativity' involves innovation and it involves development. I believe that LCC can be fostered, indeed that children need to be initiated into it, and thus that there is an important role for education to play here;
- being unable to operationalize LCC may affect a person's ability to cope with basic challenges which life throws at them, through an inability to pose questions which may lead to possible ways around blockages or problems;
- a person's ability to operationalize LCC may vary at times through their life and the cultural context may have an interaction with this;
- although LCC may appear to offer a counter-position to a technical–rationalist approach to life, it is not a 'political' concept in intention;

- that LCC can be understood from the tripartite perspective of agents, processes and domains;
- that nine features are necessary to LCC. I have also suggested that they may be interrelated in a way, which could lead to a simpler structure of two clusters of necessary features, which may bear future investigation;
- the attempt to identify an holistic framework for understanding LCC is, it seems to me, essential if we are to have a grip on how to enable individuals in route-finding, in the twenty-first century.

ACKNOWLEDGEMENTS

I am grateful to my previous and current co-authors as well as to staff and students in the Department of History and Philosophy of Education at London University Institute of Education, for discussions of these ideas over the past several years. In particular I would like to thank Professor John White, my PhD supervisor, for encouraging my study and critique of the concept of LCC through the lens of philosophy of education. Thanks are also due to my two co-editors, Bob Jeffrey and Mike Leibling, for close and constructive criticism of the ideas in this chapter. I hope I have done justice to issues raised by all of these readers.

NOTE

1. Both ends of the spectrum may be affected by the agent's perception of the role of probability in any potential action they may take. Perceptions of probability are in turn likely to be influenced by previous behaviour patterns and past experience, which contribute to the way in which the agent perceives themselves.

REFERENCES

Abraham, R., McKenna, T. and Sheldrake, R. (1992) *Trialogues at the Edge of the West: Chaos, Creativity and the Re-Sacralization of the World.* Santa Fe, NM: Bear and Co.

Bohm, D. and Peat, P. D. (1989) *Science, Order and Creativity.* London: Routledge.

Craft, A. (1988) 'A Study of Imagination'. Unpublished MA thesis, London University, Institute of Education.

Craft, A. (1996a) 'Nourishing educator creativity: a holistic approach to CPD', *British Journal of In-service Education,* **22**(3), 309–22.

Craft, A. (1996b) *Proceedings of Creativity in Education Colloquium on Multiple Intelligences and Creativity with Professor Howard Gardner, July 1997.* Milton Keynes: Open University School of Education.

Craft, A. and Lyons, T. (1996) *Nourishing the Educator.* Milton Keynes: The Open University Seminar Network Occasional Paper Series.

Craft, A. (1997a) 'Identity and creativity: educating for post-modernism?', *Teacher Development: An International Journal of Teachers' Professional Development,* **1**(1), 83–96.

Craft, A. (1997b) 'Nourishing the educator'. Paper presented at the 7th International

Conference on Thinking, Session 3.1.9, Singapore, June.

Craft, A. (1998a) 'Holistic postgraduate learning: evaluation of a UK-based innovation', *Analytic Teaching*, **18**(2).

Craft, A. (1998b) 'UK educator perspectives on creativity', *Journal of Creative Behavior*, **32**(4), 244–57

Craft, A. (1999) 'Creative development in the early years: implications of policy for practice', *The Curriculum Journal*, **10**(1), 135–50.

Craft, A. with Dugal, J., Dyer, G., Jeffrey, B. and Lyons, T. (1997) *Can You Teach Creativity?* Nottingham: Education Now.

Dearden, R. F. (1968) *The Philosophy of Primary Education*. London: Routledge and Kegan Paul.

Feldman, D. H., Czikszentmihalyi, M. and Gardner, H. (1994) *Changing the World: A Framework for the Study of Creativity*. Westport, CT and London: Praeger.

Gardner, H. (1993) *Creating Minds*. New York: Basic Books.

Gardner, H. (1997) *Extraordinary Minds: Portraits of Four Exceptional Minds and the Extraordinary Minds in All of Us*. New York: HarperCollins.

Glover, J. (1988) *I: The Philosophy and Psychology of Personal Identity*. London: Allen Lane, Penguin Press.

National Advisory Committee for Creative and Cultural Education (NACCCE) (1999) *All our Futures: Creativity, Culture and Education*. London: DFEE.

Tobin, B. (1989) 'An Aristotelian theory of moral development', *Journal of Philosophy of Education*, **23**(2), 195–211.

Warnock, M. (1977) *Schools of Thought*. London: Faber & Faber.

Chapter 4

Creative Literacy

Peter Woods

'I love reading', my 90-year-old mother-in-law is always reminding us. She needs to repeat it occasionally as if to reinforce the point with herself. Her life is sustained by reading, whether it be a quiet, programmed read during the day, or an activity to occupy and restore her mind when she cannot sleep at night. 'It's better than the pornographic films they have on TV in the night,' she says. 'They make you feel worse.' Her favourite television programme is snooker, because she can read at the same time. Snooker, like cricket, creates a nice ambience for reading. She is a regular visitor at the weekly library van, changing the six heavy large-print books she has read over the last week. It is a slight problem when we go on holiday. 'What have you got in this case, Nan?'

'Where's Jack?' Thomas, my 18-month-old grandson, has had his bath, his hair is combed, face shining, fingers in mouth, he smells, unusually, of cleanliness, and he is uncommonly quiet and still. He studies the book intently. Jack is getting ready for bed. He's looking for his slippers. Thomas lifts a flap on the page to reveal the missing objects. Now Jack wants his dressing gown, and lo, there it is hanging in the cupboard. Now some toys . . . Thomas loves reading. I do not know what is going on in his head but his concentration, his apparent ability to follow the narrative, and to interact with the book as if sharing in the making of the story is remarkable. Sometimes he insists on a marathon session, bringing you all the books from his considerable library, one after the other, for you to read with him. Some of them are so good we have to have several immediate repeat readings. Thomas loves reading.

Books can sustain you. They are a lifeline. I remember as a child a book we had in our house called *The World in Pictures*. It had no covers, just the sepia pictures, of things like New Zealand geysers, and a man in funny dress blowing an alpenhorn on a Swiss mountainside. We had very few books, so this to me was a masterwork, a transportation to the whole wide world, at times when you seemed most constrained, as on cold, wet afternoons. 'What can I do?' I was always asking my mother. This book was one of her main resources. I recently visited New Zealand to visit my daughter. When she asked me what I would like to see, I said: 'I'd like to see some geysers.' I have not been to Switzerland, but I would certainly be looking for an alpenhorn if I went.

The book I remember most vividly reading at school is *Silas Marner*. I must have been in the second form at grammar school, aged 12 or 13. This was the first classic text that I read. The teacher instructed us to read a chapter for homework each week, and then answer questions on the chapter in class. I finished the book in the first week, and found it hard to answer the questions the teacher set specifically on the first chapter. Some of the questions involved speculating about what might happen, but of course I already knew. I was reprimanded. How could I ever appreciate literature to the full if I ignored the teacher's instructions? This was my first introduction to a debate that still continues and is as keenly contested as ever.

CREATIVITY AND THE NATIONAL LITERACY STRATEGY

The current manifestation of this debate appears around the National Literacy Strategy (NLS), introduced by the government in 1998 with the aim of raising standards of literacy in all primary schools in England. Here, the two sides adopt polarized positions; in this case, one arguing the overwhelming need to concentrate on the acquisition of the basic skills of reading and writing; the other arguing the merits of appreciation, imagination and critical capacity. Too heavy an emphasis on the latter might delay the acquisition of technical reading skills; too much on the former, which is where the weight of the rhetoric lies at the moment, might obstruct the development of critical skills. The official definition of literacy puts the emphasis on skills, though it is noted that, among other things, literate primary pupils should:

- be interested in books, read with enjoyment and evaluate and justify their preferences;
- through reading and writing, develop their powers of imagination, inventiveness and critical awareness (Standards and Effectiveness Unit, 1998, p. 3).

These, however, come at the end of the list, and in practice are in danger of becoming lost in the demands made on teachers to teach grammar, punctuation, parts of speech and to deconstruct texts in the so-called 'literacy hour', that currently occurs daily in primary schools. The general model appears to minister to the education of the individual to fit into society, and to enhance the nation's economic performance, not to engage with it, ask questions about it, challenge it, possibly change it. Some feel that the Literacy Framework (Standards and Effectiveness Unit, 1998) which guides the NLS is heavily weighted to the former. Henrietta Dombey (1998, p. 130), for example, finds:

no sense of the rich texture of classrooms where literacy learning is urgent and purposeful; no sense of the vital part that literacy can play in the social and emotional lives of young children; no sense of the lessons learned through the imaginative exploration of painful experiences in the company of gifted authors and artists; no sense that writing about an experience can help a child to order it and come to terms with it . . . no sense of reading and writing put to work, enabling children to encounter other times, places and points of view – rather than remain imprisoned in the here and now.

Nor is there any mention of children's motivation to read, reading as an enjoyable activity, encouraging pupils to be enthusiastic and reflective readers, reading for their own interest (see also DES, 1989 and 1993; Furlong, 1998). Dadds (1999) has shown that many teachers are concerned about 'the apparently imbalanced emphasis on literacy skills at the seeming expense of purposes and creativity' (p. 16). In many of the training video extracts (DFEE, 1998), 'we see the dominance of preset objectives determining an unresponsive, convergent teaching style' (p. 17). Burgess-Macey (1999, p. 120) is concerned that the literacy hour

May exclude (children's) personal encounters with literature, give children less choices about their reading and writing, especially of texts based on popular cultural forms, give them little space and time for their own story-telling and story writing. In addition, children may have less opportunity to work on drawing and composing with their friends and less chance to have fun and to play with the ideas, images and language which stories can open up.

She feels strongly that 'we must create those spaces and defend those practices which make critical literacy possible, in order to remain sensitive "to the unique quirkiness and creativity of young children's responses, experiences and feelings about learning and literacy"' (Whitehead, 1999; Burgess-Macey, 1999, p. 125). Even where teachers are generally supportive of the NLS and its aims, there are problems about those 'spaces' which creativity needs in order to thrive. Fisher and Lewis (1999a) for example, found more positive reactions to the NLS among teachers than they expected, but did note a major problem of manage-ability, which in itself can curtail creativity (see also ATL survey in Byers, 1999). Similarly, Smith *et al.* (1999), while concluding that teachers are generally supportive of the NLS, did find a general concern with the lack of creativity in writing, and that 'nowhere in the literacy hour is there any reading for pleasure'. Fisher (2000) points to the lack of developmentally appropriate practice in the early teaching of literacy, the NLS treating all children from 4 to 11 years of age the same, laying down what and how they should be taught. It provides 'an inflexible model for teachers to work with: it does not acknowledge that the needs of children may be different or that the teacher may want to adapt her

teaching to the needs of her class' (p. 65). 'The greatest danger in the implementation of the NLS', she concludes, 'arises when teachers, feeling deskilled by a
plethora of initiatives to improve their teaching, follow the format of the NLS
rather than the principles behind the model of teaching' (p. 67; see also
Whitehead, 1999).

Why does this remind me of *Silas Marner*? How many pupils of the current
generation will be able to say, like my mother-in-law, 'I love reading'? For how
long and to what extent will children, like my grandson Thomas, be encouraged
to interact with texts, and not just absorb them?

What is being missed in the NLS? Why is creative reading important, and
what does it consist of? In what follows, I draw on some of my researches of
recent years that bear on this issue. They provide examples of creative practice
in reading, of the creative potential in learners, and of creative literacy – literacy
that brings about personal change, and that empowers and enriches. I conclude
by reconsidering the NLS, and some successful attempts to teach creatively
within it.

PERSONAL CHANGE THROUGH READING

In this section, I give two examples. In the first, a headteacher reflects on the
importance to his own identity of self-discovered reading in later life, and how
this conflicts with his experiences as a pupil at school which were distinctly
uncreative. The second shows more positive experiences at school among some
young bilingual children.

Finding your identity

Books can change your life. A teacher on my research into creative teaching
(Woods, 1995, pp. 145–9) told me how his life had been given shape and
meaning by certain authors. He had not enjoyed his own schooling, and had
fallen into teaching by default. Ironically, however, it was in teaching that he
found his redemption. Books played a major part in this. William Walsh's book
The Use of Imagination: Educational Thought and the Literary Mind, for
example, helped him to understand the didacticism of the teaching of his youth,
and the Victorian model on which it was based. By knowing it, he freed himself
from it, and cleared the way for a more interactive style which valued children's
own knowledge.

Above all, perhaps, for this teacher, was the identification of self Peter
discovered through reading the works of the English novelist, Leo Walmsley.
Walmsley's account of his childhood in *Foreigners* for example, captured the
essence of Peter's recollections of his own. The book recounts the experiences of
a young boy in a seaside town where his family has recently taken up residence
and whose members, therefore, were, to the locals, 'foreigners'. The feeling of
isolation and separateness, and the opposition of alien forces were things well

known to Peter. Like him, Walmsley 'hated school, because it stopped me doing so many things I liked'. Peter commented that one of the reasons why he can relate so readily to Walmsley's writing is that 'he has demonstrated that the gap between fact and fiction, between reality and the literary creation, is less real than imagined. His was a very holistic approach to life and experience.'

Here is one of Peter's favourite passages in *Foreigners*, with his own commentary following:

> At the best of times I hated school. The room itself, which was under the chapel gallery, was small and dark, and its windows were heavily barred, for the narrow playground that separated it from the edge of the cliff was actually above the level of the floor, so that really we were half underground, and it was gloomy as a prison. Through the bars you could see patches of sky, so that you always knew whether the sun was shining or not, but the sun itself, even in summer, never entered the room, and while you could hear the sea breaking on the cliff foot, or on the scaur ends if the tide was down, it was not visible. I could always think of a hundred places where I'd rather be than in this gloomy room. I hated having to sit still. I hated writing, and doing sums, and learning poetry off by heart, and learning about nouns and pronouns, and history. I liked looking at maps, and imagining I was seeing the places marked on them, but I hated having to learn off by heart the names of capes and rivers and mountains. I liked reading, but you only got one reader a year for the standard you were in, and you could read it through by yourself in one lesson (skipping the poetry) so that even the interesting bits became dull when you had to go through them word by word, spelling the difficult words out aloud, or writing them on your slate. And while you sat in school you heard all the time the sound of the sea, and the cries of the gulls which often would alight on the playground railings, and stay there, making a queer laughing sound, just as though they were laughing at you, and mocking you because you had to stay in. No matter what time of the year, there was always something exciting to do at Bramblewick. (Walmsley, 1935, pp. 24–5)

Peter comments:

> Whilst Walmsley's works contain numerous passages which have made a lasting impression on me, this is one of the most meaningful. I think that it beautifully conveys the manner in which so-called educational experiences can exclude the real world (and hence relevance). All the boys in that Edwardian classroom knew that the sun was shining outside, but inside gloom and darkness prevailed – through the exclusion of the light of practical experience and relevance. They could hear (but not fully appreciate until they escaped from that environment) the cry of the gulls and the sound of the sea – the living and the elemental worlds. Walmsley also manages to capture the manner in which that drabness is transferred to such learning as takes

place. Throughout this short passage we see the dichotomy of thoughtless repression on the one hand and untapped enthusiasm on the other – note how the passage begins in a negative way, 'At the best of times I hated school', and how it ends with a note of affirmation, '. . . there was always something exciting to do at Bramblewick.'

Against those things he did not like doing – arithmetic, grammar, history, learning poetry and the names of geographical features by rote – he sets down those things which he did enjoy – reading and studying maps. Here is another example of someone searching out those elements in an adverse experience which could provide the foundations for an alternative personal development. Here we see a determination to survive against all the odds. Here we have a child who, whilst at primary school and secondary school, loathed poetry and grammar and history, and probably writing too, who – through *real-life* experiences – was to develop into a fine novelist with a deeply rooted interest in archaeology and things historical. This poses an important question, 'How did Walmsley acquire his literary talents and his lasting fascination with the ancient world?' It was certainly not through the conventional education which he received in the Bay Wesleyan or the Scarborough Municipal Schools. This was the question which I decided I had to resolve for myself those many years ago. If Walmsley had not acquired his education in a typical classroom context was there not some other alternative, and much more relevant, approach that we ought to be considering? This was really the starting point of the educational journey which I have made in my post-formal schooling years and which has gradually given rise to that educational philosophy which I hold today (and which is still evolving). My point of departure was not one without hope of successful resolution. Although I did not articulate it at the time, I probably received some kind of inner encouragement from the unexpressed belief that if Lawrence and Walmsley could survive – *so could I!*

Child development

Peter represents an example of adult discovery of self following childhood suppression. But not all schooling is negative. In more conducive circumstances the benefits of creative literacy to individual development are evident. We did some research recently in a multi-ethnic school containing a number of bilingual children, some of whom spoke English as a second language (Woods *et al.*, 1999). Many of these come from an oral culture, where stories are passed down by word of mouth from one generation to the next. The children had developed the habit of 'storying', making up stories of their own, and these provided a link between home and school, and integrated different forms of knowledge. For Rushan the experience of the nursery took the form of observing and re-enacting the role which he had seen the teacher play from day to day:

Sometimes he get his book and he make up stories and just like one of the teachers do at school he'll pretend that there's some kids sitting there and he'll get the book and start reading the story out, but he can't read the words but he makes it up. (p. 9)

Children sometimes used storying in a form of role-play to re-enact at school experiences they had had at home. This form of 'story play' (Meek, 1991, p. 108) enables children to 'be themselves in a real world or in an imaginary world. Or they can be imaginary people in that world, or imaginary people in the real world.' Stories read and told to children can also offer them a means of personal discovery and exploration of ideas (p. 113).

These creative functions were promoted in a 'Rainbow' story project that took place in the lower school (see Woods *et al.*, 1999, pp. 93–100). Over a period of several weeks, teacher and children developed a story about a giant and a rainbow. The sessions included oral storytelling, drama and artwork, and culminated in the children presenting the story to the whole school. The project provided excellent opportunities for language development, conceptual development, and social, emotional and cultural understanding, and notably for *all* students.

Reading assisted the children's own storytelling abilities. The most frequent reaction when the children were asked to *tell* the researcher a story was that they did not know any, but they could *read* a story. Thus, when Fouzia, in her second year at the lower school, was asked if she could tell a story from Pakistan, she went to the bookshelves, and came back with *The Gingerbread Man*. Fouzia began the story in Panjabi, but seemed to get stuck translating. The researcher suggested she use the pictures in the book to help her. As soon as she began to use the pictures, Fouzia told the story mainly in English:

Mummy said to the children and the man, 'We want something to eat for tea'. The mummy baked a, em, gingerbread man, (*unclear*). The the old woman, hey, phir (*again*) old woman she tooked it out. Then it baked. Then after she, er, she, er, she tooked it out from the oven. Then, then, gingerbread man runned out, then out the farm (*unclear*), then he, the old woman, the old woman says to the gingerbread, 'Stop'. Then the man said to the old woman, he seed a little puppy, and em, 'Stop little em gingerbread man'. The gingerbread man he jumped on, on the, on the leaves. Then then he runned under the log, he said, 'Hey little gingerbread man'. Then he ran and he ran, then he ran. Then, then he stopped and he a little stop, right, then, then, then, the horse now he says, then the horse now he says 'Stop little gingerbread man', then he carries on running. Then he stopped again then the cow says, (*deepened voice for this part*), 'You look nice for my tea', the cow says 'Ma tanu kha lana ha (*I will eat you up*)'. Then he ran, and then ran. All a sudden and then little dog goes, 'Hey little gingerbread man, nice to eat'. Then he ranned and ran and oh no, gingerbread man uh billy labhda si (*he was looking for a cat*) and he stopped again, he stopped uh billy labhda si (*he was looking for a cat*) and he ranned in the river, and he ranned in the river, and he went, and the fox came and he said, 'You need, I'm just going to talk to you'. Then he said, 'Come back on my tail'. Phir una billy labhda si phir una kha lia si (*Then he found the fox and cat and ate it*).

The repetitions, the uncertainty of what to say next, the experimentation with tense, and the incidents of code switching during this telling, all indicated Fouzia's language development in both English and Panjabi. She began by switching from Panjabi into English, possibly because English was the language she has heard the story told in, and perhaps also because she realized that the researcher did not understand Panjabi, showing an awareness of audience (Rosen, 1982). Fouzia remembered the structure of the story well, and used the pictures for contextual clues. Much of the language she used could be described as storybook language (Fox, 1993), 'Then he ran, and he ran, and he ranned.' Fouzia also borrows language directly from the story, for example, 'you look nice for my tea', and 'Stop little gingerbread man.' In many ways, as noted earlier, the written word of the story can provide a strong language scaffold for children learning English as an additional language. It is not surprising therefore that she initially wanted to read the story rather than tell it. Where Fouzia did not have the English language skills to express herself, she switched to Panjabi, using expressions that perhaps best fitted what she was trying to say, a common feature among bilingual children (Baker, 1996; Blackledge, 1994; Romaine, 1989).

READING AS EMPOWERMENT

Finding a voice

Reading is empowering and self-determining to the active and critical reader. It gives readers a voice. Books give shape and substance to feelings, thus enriching experiences; they provide more of the narrative to sections of one's own life which have become submerged under the pace of modern living, and at the same time strengthen the connections with others. They provide a 'window on the world' (Greenhough and Hughes, 1998, p. 394). 'Gifted writers help us to see, to learn from and to enjoy the learning, better than we can manage ourselves' (Hoggart, 1998, p. 68). Seamus Heaney argues that

the world is different after it has been read by a Shakespeare or an Emily Dickinson or a Samuel Beckett because it has been augmented by their reading of it. In a sense, their writings are larger than life while still being true to it. It is because of Beckett's 'transformative way with language, his mixture of word-play and merciless humour, that Beckett the writer has life, and has it more abundantly than the conditions endured by Beckett the citizen might seem to warrant'. (1995, p. 159)

Evocative narratives of the self empower writer and reader alike. In Frank McCourt's (1996) autobiography *Angela's Ashes*, for example, he conjures up the feel and smell of the prevailing condition of his childhood, the wetness and dampness of it, the discomfiture, and whole areas of activity that many of us can identify with. He makes clever use of metaphors, onomatopoeia, imagery, rhythm and cadence of sentences, pathos and gentle ironic humour. There is music and poetry, clever choice of words and sentences, artfully arranged. There is possibly some slight exaggeration in places, but it contributes nonetheless to the general truth, adding to the humour and humanity of the work. Basically, it is a celebration of humanity, of the triumph of the human spirit against the odds, of making common cause with others across national and generational frontiers. Interestingly, McCourt had to write several drafts of the text before he found 'his own voice'.

Chris Searle's (1998) mission in life is to give voice to those in disadvantaged areas and circumstances – people who are usually on the receiving end of others' power. He demonstrates the power of literacy for both children and their elders in his account of his teaching in inner-city areas over 25 years. A Muslim girl comments, 'words are my friend'. An old woman, long since mute, and treated impersonally by staff, dies, and a nurse finds a poem in her locker. It ends:

> But inside this old carcase
> a young girl dwells,
>
> And now and again
> my battered heart swells.
>
> I remember the joys,
> I remember the pain,
>
> And I'm loving and living
> life over again.
>
> I think of the years
> all too few – gone too fast,
>
> And accept the stark fact
> that nothing can last.
>
> So open your eyes nurses
> open and see,
>
> Not a crabbit old woman,
> look closer, see ME.

Unsurprisingly, Searle's students display an 'empathy for the old', epitomized in the way a group of them 'adopted' an ex-boxer, pensioner Stephen Hicks, who had submitted poems to Searle for one of his compilations. Literacy here is not only empowering individuals, but the community in general, strengthening the relationships among them.

Critical literacy

Searle is clearly a supporter of 'critical literacy', which Richard Hoggart sees as 'literacy which is critically aware, not easily taken in, able to "read" tricks of tone, selectivities, false ad hominem cries, and all the rest' (Hoggart, 1998, p. 58). It is a literacy 'alert to the manifold deceptions – carried mainly in language – by which persuasion operates in the open commercial society'. Literacy unrelated to the way language is misused in our society, argues Hoggart, becomes simply a way of further subordinating great numbers of people. (p. 59). So we cannot just settle for literacy and reading. We need 'creative reading' whereby readers create a response to what they read, and by so doing make it their own, not that of the author. In this, there has to be recognition of cultural contexts. As Barton and Hamilton (1998) demonstrate, people's everyday lives are lived and sustained by literacy. Literacy is not just a collection of techniques that simply resides in the head as an autonomous skill. Rather it is an accomplished practice, when, in effect, it becomes many literacies, operating at many levels with many different functions and meanings depending on the social relationships within which they are embedded. Barton and Hamilton explore the practices of some of their sample and their 'ruling passions'. Harry's is authentic war stories – they help him make sense of his own experiences. Shirley's are fighting injustice and making changes, and getting things done in the community. In these case studies, the human factor – and voice – comes across very strongly, and the ways they make sense of their lives through myriad forms of literacy, involving, for example, war stories, newsletters, books, newspapers, magazines, leaflets, cards, lists, maps, diaries, road signs, posters, graffiti, but also other media as well as print. The strengths of out-of-school literacies becomes even more evident when considering the 'web of literacies in local organisations' such as 'The Allotment Association' and the 'Housing Action Project', neither immediately evident as literate environments. But there are meetings literacies, campaigning literacies, literacies in groups, and in these respects literacy is a communal resource, not simply an individual skill. The authors were impressed by the extent of local organizations, the range of literary practices they support and encourage, and by the sheer extent of knowledge in the community. Drawing on and creating local knowledge in such matters as home economics, repair and maintenance, gardening, pets, people create vernacular literacies in organizing life, personal communication, private leisure, documenting life, sense-making, social participation. These are learned informally, continuously throughout their lives, often through community networks. Yet they have low formal status, being little valued by schools.

Literacies are hierarchically ordered. According to Colin Lankshear (1997), this includes the 'official' literacy of school, established by dominant social and cultural groups (Heath, 1983; Woods *et al.*, 1999). Critical literacy involves considering questions such as what reading practices are characteristic of particular social groups; how reading material is produced, in what form, by whom and how it acquires influence; and what influences the interpretation of texts in particular circumstances. Lankshear gives examples of texts that 'can be seen as involved in the discursive production of unduly passive and underinformed citizens' (1997, p. 60). Rather, the educational quest is for the development of a critical consciousness that is aware of power in society and how it is used and distributed; can get beneath surface appearances, recognize and challenge myths and values learned in mass culture; desocialize oneself from such prejudices as racism, sexism and homophobia; and take part in initiating social change.

Reading as therapy

Books are also therapeutic. They make you feel better. Primary teachers know this very well. One headteacher at a school read the pupils Philippa Pearce's story *The Lion at School* – about being brave. A teacher in a school of one of my researches (Woods *et al.*, 1999, pp. 71–3), confronted by 5-year-old Saadia who had cut her finger, chose a story which she felt might help her feel better – *Don't Cry Little Bear*, about a small bear who hurts himself. She compared Saadia's story to that of Little Bear, and used her name card to place over the words 'Little Bear' in the text when she wanted to refer to Saadia's story. The following extract is from the start of the story:

T	Ssh, Nora, you come and sit near me, you're being silly. You sit near me. This is to make Saadia feel better. *Don't* cry Saadia. What sound does this make? (*points to letter 'c' in cry*)
Pupils	C, C, C.
T	(*Turns page*) Let's see what's on this page. (*T. points to writing on book, putting Saadia's name over words 'little bear'*) What's the story called?
Pupils	Don't cry Saadia. (*Attiqa is the leader of this*)
T	*Don't* cry Saadia. Did Saadia fall off her bike? (*picture in book shows little bear falling off his bike*)
Pupils	Yeah.
T	Did you fall off your bike Saadia?
Saadia	(*Shakes head*)
T	No, I don't think she did. What did Saadia hurt?
Nadia	Her leg.
T	No, not her leg.
Pupil	Arm.
T	Her *finger*. Saadia hurt her finger. What did little bear hurt?
Attiqa	Arm.
T	His arm, good. Who's this coming? (*picture shows Little Bear's mother coming to help*)
Pupils	Mum.

T	Mum. What did mum say to little bear? She said 'Don't cry little bear.'
Pupils	Don't cry little bear.
T	What do we say to Saadia?
T & Pupils	Don't cry Saadia.
T	Mum said 'I will pick you up.' Who picked Saadia up?
Pupil	Her mum.
T	No. Who picked Saadia up?
2nd Pupil	Mrs Boyle.
T	Mrs Boyle. Mrs Boyle said 'I will pick you up.' She said 'So *don't* cry. Don't cry Saadia.'
Alia	Little, Saadia.

We see within this small extract a considerable amount of learning developing. There is some attention to phonics in the opening stage. Throughout the telling Chris pointed to the words 'Don't cry Little Bear/Saadia' as she and the children read them out, encouraging the children to become 'partners' in the reading process. There is the early development of scientific understanding, labelling parts of the body, leg, arm and finger. The story also provides a strong scaffolding process for English language development. The repetition of phrases throughout the story enables all the children to join in, even those who may have little English. Further, because this story was well known to the children, new language could be brought by telling in parallel Saadia's experience, while maintaining the basic structure of the story. Later in the story, other children began to talk about their experiences of falling over or being hurt. However, the lesson did not end with the completion of the story. Chris asked the children if they would like to make a class book of Saadia's story, and the children agreed enthusiastically. They drew the pictures and 'wrote' out the story, and the book was placed in the reading corner of the classroom. Mari observed the children on several occasions reading the book in class. Later in the term the book was used by the class as the focus for their class assembly and they shared Saadia's story with the rest of the school.

This example shows the pedagogical advantage that can be gained by recruiting children's feelings stirred by things that have actually happened to them or to a friend or colleague. It illustrates what can be achieved when teachers are creative in finding relevant opportunities within everyday occurrences. This had not been the planned morning activity. The book had been the key resource.

READING AND WRITING AS ENRICHMENT

Consider the following poem:

Happiness

Happiness rumbles in your tummy like thunder,
You feel it is going to pop out any minute,
Big smiles appear on your face.
It feels as if you are going to leap into the air and shout out loud
And giggle until your eyes pop out.
Life becomes bright as if you had pulled the curtains.
When you are happy you go quite red in the face,
You feel like a sausage sizzling in a pan
Ready to spit and pop.
You get excited and don't know what to do.
You feel like crying.
You get out of bed and kick everything over.

(Oliver Muddiman, aged 8, Earls Barton Primary School.
Published in *Once Upon a Celebration*, Northants CC Education
Department)

To me, this poem conveys joy, energy, enthusiasm, and an irrepressible dynamic spirit that is not just a quality of this young boy, but of the entire human race. There is no accounting for it, and it is difficult to put your finger on what this quality is exactly. The poem says just this, but says it in such a way and in such a form that it aids recognition, and in the recognition comes renewed resolve of one's own, and a sense of companionship. It is an example of the way in which 'poetry brings human existence into a fuller life' and how it promotes 'excitements and transformations' (Heaney, 1995, p. xvii). Heaney argues that

poetry becomes another truth to which we can have recourse, before which we can know ourselves in a more fully empowered way. In fact to read poetry of this totally adequate kind is to experience something bracing and memorable, something capable of increasing in value over the whole course of a lifetime. (p. 8)

He goes on to talk of

the fluid exhilarating moment which lies at the heart of any memorable reading, the undisappointed joy of finding that everything holds up and answers the desire that it awakens. At such moments, the delight of having all one's faculties simultaneously provoked and gratified is like gaining an upper hand over all that is contingent and . . . inconsequential. There is a sensation of arrival and of prospect, so that one does indeed seem to 'recover a past' and 'prefigure a future', and thereby to complete the circle of one's being. (p. 9)

There is nothing like writing a book to sharpen the edges of one's critical appreciation. Margaret Meek (1998, p. 123), for one, is convinced that 'the best evidence of reading progress comes from the observations of good teachers who take time to discuss reading with their pupils and who teach them to write'. One of the best examples I saw of this involved the writing of *Rushavenn Time*, a book written by a group of primary children, guided by their headteacher and a children's author, Theresa Whistler. It won a prize for being the best children's book of its year. The process of its writing I saw as a 'critical event' in the children's education – one involving pronounced and remarkable change in their development (Woods, 1993).

As a direct result of the experience, pupils' attitudes towards learning changed markedly. Increased or new-found confidence in oneself was frequently mentioned, leading to a willingness to talk and to risk expression of ideas, heightened motivation, a growth in sense of self-worth and self-esteem, and a feeling of control of the learning process. Rushavenn, for example, gave Stephen 'confidence to write, whereas before writing was like maths, number crunching. It taught me there's no point in writing something down if you're not going to mean what you say . . . you've got to feel inside that you're telling the truth' (Woods, 1993, p. 16). Sarah told of her excitement at the discovery that 'her own thoughts and feelings that she hadn't put into words before were of real value'. It gave her a lot of confidence, 'speaking in a group and telling people her ideas', and made her feel 'her pieces of paper weren't inferior to anybody else's' (p. 17). Students discovered new ways of learning, new ways of expressing themselves, creative and critical powers, the strength of teamwork, and the huge potential of strong motivation. The construction of Rushavenn, therefore, gave pupils new knowledge of the self, contributing to both personal and social development, and refined their learning skills in new ways. For the teacher, it was his most gratifying achievement as a teacher in his long career.

CONCLUSION

We have noted in our researches that creative teaching is characterized by innovation, ownership of knowledge, control of teaching processes and relevance to the learner. Creative learning has the same properties. These are all evident throughout the examples here of creative reading. Reading can change your life, it can inform, motivate, inspire and elevate; but it must be reading you do for yourself, at your own pace, in your own way, and that has a bearing on your own background, interests, values, beliefs and aspirations. Reading that is forced on you in a mechanistic way and formally assessed may have the reverse effect, the major purpose becoming pleasing the teacher and passing tests, and a preoccupation with form rather than substance.

In order to prosper, creativity needs opportunity (Woods *et al.*, 1999). Certainly, creative teachers can often turn constraint into opportunity, but there are limits. How does the NLS now stand on these criteria after two years of operation?

There is one interesting finding. It is that the most successful teachers of literacy within the strategy in terms of the objectives of the NLS are indeed creative teachers. Thus, Wray *et al.* (1999) found that the effective teachers in their research had a coherent set of beliefs about the importance of meaning in literacy teaching, and actively tried to help their students make connections between text, sentence and word levels. They were concerned to 'raise children's awareness of their own literacy use and comprehension', and were experts at 'scaffolding' children's learning (p. 20). They put their teaching into a wider context, used whole texts as a basis, were clear about purposes, and put a 'heavy emphasis on literacy in the environments which had been created' (p. 21; see also Wray *et al.*, 2000). Medwell *et al.* (1998) also found that effective teachers of literacy 'placed a greater emphasis on children's recognition of the purposes and functions of reading and writing and of the structures used to enable these processes'. Teachers 'owned' the literacy knowledge in the sense that 'they appeared to know and understand the material in the form in which they taught it to the children, which was usually as material which helped these children to read and write' (p. 76). Their pupils were 'much more heavily involved in problem-solving and theorising about language for themselves rather than simply being given facts to learn' (p. 77). To these teachers, the creation of meaning in literacy was crucial. They did not ignore technical skills, but sought to embed them within a meaningful framework. Similarly, Dawes (1999) shows how teachers in one school mediated the prescription of the NLS to their own beliefs and values. White (2000, p. 21) gives an example of how a teacher 'maintained a constructive balance in the paradox of pedagogy', that is an 'acceptable level of structure and canon', while allowing children to feel that they had 'sufficient autonomy and involvement in the creation and maintenance of the classroom culture'. Fisher and Lewis (1999b) draw the contrast between teaching as a technical activity, where pedagogy is specified, and teaching as a professional activity, where teachers have pedagogical flexibility among a broad repertoire of methods. The latter has strong support in general as a feature of effective teaching (see, for example, Alexander, 1992; Alexander *et al.*, 1995). They also found that the most effective teaching of literacy among their sample of small rural schools was well paced, discursive, interactive, confident and ambitious – the very pedagogical qualities advocated in the NLS *Framework for Teaching* (Standards and Effectiveness Unit, 1998, p. 8). The Committee on Creative and Cultural Education (NACCCE, 1999, p. 79), while noting the problems of many teachers who felt their creativity being squeezed by the literacy hour, observed:

There are schools and teachers who have used the literacy hour as a starting point for a wide range of creative activities in reading, writing, drama and in the other arts. We see great value in integrating the objectives of high standards of literacy with those of high standards of creative achievement and cultural experience . . . It would be of value to many schools to have access to materials, ideas and strategies in the imaginative implementation of these strategies.

There is nothing, therefore, intrinsically in the NLS to prevent creative approaches – indeed, there are principles within it upon which such approaches are founded. The problem is more one of pressure, overload and a certain imbalance, both within the NLS and within the National Curriculum in general, which make it difficult for many teachers to put those principles into practice. Here is yet another challenge for us all – for policy-makers not to crowd out those valuable spaces by over-prescription; for teachers to find the spaces that do exist and to find ways of taking advantage of them; and for researchers continuing to monitor the effects, and recording and disseminating examples of creative practice.

ACKNOWLEDGEMENTS

I am grateful to Anna Craft, Bob Jeffrey, Mike Leibling, Geoff Troman and Ros Fisher for their comments on an earlier draft of this chapter. For their inputs into some of the research projects featured here, I would like to thank Mari Boyle and Peter J. Woods.

REFERENCES

Alexander, R. (1992) *Policy and Practice in Primary Education*. London: Routledge.
Alexander, R., Willcocks, J. and Nelson, N. (1995) 'Discourse, pedagogy and the National Curriculum: change and continuity in primary schools', *Research Papers in Education,* **11**(1), 81–120.
Baker, C. (1996) *Foundations of Bilingual Education and Bilingualism*. 2nd ed. Clevedon: Multilingual Matters.
Barton, D. and Hamilton, M. (1998) *Local Literacies: Reading and Writing in One Community*. London and New York: Routledge.
Blackledge, A. (1994) '"We can't tell our stories in English": language, story and culture in the primary school'. In A. Blackledge (ed.) *Teaching Bilingual Children*. Stoke-on-Trent: Trentham Books.
Burgess-Macey, C. (1999) 'Classroom literacies: young children's explorations in meaning making in the age of the literacy hour', *Reading*, November, 120–5.
Byers, R. (1999) 'The National Literacy Strategy and pupils with special educational needs', *British Journal of Special Education*, **26**(1), 8–11.
Dadds, M. (1999) 'Teachers' values and the literacy hour', *Cambridge Journal of Education,* **29**(1), 7–19.
Dawes, L. (1999) 'From research to action: the Redbridge Literacy Initiative', *Education*

3–13, **27**(1), 22–7.

Department for Education and Employment (DFEE) (1998) *The National Literacy Strategy: Literacy Training Pack*. London: DFEE.

Department of Education and Science (DES) (1989 and 1993) *English for Ages 5–16*. London: HMSO.

Dombey, H. (1998) 'Changing literacy in the early years of school'. In B. Cox (ed.) *Literacy is not Enough: Essays on the Importance of Reading*. Manchester: Manchester University Press and Book Trust.

Fisher, R. (2000) 'Developmentally appropriate practice and a National Literacy Strategy', *British Journal of Educational Studies*, **48**(1), 58–69.

Fisher, R. and Lewis, M. (1999a) 'Anticipation or trepidation? Teachers' views on the literacy hour', *Reading*, April, 23–8.

Fisher, R. and Lewis, M. (1999b) 'Implementation of the National Literacy Strategy: indications of change'. Paper presented to ESRC Research Seminar 1 on Raising Standards in Literacy, University of Plymouth, May.

Fox, C. (1993) *At the Very Edge of the Forest: The Influence of Literature on Storytelling*. London: Cassell.

Furlong, T. (1998) 'Reading in the primary school'. In B. Cox (ed.) *Literacy is not Enough: Essays on the Importance of Reading*. Manchester: Manchester University Press and Book Trust.

Greenhough, P. and Hughes, M. (1998) 'Parents' and teachers' interventions in children's reading', *British Educational Research Journal*, **24**(4), 383–98.

Heaney, S. (1995) *The Redress of Poetry*. London: Faber and Faber.

Heath, S. B. (1983) *Ways with Words: Language, Life and Work in Communities and Classrooms*. Cambridge: Cambridge University Press.

Hoggart, R. (1998) 'Critical literacy and creative reading'. In B. Cox (ed.) *Literacy is not Enough: Essays on the Importance of Reading*. Manchester: Manchester University Press and Book Trust.

Lankshear, C. (1997) *Changing Literacies*. Buckingham: Open University Press.

McCourt, F. (1996) *Angela's Ashes*. London: Flamingo.

Medwell, J., Wray, D., Poulson, L. and Fox, R. (1998) *Effective Teachers of Literacy: A Report of a Research Project Commissioned by the Teacher Training Agency*. Exeter: University of Exeter.

Meek, M. (1991) *On Being Literate*. London: Bodley Head.

Meek, M. (1998) 'Important reading lessons'. In B. Cox (ed.) *Literacy is not Enough: Essays on the Importance of Reading*. Manchester: Manchester University Press and Book Trust.

National Advisory Committee on Creative and Cultural Education (NACCCE) (1999) *All our Futures: Creativity, Culture and Education*. London: DFEE.

Romaine, S. (1989) *Bilingualism*. Oxford: Basil Blackwell.

Rosen, H. (1982) *Stories and Meanings*. Northamptonshire: NATE.

Searle, C. (1998) *None but our Words: Critical Literacy in Classroom and Community*. Buckingham: Open University Press.

Smith, F., Hardman, F. and Mroz, M. (1999) 'Evaluating the effectiveness of the National Literacy Strategy: identifying indicators of success'. Paper presented at the European Conference on Educational Research, Lahti, Finland, 22–25 September.

Standards and Effectiveness Unit (1998) *The National Literacy Strategy: Framework for Teaching*. London: DFEE.

Walmsley, L. (1935) *Foreigners*. London: Jonathan Cape.

Walsh, W. (1959) *The Use of Imagination: Educational Thought and the Literary Mind*. London: Chatto and Windus.

White, C. (2000) 'Strategies are not enough: the importance of classroom culture in the teaching of writing', *Education 3–13,* March, 16–21.

Whitehead, M. (1999) *Supporting Language and Literacy Development in the Early Years.* Buckingham: Open University Press.

Woods, P. (1993) *Critical Events in Teaching and Learning.* London: Falmer Press.

Woods, P. (1995) *Creative Teachers in Primary Schools.* Buckingham: Open University Press.

Woods, P., Boyle, M. and Hubbard, N. (1999) *Multicultural Children in the Early Years: Creative Teaching, Meaningful Learning.* Clevedon: Multilingual Matters.

Wray, D., Medwell, J., Fox, R. and Poulson, L. (1999) 'Teaching reading: lessons from the experts', *Reading,* April, 17–22.

Wray, D., Medwell, J., Fox, R. and Poulson, L. (2000) 'The teaching practices of effective teachers of literacy', *Educational Review,* **52**(1), 75–84.

Chapter 5

Creativity as 'Mindful' Learning: A Case from Learner-Led Home-Based Education

Leslie Safran

INTRODUCTION

This chapter first defines mindfulness, looks at creativity as mindfulness, and goes on to discuss mindful learner-led education. A definition of the mindful teacher and the role of the teacher will be examined. In the second part of the chapter my own journey towards a learner-led approach in home-based education will be described, followed by other examples, drawn from my own experience and that of other home educators, to illustrate mindful learner-led education.

Creativity as mindfulness

In her book *The Power of Mindful Learning*, Langer (1997) defines mindfulness as 'the continuous creation of new categories; openness to new information; and an implicit awareness of more than one perspective' (p. 4). Mindlessness, on the other hand, is characterized by 'entrapment in old categories; by automatic behaviour that precludes attending to new signals; and by actions that operate from a single perspective' (p. 4). In fact the direct opposite of the mindful categories.

A mindful person takes an active, open, interested approach to life. Being mindful is an attitude towards life. People do not need to be conscious that they have this approach to life. Our perspectives are often unconscious; for example, when we make what we think is a rational decision we might actually be acting out of some other motive, such as fear. Prejudices, too, are often unconscious. We say we do not have prejudices yet we act in a manner that belies an unconscious prejudice. A person does not have to be aware that mindfulness is their approach to life in order for them to be mindful and to act mindfully, according to Langer's definition. In fact 'implicit awareness' is part of the definition.

Mindfulness encompasses creativity as it includes the notion of making something new or putting things together in new ways. It also includes being open to new ideas and seeing many points of view. It is not just about making new connections but continually thinking about any part of life, consciously or unconsciously, looking around life from all angles, and asking questions about what one finds.

I have chosen to use the idea of mindfulness over other definitions of creativity[1] as it seems to me that Langer's definition fits well with the theory of learner-led education and with the home-based educating process.

LEARNER-LED LEARNING AND MINDFULNESS

I concentrate on the learner and learning aspect of education in this chapter, because my belief is that whether learning takes place depends on the learner. There also has to be something to be learned but the activity of learning and the content of the subject matter are up to the learner.

Learning is the attainment of knowledge, a skill, or information, either by yourself, through study and experience, or through a teacher. Mindful learning is a state of mind. While attaining knowledge or a skill the mindful learner is open to new information, trying to create new categories all the time and recognizing that any perspective is one among many. The mindful learner reflects on the subject matter, turning it over and seeing it from many angles while processing the information. The information is then taken in by the learner in such a way that he or she can use it in a new context or change it to fit an old one – or, indeed, change the context to reflect or fit the learning.

Learner-led education can easily accommodate different learning styles. Different people find they are better able to learn in different ways, some through activity, some through visual displays, some through aural, or written and/or various combinations. Whether one finds a noisy active atmosphere more conducive to learning, or a quiet one; what physical position he or she takes up; and how long he or she keeps up the activity can all be determined by the learner.

There is an emotional dimension to learner-led learning that crucially means being interested in a subject and desiring information about it. The learner is then motivated to seek out the wanted information and to internalize it, to take it in. Normally the original wish to obtain the information facilitates the consequent absorption.

The bonus here is that by being emotionally involved the learner makes the learning process his or her own. The learner can feel active and responsible for initiating the activity. They feel proud and satisfied when the outcome of the learning is successfully achieved. Generally this is an empowering experience which itself can multiply further forays into areas of learning. This wish to learn is potentially present in all children; developing and retaining it is the issue.

When a learner is motivated, interested and wants a particular bit of information, and he or she seeks the satisfaction of attaining some information, then he or she is in a state of mindful learning. Mindful learners control consciously or unconsciously what they want to learn, when they want it, where they want it, how they take it in and how much they want. There may, at times, be tremendous frustration and difficulty for the learner and many blind alleys towards a particular subject but the desire by the learner for the knowledge or skill can drive them on through the difficult times.

TEACHING AND LEARNER-LED MINDFUL LEARNING

In defining 'to teach' I draw on its original meaning 'to show'. I propose that a fuller definition of 'to teach' would be 'to enable a person to do something by showing, explaining, or passing on a skill or knowledge'.

Mindful teaching facilitates learning by showing, explaining or passing on a skill or knowledge while being mindful of the subject matter, open to new information, creating new categories and being aware of many perspectives within the subject matter. More importantly, the mindful teacher is also mindful of the learner, that is open to their perspectives, and receptive to information from the learner.

The mindful teacher is therefore learner-led. A mindful teacher begins from where the learner is and opens up the unknown, showing new possibilities to the learner at a pace appropriate to them. The learner sets the pace which the teacher works to. The mindful teacher makes critical thought possible for the learner through questioning the learner, showing them areas and avenues the learner may not yet have discovered for themselves. But teaching is only one possible way to mindful learning for the mindful learner.

Learner-led mindful learning

In mindful learning it is the learner who controls the relationship between him or herself and the subject matter. The practice of teaching is secondary in learner-led learning. If a teacher is involved in the learning, the teacher role is more like that of a facilitator.

Mindful learner-led education is not symmetrical for the teacher and the learner. The learner sets the agenda of what is to be learnt. The mindful teacher's role is to follow the mindful learner's interests and learning style and facilitate them by mediating between the subject matter and the learner. Mindful teachers do not think primarily about themselves, time constraints or meeting outside requirements of subject matter.

There can be mindful learning without teaching. In learner-led situations, frequently there is no other person doing the teaching. One is learning *by* oneself, *for* oneself. For example, a person lazing around happens to see a bricklayer across the street laying bricks skilfully. The person becomes interested and watches intently. As the learner watches, he is both teaching himself and learning at the same time. The person then uses that 'lesson' later when trying to do some bricklaying for himself, eager to try out what he took in.

In mindful learning, often the teaching and learning are done when no one, neither the learner nor the teacher, is aware of it or intends it consciously. Through conversation, observation, interaction with the world in all ways we are teaching others and ourselves all the time.

These processes of mindful learner-led learning and mindful teaching with or without a mindful teacher go on all the time, whether intended or unintended. When we need help with a recipe, a new idea for a party, a dress design or any project or problem and we talk about this with a friend, family or colleagues, then the ideas start to flow and mindful learner-led learning takes place.

Mindful learning happens at any time and at any age. It is not confined to a particular place or situation, nor to the constraints of any curriculum. It is lifelong, from the child watching a spider on its web to someone learning to play an instrument in retirement.

'Mindfulness', as discussed so far in this chapter, is the mainstay of much home-based education practice although the participants may not be conscious of this. The idea of 'following the child' to which many home educators aspire, in itself sounds rather limp but directly refers in practice to mindful teaching and learning. By allowing the child to initiate the learning activity, and following as long as the child wants, wherever the child wants to go, in itself allows mindful learning to be developed.

I will now look at how this view of mindful learning and learner-led practice is involved in home-based education.

MOVING TOWARDS MINDFUL LEARNING: A CASE FROM HOME-BASED EDUCATION

I would like to begin with a brief story to show how I began, through my life experience, to move towards learner-led mindful home education.

When my son was 4 I thought it was about time he learned to read. I had read to him voluminously since he was old enough to understand a story when he was about 8 months old. We visited the library twice a week and took out fifteen books each time (we were living in Canada at the time and that was allowed). By the time the books were returned to the library each book had been read several times. We also had a house full of books. But still I was worried and anxious about the adequacy of this education, wanting a head-start for my son. He would be starting school soon and I did not want him to be behind. It is a tough world out there. It was time he learned to read. We sat down every morning with a 'Dick and Jane' reader. Each book had several words on the page. You may remember them: 'See Jane run. Run Jane run.' We looked at these every morning for four days. He seemed to be struggling through. Oh no! Late reader, slow learner, dyslexia. On the fourth morning he said 'Reading is boring . . .' we stopped there. I was in shock. Had I closed his emotional openness to this important ability? Would he hate books for ever, never learn to read and be a misfit all his life? We went back to the old way of my reading to him while I tried to think of a new strategy to teach him to read.

Just before Christmas, about six months later, early in the morning he was up playing in his room. I heard him saying aloud a Dr Suess book *Green Eggs and Ham*. It was a new book so I knew he had not memorized it. I went in and watched him *read* this book to himself and for himself. He had learned for himself one of the most respected skills in our society.

Here was for me a very important lesson in mindful teaching in terms of letting the child learn what he needs when he needs it. It was this experience that gave me the confidence to try home-based education for what I thought might just be a little while.

I was still worried about those subjects in which I had no interest or expertise. How was my son to learn to divide fractions, how a river is formed and the causes of refraction?

September 5, 1988, was the start of home-based education proper for us. I woke with total panic and thought I had better get up and do chemistry! I was so panicked I could not do anything. We went to the park. We did bark rubbings (art, biology). At the café my son bought the tea and got the change (maths and social skills) and then we went shopping (life skills, more maths) and went home and baked a cake (chemistry!, more maths, reading). It was dawning on me that he did not need a teacher with the relevant professional skills in each subject. He could attain a great deal of knowledge from the world in his daily activities by himself.

What a relief to discover that many topics arise naturally in the course of everyday activities. I had overestimated my own role and underestimated everyday life and my son. In addition topics he might not come across in the course of everyday life could be explored through other resources available in society, such as libraries, museums, public lectures, the media, etc.

But I still feared I would need to teach him things he would not come across in everyday life so that he would not fall behind in the modern world

Having survived our first day I gained enough confidence to set up an 'educational' programme of our own. We did three academic subjects each morning as well as violin practice. In the afternoons we would go on outings.

However, I was still thinking I had to put certain prescribed ideas into his head. I was somewhat patient but also felt frustrated at times and we often seemed to be doing the same thing over and over. At other times my son would understand everything quickly and retain the information gained on first acquaintance. Violin practice was the worst time. It invariably came at the end of the morning and by the end of the practice I would be shouting and he would be crying. This was exactly what I was trying to avoid. I decided to try an experiment for a month remembering the experiences we had had with reading. I would not practise with him at all. If he chose to practise fine, if not, that would be fine too. I would wait and see what his violin teacher made of it. The violin teacher never noticed. My son progressed very quickly. I never practised with him again. He is now 16 and a very good musician, playing three instruments. He never needed to 'learn' about learner-led learning. He was open to new information and perspectives on his own.

This letting go and following my son, trusting that he would know what he wanted and being the mindful teacher he needed quickly extrapolated to all areas of our life. I gave up teaching and learning in the traditional sense and lived life with him, doing lots of things! As a mindful learner in these situations he had a multitude of options ranging from taking in the information on one hand to not interacting with the situation at all. If the latter were the case, that activity would be dropped.

We did volunteer work – running stalls at fairs to raise money, working in the local library and helping out in the offices of a huge London charity to name a few. We also did projects with other families. We looked at the Middle Ages for a year, acting out the feudal system, re-enacting the fight between Henry and Thomas Beckett in the playground, drawing characters from the *Canterbury Tales* Prologue, writing and performing several times a play of one of the tales, culminating in a week at Canterbury where we wrote our own tales and spent hours in the cathedral drawing and making things. We all, children and adults, had a great time and all learnt a great deal. The added result was we built up our confidence and good emotional relationships to learning situations. These children are now young people and we all remember that year with much fondness.

Mindful learner-led home-based education

There are many aspects of home-based educational learning that directly reflect mindful learner-led learning. First, as there is no required curriculum in home-based education, the child can follow his or her own interests and thereby the interests are directly acknowledged and given importance. The child has complete ownership of the practice, including the information wanted and learning style. Also the whole of life is viewed as an encyclopaedia and as an educational experience. He or she feels empowered and both the child's self-esteem and confidence are developed. The children's interest in any particular topic is allowed to flourish.

Second, there is scope within the home-based education movement for a tremendously mindful education, because there is no particular 'way to do it', no rules on how to achieve education. Each family can find a path that suits them. There is a built-in need for constant flexibility in response to the changing situations of the family. This means being continually malleable, reflecting the changing and complex needs of every family as they grow and develop. Each family almost automatically becomes open to new information, ideas, techniques and perspectives, acknowledges the changing needs of each child.

We can see these features illustrated in an example. An adult might begin reading a book on Indian folk tales to the child. The adult might have ideas of then looking at where India is on the map, making some Indian food, and going to interview an Indian friend about their childhood, etc. This project could be extended as long as the child and adult liked. But what often happens is the child will take the ideas somewhere else entirely and the adult will follow. For example, the child might love one vision in the folk tale and decide to make a sculpture of that and spend the rest of the day doing that despite the adult's wishes to do something else.

The facilitator has to learn to be flexible, not to push the seemingly more broad 'educational' path on to the child and allow that, although it is not obvious to the adult what the child is getting out of their endeavours, her learning projects are far more important than the specific content of the topic at hand that the facilitator had in mind. More important, because the learning is meaningful to the learner and is emotionally satisfying, mindful learning can flourish.

The learner, as seen in the example above about the project on India, leads the learning. The learning is continuous. There is no imposed timetable to stop or start an activity. There is no obvious split of 'work' and 'play' in the traditional sense. There are just activities. Children can spend hours on a project that many would call work and not even need to rest. They are filled up by this activity and do not see it as tiring. Similarly, children may spend many hours apparently just playing, but mindful learning is going on.

There is enormous importance given to childhood and children in the home-based educating family. Having chosen to home educate and base life around the family's needs, the child is usually given equal place in the daily running and decisions in a natural self-regulating way. There do not have to be family discussions or contrived times when families meet together to discuss the day or share problems. They are living together in a continuous and organic way. They do not spend all their time together but there are plenty of times for talking about what has happened during the day. The family knows each other's circumstances so they can relate to each other's stories with ease. This leads on to a huge part of home-based educational learning – conversational learning.

Conversational learning

'Conversational learning' is central to home-based education. It is well documented as a form of learning for the under-5s, and Alan Thomas in his book *Educating Children at Home* (1998) talks about how this is extended in home-based education. The home-educating parent can dovetail exactly with their child and facilitate their progress. There is tremendous scope for the child to initiate conversations and control the amount of information they need and want to take in.

It is common to talk about the 'eyes glazing over' syndrome of children. The child asks a question and after receiving as much information as they want the eyes tell you the child is 'gone'. In other circumstances this might be interpreted as not paying attention or not concentrating, not learning. But in conversational learning the mindful teacher realizes the child has got the information they required for that question and will end the session. Thus the mindful teacher actually recognizes that the child has reached this state and is not just passive and 'unmindful'.

There can be temptation to offer 'help' that can turn an activity into an unmindful teaching session. Holt (1981) gives a good example of this. He was reading aloud to a 4-year-old child and thought

> that by moving a finger along under the words as I read them I might make more clear connections between the written and spoken word. It didn't take the child very long to figure out what had begun as a nice friendly, cosy sharing of a story had turned into something else, that her project had by some magic turned into my project.

After a while the child takes Holt's finger away from the page. He remarks 'I gave up "teaching" and went back to doing what I had been asked to do' (p.143). Holt became a mindful teacher by allowing the child to learn in their own time and style.

Further features of home-based education

In home-based education there is no need for age-related boundaries. If a learner is good at something they can carry on to whatever level they feel able. Conversely if they are not ready for something they can wait until they are. Consolidation of what you are learning can take place unexpectedly, not only during an activity but sometimes long afterwards, having taken a rest and by *not* doing that activity. For example, my son never enjoyed visual art from the moment he could hold a pen. He did it but was not interested in it. At playgroups he would paint when told to do so. We had the equipment at home but he never asked to do it and would say no to my suggestions. When he chose an activity he would never choose to paint or draw. But over the years, despite his lack of practice, whenever he did a painting or drawing they changed, in the sense that they resembled a painting or drawing of any other child his age. This has been true even more importantly with regard to his musical education where he was able to improve without a lot of practice.

One aspect of the emotional side of learning in home-based education is the huge variety and ages of the people you spend time with. In meetings of home-based educators there are children of all ages. It is remarkable to see young children showing each other a skill at one time and 'taking in' from another child at the next moment, going off in imaginative play, rolling on the floor with a baby, 'being' a baby and then back to another game all in a short space of time. The enhancement of children's general psychic health is achieved by allowing children to listen to and act on their immediate emotional disposition. Their emotional contentment is apparent in the busy but calm atmosphere of these social gatherings.

Another facet of emotional health which is very important for the 'taking in' process is the ability to deal with uncertainty. Holt wrote

> We are all of us, no matter how hard we work, no matter how curious we are, condemned to grow relatively more ignorant every day we live, to know less and less of the sum of what is known . . . I expect to live my entire life in uncertainty, about as ignorant and uncertain and confused as I am now, and I have learned to live with this, not to worry about it. I have learned to swim in uncertainty, the way a fish swims in water. (1971, pp. 142, 144)

That is truer today than it was when Holt wrote it in 1971. Problem-solving at all levels requires people to face uncertainty, to be open to all sorts of solutions and to be uncertain about the answers they are looking for. Being 'mindful' involves tolerating the uncertainty of unknowing, of failing and not knowing the future. In home-based education life is lived with little structure. Uncertainty is part of the joy and excitement of the learning experience.

In home-based education mindful learning/teaching is undertaken continually every day. The role of the home-educating parent and any other person involved in the child's life is to 'show' the world to the child. The home-educating parent does not have to learn about anything that they are not interested in, as I had feared. But that does not mean the child does not ever get to know about these things. It is the role of the home-educating parent to find opportunities for any experience for the child. To some extent this happens naturally. When people hear a child is educated out of school, they often offer to help the child along. In our case alone I can think of countless offers. Specifically, a baker friend came and taught my daughter to make bread; another friend took both my children to help volunteering; we have been offered tickets to concerts; neighbours currently teach sewing; and grandparents play a huge role sharing their skills when the children are interested.

An unintended consequence of home-based education that underpins its inherently creative and mindful nature is that the home-educating family is departing from the normal life pattern in society. Home-educating families have to deal with this personally on a day-to-day basis as they are constantly asked about home-based education. How you are judged by the outside world, your vision of your own future and life choices, as well as those for your children and their own choices for themselves, are all called into question. The home-educating family is constantly called upon to justify being outside society. This can be a repetitive nuisance but it also helps one to review and re-evaluate life, as well as to articulate and clarify to yourself what you are doing.

There is no prescribed path once you have thrown out the normal social steps. A common pattern for families is to find that almost as soon as life has settled down, someone in the family will move subtly and the mosaic shifts again. The regrouping and speaking to the ever-changing needs of the people in the family is what life is. It is a natural movement of life.

The process described earlier, of moving away from accepting the 'norm' and moving towards a home-based mindful learner-led approach requires reassessing the role of learning and teaching. This evolves over some time.

Given how ingrained and unquestioned the traditional way of thinking is, it is nevertheless surprising how quickly the change occurs. The unfolding of the child's own abilities, joy, education and quality of life is continual proof and encouragement that this is a highly effective way to educate children, and often speeds along the process of developing a way of life that suits the family.

An example of mindful learning at home

For her tenth birthday Mary (a pseudonym) decided to give a party around an imaginary planet that she would 'visit' before the party date and then have the party in its honour. The invitations featured a spacewoman saying she had just returned from Zonky and would like to tell the guests about her trip. If the guests were very lucky, a visitor from Zonky might be able to come to the party too. They were invited to come in Zonky's national colours (the colours that Mary had just used when redecorating her room). When they arrived the children were shown photos from Mary's trip. Unfortunately, they were told, in the heat of the trip back to earth, a chemical reaction had changed them from photos into drawings. A map on the wall showed where Zonky was in relation to the earth and the national anthem was taught to the group.

The food at the party was as near as Mary could find on earth to the food Zonkians eat; blue spaghetti eaten from a glass with one chopstick and special fruit punch. The party then retired to another room to await the visitor from Zonky. While they waited, Mary taught her guests the special tune to 'Happy Birthday' as sung on Zonky and they sang it in a round. Mary had planned for months an elaborate costume for the visitor (actually her mother dressed up) to wear. Mary had chosen special gifts to suit each person coming to the party which the visitor from Zonky would hand out as if from that planet with an appropriate story about what each item represented on Zonky and why it was considered appropriate for that particular friend. Only Mary could speak Zonkian so she had to translate what the visitor said.

After the visit, a fleeting one, as Zonkians could not afford to let anyone stay away for too long, the party retired to the kitchen for a special birthday treat left for Mary by her Zonkian friend. 'Happy Birthday' was sung in the usual way and in the Zonkian way several times.

Mary made up this entire scheme. She designed the invitations on the computer, wrote the tune to be sung, bought specific presents for each child, drew the map and 'photo album' of her trip, cooked the food, designed and made the punches, made up the customs for Zonky and created the Zonkian person. Her mother helped whenever needed but mostly this took the form of practical support with shopping.

Hopefully the creativity and mindful learning in this scenario are easy to see. The amount of traditional learning involved was also quite considerable. All the factors I described earlier can be seen in this example; trusting that the child will learn, and supporting her in her endeavours being top of the list. The whole enterprise was full of mindfulness, being open to new information, creating new categories and seeing more than one perspective. There was no timetable, although there was a deadline and a natural structure to the event. Being flexible and supporting Mary in her ideas included talking and encouraging, conversational learning and problem-solving. Mary's description and plans for Zonky also mirror the traditional subjects that would be covered in studying a foreign country. History, culture, music, art, language and geography of that area are all represented, although Mary had never been specifically taught any of these disciplines.

This is not an experience that is unique to home-based educators. Learner-led education is not something mysterious. It happens in most households. Home-based education involves helping children to be creative and feel confident, to encourage and enhance human life, to allow each person through the mindful development of their character and mental powers to do what they choose. These are things learner-led home-based education can easily fulfil. But the basis of this process is also practised widely in many homes whether explicitly recognized or not. Dinner conversation, family outings and holidays are examples of how mindful education is possible for anyone. Extending these practices and acknowledging their educational importance is possible in every family.

CONCLUDING WORDS

I have tried to show in this chapter how the mindful teacher's role is secondary to the hard work of learning, which is performed by the mindful learner. Mindful learning allows the learner to develop self-knowledge and self-confidence. This provides a foundation for wanting to learn, having the confidence to do whatever is necessary to learn and asking for help when it is needed. If the learner is able to experience this type of learning, he or she has gained a way of being which is useful throughout life. Mindful learning is not confined to the young. It is a life attitude, relevant at any age. Anyone can become a mindful learner and thereby enrich an entire life.

NOTE

1. I am wary of some definitions of creativity. For example, the one given in the NACCCE Report (NACCCE, 1999, p. 29) which defines creativity as 'imaginative activity fashioned so as to produce outcomes that are both original and of value'. The need for outcomes that have value makes the creative act constrained and narrowed to what is defined as original and as valuable, and to whom. Also having to attain an outcome is not what creativity is primarily about, in Langer's sense. Langer is concerned with a general approach to life no matter what the outcome, and therefore is consistent with unintended consequences.

REFERENCES

Holt, J. (1971) *The Under Achieving School*. Harmondsworth: Penguin.
Holt, J. (1981) *Teach Your Own*. Liss, Hants: Lighthouse Books.
Langer, E. J. (1997) *The Power of Mindful Learning*. Reading, MA: Addison-Wesley.
National Advisory Committee on Creative and Cultural Education (NACCCE) (1999) *All our Futures: Creativity, Culture and Education*. London: DFEE
Thomas, A. (1998) *Educating Children at Home*. London: Cassell.

Part Two
CREATIVITY AND PEDAGOGY

Chapter 6

Creativity and Knowledge

Margaret A. Boden

Creativity and knowledge are not opposed to each other, even though an overemphasis on current knowledge can sometimes smother creativity. On the contrary, creative thinking cannot happen unless the thinker already possesses knowledge of a rich and/or well-structured kind.

Creativity in general is the ability to come up with new ideas that are surprising yet intelligible, and also valuable in some way. This is true for all cases of creativity, whether within science, art, politics, cookery, whatever.

This definition is ambiguous, because a 'new' idea may be:

- new with respect to the whole of human history; or
- new with respect to the person's previous ways of thinking.

For our purposes in this chapter, the second type of novelty – which of course includes the first as a special case – is the more important. Teachers and psychologists need to know how children and adults can think up valuable ideas that they had not thought of before (perhaps even *could not* have thought of before), and how they can be helped to do so. If some of those ideas are also new in the historical sense, and even valuable enough to be recorded in the history books, all well and good. But the fundamental process we have to understand is the creativity of the individual mind.

To speak of the 'individual' mind, here, is not to deny that interpersonal and cultural influences are enormously important (Csikszentmihalyi, 1999; Schaffer, 1994). On the one hand, the knowledge that leads to creativity is largely assimilated from the person's national culture, their various peer groups, and their particular family circumstances. On the other hand, their readiness to think creatively, and to persist in doing so in the face of criticism and failure, is strongly affected by their self-confidence, which in turn reflects their family and wider social situation.

The psychology of motivation is as important as the psychology of cognition in understanding creativity (Collins and Amabile, 1999; Perkins, 1981). The key creators – people such as Einstein, Gandhi, or T. S. Eliot – are almost selflessly (and certainly selfishly) committed to their creative work, leaving little room in their lives for anything else (Gardner, 1993). But even you and I need self-confidence to think in unusual ways, and commitment to follow up our apparently outlandish ideas.

The cognitive psychology of creativity asks where those new ideas come from, and what mental processes are responsible for producing them. It is generally accepted that there is no special faculty here, still less one restricted to a tiny élite. On the contrary, creativity is based in everyday properties of our general intelligence (Perkins, 1981). But it is possible to distinguish three different types of creative thinking: combinational, exploratory and transformational (Boden, 1990; 1994). All are grounded in previous knowledge, but the way this knowledge is used differs in each case. It follows that the way to encourage them – or to smother them – differs, too.

Combinational creativity produces new ideas by combining (associating) old ideas in unfamiliar ways. Poetic imagery, the technique of collage in visual art, and the use of analogy in science or rhetoric are familiar examples. This type of creativity requires not only a rich source of 'old' ideas, but the ability to make associations of many different kinds. It also requires the capacity to make associations that are unexpected – yet intelligible, or valuable. That mental flexibility can be inhibited by lack of self-confidence, as well as by having a sparse collection of ideas in the first place. The more diverse types of knowledge (concepts, not just 'facts') a person acquires, the richer their mental source for making novel combinations of ideas.

Both exploratory and transformational creativity require knowledge of a rather different type. Namely, they arise out of some culturally accepted style of thinking, or structured conceptual space, that the person has learnt – and, to some extent, mastered. Examples of conceptual spaces include the various styles of dancing, painting and music; systems of geometry; theories in chemistry and geology; and rules of accountancy – or cookery. One cannot become a competent cook or accountant in five minutes: in general, learning how to move around in a particular conceptual space (how to respect its rules) always takes some practice, and may involve years of study or apprenticeship.

Exploratory creativity can happen once the person has learnt (some of) the relevant rules. Countless people earn their living by means of exploratory creativity: run-of-the-mill lounge-pianists and graphic artists, mundane jazz-musicians, and many workaday scientists too. Basically, this type of thinking investigates the possibilities inherent in the space: just what do the rules enable one to do? Even that can often generate surprises (think of chess).

There is a strong analogy, here, with the exploration of a pre-existing geographical space. Dr Livingstone, for instance, found new places (rivers, mountains) he had not visited before, and whose existence he had not suspected. Likewise, someone exploring a certain jazz style will come up with many improvisations he or she had not produced before, and someone doing geometry will often prove theorems they had not proved before. Moreover, they may be surprised to find that a certain theorem *can* be proved, or that a particular jazz sound *can* be improvised by following the accepted rules. Similarly, one may be surprised by a particular move in a game of chess.

But there is also an important disanalogy, which is that mental spaces are easier to change, or adapt, than physical spaces are. In other words, in exploring a given style of thinking the rules do not have to be (though they may be) followed to the letter. They can be stretched, tweaked or even significantly changed. Dogged exploration shades into playing around, and playing around can sometimes result in fundamental transformation of the space concerned.

Transformational creativity, then, involves some significant alteration of one or more of the rules of the current conceptual space. This enables certain ideas to be generated, which simply *could not* have been generated before the rule change. And the more fundamental the rule that is transformed, the more shocking or 'impossible' the new ideas will seem to be.

For instance, if one accepts the view that all chemical molecules are (open-ended) strings, one cannot imagine that some molecules may be (closed) rings. To transform the space of chemical theory by changing 'string' to 'ring' is to make possible a whole new class of chemical hypotheses. Similarly, to change one's painting technique from 'brush-stroke' to 'brush-dot' may be to create a new style of painting.

Most of the creative ideas that get into the history books are cases of trans-formational creativity. (The two examples just mentioned recall the origins of aromatic chemistry and pointillisme, respectively.)

Changing rules, whether by transforming or merely tweaking them is relatively easy – though even this cannot be done if one does not know the rules in the first place. (One need not know them consciously, although if one does then one can deliberately consider changing them in a variety of ways.)

But changing them in a way that will produce valuable ideas, as opposed to nonsense, requires considerable knowledge – and self-discipline. Some novel constructions will be 'worthless', no doubt. That does not matter, provided that the person (either alone or with help from others) can tell the wheat from the chaff. Judgement, as well as playfulness, is needed.

The creative thinker (potentially, every one of us) has the ability not to be rigorously limited by the pre-existing rules. But that is not to say that the rules are irrelevant. They are, after all, the source of the new ideas. Moreover, if some stylistic rules are fundamentally altered, others remain. If that were not so, the new idea would not be intelligible, and therefore would not be valued. If one is to be persuaded of the value of a shocking new idea, it must be thought of in relation to the older ones. A totally novel concept (even if it were possible) would be unintelligible and therefore valueless, so would not count as creative.

To encourage exploratory and transformational creativity, then, we should give children and more mature students the chance not only to practise the relevant style of thinking, but also to analyse it, to play around with it, and even to transform certain aspects of it. The better the person's grasp of the conceptual space concerned, the more likely that they will be able to judge the worth – or worthlessness – of new ideas.

This helps explain why expertise is essential for creativity, yet why 'experts' are commonly thought of as hidebound and uncreative. Unthinking expertise, or blind rule-following, excludes creativity. Self-aware, self-critical expertise is different. But self-criticism requires self-confidence. The parent or teacher who ridicules the child's attempts to master a new skill, or to play around with it, teaches a highly destructive lesson: that creative thinking is foolish, fruitless and even dangerous.

So much, then, for the theory. What about the practice? What are the educational implications of what we know about the psychology of creativity?

It is easy enough to say what will smother creativity in the classroom: three things, above all. First, an unbending insistence on the 'right' answer, and/or on the 'right' way of finding it; second, an unwillingness (or inability) to analyse the 'wrong' answer to see whether it might have some merit, perhaps in somewhat different circumstances (think of the 'failed' glue recipe that led to Post-it Notes); and third, an expression of impatience, or (worse still) contempt, for the person who came up with the unexpected answer.

Whether the classroom be in a primary school, an apprentice's workshop, or a university, these attitudes on the part of the teacher can nip creativity in the bud. For they tend to undermine the person's self-confidence, stifling their impulse for questioning and mental play. Only the strongest pupils will survive a lengthy tutorial regime of this type with their self-image intact and their adventurousness undimmed. Some tender souls will withdraw into their shells after even a brief experience of it, requiring careful nurturing in the future if they are to recover.

The classroom, of course, is not the only important influence. Parents and peer groups are crucial too. The more that the value of creativity is recognized in society at large, the more likely that individuals will have the inclination – and the courage – to risk it. In principle, then, a societal commitment to creative thinking could counteract the deadening influences that the more unfortunate children may encounter at home. Instead of being a place where the young child's curiosity is dampened down, or guided into highly restricted channels, the school could be a stimulus and a liberation. (Many schools already are.)

Fears have been expressed, recently, that the introduction of the National Curriculum has left little time for exploratory teaching, less for non-core subjects such as history, and still less for subjects perceived as marginal, such as music and art. In addition, the culture of testing emphasizes content at the expense of process, and especially thought processes that cannot be relied on to give the expected answer. A recent report published by the National Advisory Committee on Creative and Cultural Education (NACCCE, 1999) suggests some timetable changes that could help. More to the point, however, is the spirit in which the teaching is done. Overall, the report recommends that teachers, and teachers' training colleges, deliberately promote creative thinking, from the earliest primary years. While this includes 'the creative arts' (e.g. music, painting, pottery), it also covers teaching curricular subjects in an imaginative way. History and English, and even chemistry and maths can be taught in ways that encourage children to learn from experiment – whether in their minds or in a test tube.

Most important of all, here, are the primary school and the early years of secondary school. To foster the natural creativity of the child, and to avoid damaging it by premature criticism, the teacher should aim to encourage 'an appropriate attitude towards imaginative activity – a sense of excitement, respect, hope and wonder at the potential for transformative power that is involved, accompanied by a sense of delayed scepticism and distance' (NACCCE, 1999, p. 91). And this 'appropriate attitude' should be held by teacher and child alike. If it is held by future generations of parents too, so much the better. (Future parents are today's children: societal creativity cannot be built overnight.)

As for just how this can be done, that is more problematic. There are no guarantees on how to foster 'imaginative activity', despite the huge amount of research that has gone into it (for a useful review, see Nickerson, 1999). But the good news is that, as explained above, everyone has creative potential. And if we bear in mind the three different ways in which creative ideas are generated, we can see how various types of educational experience can be helpful.

Combinational creativity is the type of creative thinking on which most psychologists and educationists have focused in the research literature. And popular 'practical' techniques for creative thinking, such as those of Edward de Bono and Tony Buzan, exploit this type of imaginative thinking, too. Both these writers have published many books on creative techniques, most – but not all – aimed at older children, university students and people in business (see, for instance, de Bono, 1992; Buzan, 1995).

Combinational creativity depends on the person's having knowledge of 'disparate' things, and sensitivity to relatively subtle similarities. It follows that children, from their earliest years, should be introduced to as many domains of knowledge, as many different forms of experience, as possible. Moreover, these should not be presented in a rigidly compartmentalized fashion. Some of the items being studied in science classes, for example, could feature also in English lessons (there are many poems about animals or flowers, and some about sun, stars, sea, and even gold and silver). As for cultural differences, children who are enlivened to the existence of different cultures will be less ready to assume that there must be only one way of thinking about family relationships and the world around them.

'Storyboards' (and carefully chosen storybooks) can be an excellent way of helping a teacher to present a wide range of knowledge. A single board may trigger discussion of a cultural myth, or historical legend; ideas about social relationships, including familial obligations; work experiences of many kinds, from farms to factories; scientific theories about the solar system, or the biology of the animals featured in the story, and so on.

One way of encouraging children to combine specific ideas that are normally kept apart would be to give them (or let them pick out of a hat) pairs of 'unrelated' words that they then have to combine in some sensible manner. They could form a sentence mentioning both; they could tell a story in which both things play a key role; they could give three ways in which they are alike (and three in which they are different); and the like. Jokes that rely on combinational creativity, such as puns of various kinds, could help too – especially if the children were helped to analyse as well as to enjoy (joke books list many examples).

The other two forms of creativity are less commonly recognized, and more difficult to teach. Both exploratory and transformational creativity depend on the person's having already acquired a culturally accepted style of thinking, or structured conceptual space. In addition, they involve the individual's making judicious evaluations of the novel ideas they produce. Neither of these psychological abilities comes in the twinkling of an eye, for both need time – and application – to mature.

Even relatively young children, however, can be introduced to simple 'styles' of thought. Rhyming verse is one example, colour co-ordination another, dance yet another. So are familiar story structures, such as Goal–Problem–Help–Gratitude–Reciprocation, or Goal–Interference–Revenge. Each of these conceptual spaces can be explored, so that the child gradually learns what lies within them and what does not. ('Gradually' is well chosen here: learning even such simple spaces takes time, and practice.)

Later, more richly articulated artistic styles and scientific theories will be added. A child who knows that atoms of different elements have different numbers of 'hooks' (valences), for instance, can be encouraged to explore the space of possible molecules in an imaginative way. If equipped with the chemist's periodic table, which explicitly identifies many dimensions of 'chemical space', this exploration can be both more disciplined and more imaginative. After all, it was the gaps in the periodic table which alerted chemists to the possibility of unknown elements of predictable kinds. Likewise, the more children know about the 'space' of musical rhythm and harmony, the more adventurous they can be without risking falling into musical nonsense.

What counts as nonsense, however, is a delicate question. Even exploratory creativity is often more than merely following the rules – though learning to follow the rules must always come first. For this type of imagination allows one also to tweak the rules, to make small variations in the usual way of thinking so as to discover what that style allows – and, crucially, what it does not. And transformational creativity, by definition, always breaks some of the rules. Sometimes, it breaks fundamental stylistic rules (such as molecules being open-ended strings, or musical compositions being based on a home key or tonal scale). Deciding whether the resulting structure of thought is a creative insight or outrageous nonsense is never simple, and always requires knowledge and sensitivity on the part of the person (teacher or child) concerned. Here there are no guarantees.

How can teachers encourage children to explore and, eventually, even to transform their ideas? And (even more difficult) how can they help them learn how to assess the value of their new ideas? The best way is to alert the children to the fact that there are systematic *styles* of thinking, which provide guidelines relating countless specific ideas. Our minds do not consist only of isolated thoughts, or even of groups of loosely associated thoughts (which are highlighted in combinational creativity). To the contrary, many of our thoughts are integrated within culturally accepted structures, of more or less complex kinds. And, in principle, these structures can change.

Much of our knowledge of familiar stylistic structures is intuitive, not explicit. Most of us can recognize an 'Impressionist' painting, but only art historians can say clearly what counts as Impressionism. But the more we can make our knowledge explicit, the more we shall be in command of it. The child who can say what a rhyme is, or even tell us whether *this* rhymes or *that* does not, is probably in a better position to play around with rhyming than one whose appreciation of this verse-style is purely intuitive. The same goes for rhythm, and for molecules. Only someone who knows the rules of chess can suggest an alternative version (two queens, or none; three-dimensional, or played by correspondence).

Likewise, only someone who knows the previously accepted style will be in a position to evaluate the new style in relation to it. One can compare the ways in which the two are similar (both rhyming and blank verse have metre, and both can employ imaginative – 'combinational' – imagery), while also identifying the ways in which they differ (the 'liberation' from the constraint of rhyme, which makes the poet's choice of words much more open). Whether the one or the other is held to be 'better' may be a hotly contested, indeed undecidable, issue. But whether – and why – the new style is at least sensible, perhaps even interesting, can be discussed more fruitfully.

There's a danger here, of course. There are usually other 'rules', other 'guidelines', at work which not even the style expert can make explicit. So we should not let the child believe that there are strict recipes for rhyming, still less for playing around with rhyming. (What counts as an outrageous or cheeky rhyme, and how does this differ from a failed rhyme?) Even recipes, as any practised cook knows, do not say everything – and can be creatively altered in many different ways. Indeed, cookery classes are yet another opportunity for getting children to analyse the structure of what they are doing and to suggest amendments to it. ('What if we used raspberry jam instead of bramble jelly? And what if we used mustard?')

All of this puts high demands on the teacher, not least on his or her own creativity. The teacher who lacks the relevant knowledge, who thinks in rigidly prescribed fashions, who cannot try to make their intuitions explicit, and who lacks the self-confidence to say 'Let's try this!' or 'I don't know' will feel helpless and threatened if asked to teach in the ways sketched above. All the more reason, then, why this approach must be simultaneously introduced into the training colleges as well as the schools, and why we should not expect overnight success in changing the way people think about creativity.

Still less should we let the child (or the trainee teacher) think that rules do not matter. Both exploratory and transformational creativity can take place only from a firm bedrock of stylistic familiarity, grounded in practice. Even Mozart had to familiarize himself with the contemporary musical style for ten years before he came up with anything interestingly new, as opposed to merely competent – and in this he was like other leading composers (Hayes, 1981). Creativity and knowledge are two sides of the same psychological coin, not opposing forces.

In sum, the 'freedom' of creative thought is not the absence of constraints, but their imaginative – yet disciplined – development. 'All work and no play' does indeed make Jack a dull boy (and Jill a dull girl, too). But 'all play and no work' is just as sterile. Creativity is not the same thing as knowledge, but is firmly grounded in it. What educators must try to do is to nurture the knowledge without killing the creativity.

REFERENCES

Boden, M. A. (1990) *The Creative Mind: Myths and Mechanisms*. London: Abacus.
Boden, M. A. (1994) 'What is creativity?' In M. A. Boden (ed.) *Dimensions of Creativity*. Cambridge, MA: MIT Press.
de Bono, E. (1992) *Serious Creativity: Using the Power of Lateral Thinking to Create New Ideas*. New York: HarperCollins.
Buzan, T. (1995) *The Mind Map Book*. (Revd edn). London: BBC Books.
Csikszentmihalyi, M. (1999) 'Implications of a systems perspective for the study of creativity'. In R. J. Sternberg (ed.) *Handbook of Creativity*. Cambridge: Cambridge University Press.
Collins, M. A. and Amabile, T. M. (1999) 'Motivation and creativity'. In R. J. Sternberg (ed.) *Handbook of Creativity*. Cambridge: Cambridge University Press.
Gardner, H. (1993) *Creating Minds: An Anatomy of Creativity Seen through the Lives of Freud, Einstein, Picasso, Stravinsky, Eliot, Graham, and Gandhi*. New York: Basic Books.
Hayes, J. R. (1981) *The Complete Problem Solver*. Philadelphia: Franklin University Press.
National Advisory Committee on Creative and Cultural Education (NACCCE) (1999) *All our Futures: Creativity, Culture and Education*. London: DFEE.
Nickerson, R. S. (1999) 'Enhancing creativity'. In R. J. Sternberg (ed.) *Handbook of Creativity*. Cambridge: Cambridge University Press.
Perkins, D. N. (1981) *The Mind's Best Work*. Cambridge, MA: Harvard University Press.
Schaffer, S. (1994) 'Making-up discovery'. In M. A. Boden (ed.) *Dimensions of Creativity*. Cambridge, MA: MIT Press.

Chapter 7

Teacher Education within Post-Compulsory Education and Training: A Call for a Creative Approach

Ken Gale

INTRODUCTION

Defining a creative approach

The approach taken in this chapter will be to encourage those involved in post-compulsory teacher education to engage in a consideration of new and fresh approaches to their professional practice. This might be achieved by encouraging a critical examination of their practices in the light of a diverse range of theoretical and research-based trends and developments that have taken place in the field of educational studies in recent years. Therefore, this chapter is designed to focus upon four theoretical models within which a creative approach to post-compulsory teacher education might be developed.

To facilitate this purpose these models are described here as:

- humanistic;
- reflective practitioner;
- critical theory; and
- post-structural.

It is important to stress that these are categories of convenience rather than fixed immutable theoretical models that might be used to define and to govern specific forms of practice, and it is hoped that these models will be used as a means of theorizing possible creative practices. Their use is designed, therefore, to encourage those involved in post-compulsory teacher education to relativize, critique and evaluate these and other models, theoretical positions and perspectives that might be relevant to their practice, with a view to developing fresh, innovative and creative approaches to their practice in the future.

Possibly the most fundamental issue that arises in relation to taking a creative approach to teacher education within the post-compulsory sector is based upon a simple question. Can a creative approach be expressed, sustained and effectively practised within the policy frameworks that establish and govern current procedures and practices? In addressing this question, therefore, the nature, character and intended purpose of a creative approach to post-compulsory teacher education has to be clearly described, defined and evaluated. It is clear that a creative approach to post-compulsory teacher education will involve teachers in coming to terms with their work as a rigorously developed professional practice. Ball articulates this emphasis in what he describes as the 'urgent role of theory in educational studies' (Ball, 1995, p. 255). He suggests ways of promoting a form of educational studies that stresses contingency, reflexivity and risk-taking over a more traditional technical rationalism. In Ball's view such an approach is designed to suggest to practitioners ways of re-examining their practices within the context of the curriculum and management pressures that currently operate within the post-compulsory education sector. Such an approach is likely to have an effect upon practices beyond the limits of the classroom itself, but it would appear that if teachers were encouraged to consolidate their professional identity and practice style then the consequences of this will also need to be carefully examined. For example, in espousing the value of narrative and life history approaches, Goodson suggests that 'Life politics, the politics of identity construction and ongoing identity maintenance, will become a major and growing site of ideo-logical and intellectual contestation' (1998, p. 4). Schon (1983), in outlining the nature and character of the reflective practitioner, was influential in alerting us to the possible effect of risk-taking and reflexive approaches upon the institutions within which they are situated:

> When a member of a bureaucracy embarks on a course of reflective practice, allowing himself to experience confusion and uncertainty, subjecting his frames and theories to conscious criticism and change, he may increase his capacity to contribute to significant organizational learning, but he also becomes, by the same token, a danger to the stable system of rules and procedures within which he is expected to deliver his technical expertise. (p. 328)

A creative approach to post-compulsory teacher education would, therefore, appear to require a rethinking and a repositioning of practice style, values and approaches that in turn may contribute to various forms of change. Woods and Jeffrey (1996), perhaps with an implied reference to the work of Kuhn (1970), in examining the nature of learning and the need for flexibility within a creative approach to teaching, suggest that 'sometimes there are extraordinary leaps . . . there is a need to recognize these when we see them'. They also notice that whilst substantial demands exist for teachers to use creative or innovative approaches in their classroom practices, they are often constrained within institutional frameworks and policy requirements that are, in fact, rigid and inflexible. It is within the context of this apparent tension that Ball has suggested that teachers must consider whether they are to be 'intellectuals or technicians' (1995, p. 255). The rhetoric contained in Ball's phrase helps to reveal the climate within which a possible creative approach to teacher education within post-compulsory education needs to take place. This is a climate that sees the role of the Further Education Funding Council (FEFC) and the Higher Education Funding Council (HEFC) playing a major and influential part, both in terms of resources and practices. The Dearing Report has also been instrumental in the emergence of organizations such as the Institute for Learning and Teaching (ILT) in higher education and the Further Education National Training Organization (FENTO) in further education. These bodies are becoming increasingly influential in setting down various standards and practice requirements within the post-compulsory sector and therefore provide an important context within a creative approach to teacher education within the sector.

THEORIZING THE NOTION OF A CREATIVE APPROACH TO POST-COMPULSORY TEACHER EDUCATION

It is within the context of these policy requirements and the institutional frameworks in which they are designed to function that a detailed, critically reflexive and closely analytical approach to the examination of creativity within post-compulsory teacher education needs to take place. Space does not provide the opportunity to examine vast numbers of theoretical expositions on the nature of creativity; however, it will be possible to identify and briefly examine four major areas in which a creative approach may be applied with relevance and apposition to post-compulsory teacher education.

The humanistic model

A humanistic model of post-compulsory teacher education would be based upon the principles and practices of person-centred psychology as exemplified in the work of Rogers (1961; 1989) and Maslow (1954). Such a model of learning was developed in America mainly as a reaction against behaviourism which, it was argued, attempted to reduce learning to simple statements of learner behaviour. By placing the learner at the centre of the learning experience, the humanistic model focuses on the notion of the self as the essential characteristic of human existence. In Maslow's famous hierarchy of needs 'self-actualization' becomes the pinnacle of human achievement and development, the point at which needs gratification is fulfilled. This model is, therefore, based upon holistic notions of personal growth, the realization of inner potential and the satisfaction of a hierarchy of motivating needs.

The approach taken through the implementation of such a model would inevitably be student centred, placing the learner at the heart of a range of experiences that would lead to learning and personal development. So in the work of Rogers it is the processes that lead to active self-discovery that are valued rather than the behavioural responses to certain stimuli or the acquisition of particular forms of knowledge. The holism that this approach implies encourages and involves personal development, stimulation of feelings, self-initiation and self-evaluation. The teacher or facilitator of this form of student-centred learning is seen to work within a role that, according to Rogers, provides unconditional positive regard and empathy towards learners and their learning experiences. In this respect teaching does not involve controlling or directing the students towards the satisfaction of goals which are external to the learner, rather it involves providing the means by which learning can take place. This kind of model is unlikely, therefore, to be able to align itself to a set of externally recommended set of 'standards' as identified within the FENTO recommendations. Rogers claims that teaching can only be a meaningful and valuable activity in that it provides an environment in which learning can take place. In a famous passage he asserts: 'I have come to feel that the only learning which significantly influences behaviour is self-discovered, self-appropriated learning' (1989, p. 302). Learning then becomes conceived as something which is part of a process rather than as something that leads to the acquisition of a particular product; its emphasis is therefore formative rather than summative. A formative approach, therefore, involves teachers and learners in examining teaching and learning practice actually during the programme of study and will involve ongoing techniques such as question and answer routines, project work and regular and sometimes informal self, peer and tutor assessment activities. This would be preferred to a summative approach in which the emphasis would be upon what the learner might have achieved at the end of the programme of study, as evidenced by the passing of a test or the fulfilment of a range of competences or performance criteria. The teacher's role is therefore to act as a facilitator in this process, providing what Woods (1988) and others have described in a different context as 'scaffolding': a means of enabling growth.

In terms of a creative approach to post-compulsory teacher education the humanistic model suggests a facilitative rather than a directive or didactic approach; one in which the full potential of the learner can be realized. The slavish adherence and commitment to the preset goals, standards and outcomes of any external authority, it is claimed, will not help to achieve this. Rogers himself asserted that 'my experience has been that I cannot teach another person how to teach' (1989, p. 301). Such an approach, therefore, would involve the provision of a supportive learning environment. This might include:

- identifying the learning needs of the individuals within the group;
- recognizing these as a motivational force in learners;
- using these as the basis for facilitating learning;
- acting as a resource to student learning;
- becoming a participant learner and member of the learning group; and
- sharing feelings and thoughts with the learning group.

In commenting on the work of Rogers in this specific context, Schon provides a means of assessing the creative nature and potential of this approach:

> Rogers . . . has *reframed teaching* in a way that gives central importance to his own role as a learner. He elicits self-discovery in others, first by modelling for others, as a learner, the open expression of his own deepest reflections . . . then . . . as he expresses his own uncertainties and convictions, emphasizes the 'merely personal' nature of his views and invites and listens to the reactions of others, he seeks to be literally thought-provoking. (1987, p. 92)

Whilst not strictly operating within a humanistic conceptual framework, the work of Heron (1989) provides an extremely practical illustration of the way in which a creative approach to the facilitation of learning can be employed. Heron encourages an approach that inscribes the teacher as a facilitator working with groups of learners. The facilitator enters into a relationship with the group in which there is an attempt to reach all group members through a variety of facilitative strategies. He describes learning as 'having four interdependent forms, which in many ways complement and support each other' (p. 12). He places these four forms within 'an up-hierarchy, with the ones higher being grounded in those that are lower' (p. 13).

1. 'Experiential learning' involves an encounter with the world followed by
2. 'imaginal learning' which involves the learner in the identification of the patterns of form and process in the world; these then help to form the basis for
3. 'conceptual learning' and the development of language and knowledge and, finally, arising from the preceding forms,
4. 'practical learning' and the application of a range of skills.

Heron appears to give an axiomatic role to imaginal learning within his hierarchical model by providing a creative and clearly student-centred means of moving from an actual experience to conceptual learning. Within this relationship the learner is given an important and extremely active cognitive and affective capability. Concepts and personal autonomy are not framed within an authoritarian set of relationships, rather the learner is encouraged to seek out, through the agency of creative and imaginative processes, the connections that might exist between experience and the way in which these experiences might be conceptualized.

Within this broad humanistic context, therefore, it becomes clear that a creative approach to post-compulsory teacher education, crucially, is seen to focus both upon the affective or attitudinal character of learning, as well as upon the development of knowledge or particular skills.

By adopting a student-centred approach to learning, a creative approach to post-compulsory teacher education based upon a humanistic model is also a clear example of what we might describe as experiential learning. The experiences of the learners become of primary significance in the development of their own learning process.

What might be described as the reflective practitioner model of post-compulsory teacher education, is also based upon the principles and practices of experiential learning.

The reflective practitioner model

Donald Schon (1983, 1987) is widely associated with the growth and popularity of the reflective practitioner model, and the opening paragraph of *Educating the Reflective Practitioner*, through the use of a carefully chosen metaphor, neatly introduces and contextualizes the nature and role of reflective practice:

> In the varied topography of professional practice, there is a high ground overlooking a swamp. On the high ground, manageable problems lend themselves to solution through the application of research-based theory and technique. In the swampy lowland, messy, confusing problems defy technical solution. (1987, p. 3)

The use of this metaphor suggests, on the one hand, a somewhat positivistic, technical-rationalist model of practice, based upon carefully developed techniques and a 'tried and tested' methodology and, on the other, a practice which Schon himself describes as 'non-rational intuitive artistry' (1983, p. 239). It is clearly Schon's contention that the latter provides the most appropriate means of addressing those 'messy, confusing problems' that 'defy technical solution'. The use of what he describes as 'reflection-in-action', a form of thinking whilst doing, involving 'the spontaneous, intuitive performance of the actions of everyday life' (1983, p. 49) describes for Schon the artistry that will help to address these problems. 'Reflection-in-action' can be contrasted with what Schon refers to as 'reflection-on-action', where the reflection might be seen as a retrospective activity, looking back at what has been done in a rational considered manner. A frequently cited theorist of experiential learning within the field of teacher education and training, David Kolb, posits a concept of reflection similar in principle and practice to Schon's notion of 'reflection-on-action'. Kolb proposes that experience can be turned into learning experience through a 'process whereby knowledge is created through the transformation of experience' (1984, p. 38). He describes a learning cycle that moves from 'concrete experience' through 'reflective observation' and 'abstract conceptualization' to 'active experimentation'. This cycle exemplifies a technique that employs 'reflective observation' in much the same way as Schon describes 'reflection-on-action', rather than the kind of creative approach that is implied by 'reflection-in-action'. This would also appear to be the kind of technical-rational approach to reflective practice that FENTO is referring to, and which they describe in one of their eight standards within the 'Key Areas of Teaching' as 'reflecting upon and evaluating one's own performance and planning future practice' (FENTO Key Area of Teaching, 1999).

So although, as Ghaye (2000) points out: 'There are many kinds of reflection and many types of practice undertaken by different people in different contexts' (p. 6), Schon appears to offer us a kind of reflective dualism, embracing artistry on the one hand and technique on the other. He espouses the value of 'reflection-in-action' as an artistry, a creative approach to practice which, he feels, will help to address what he refers to as the 'crisis of confidence in the professions' (p. 13). In commenting upon Schon's work Usher *et al.* (1997) mention that 'reflection-in-action' will be enacted rather than applied. So that where 'reflection-on-action' tends to be retrospective, involving the practitioner in a careful, rational and applied post-activity *technique*, 'reflection-in-action' will take place within the activity, in the form of a 'non-rational intuitive *artistry*', referred to earlier, which will be immediate to and within the activity itself. They argue that Schon has failed 'to address the lessons of reflection-in-action to his own practice as a producer of text' (p. 142). They argue strongly for a greater reflexivity, to see 'how practices themselves are inscribed – including the situated practice of academic writing' (p. 143).

A creative approach to post-compulsory teacher education using the concept of the reflective practitioner as described by Schon would be likely, therefore, to focus upon the use of 'reflection-in-action' despite the criticisms that have been directed at it by Usher *et al.* and others. An intriguing question for the teacher educator remains: how might the principles and practices of 'reflection-in-action' be included within a successful teacher education programme? The answer would appear to lie, at least in part, within the context of the critical comment offered by Usher *et al.* (1997). The need for reflexivity appears to be crucial in this respect. Practitioners need to be encouraged to look in on their own practices, to turn their practices back on themselves to examine critically what these practices entail. The creativity that this approach implies can be articulated and expressed through the agency of personal narratives, practice portfolios and learning journals. Such an approach will encourage teachers and others to theorize their practices in a critical and imaginative way. In carrying this out a further and significant question is raised by Schon in relation to the idea of a creative approach to professional practice:

> What happens in such an educational bureaucracy when a teacher begins to think and act not as a technical expert but as a reflective practitioner? Her reflection-in-action poses a potential threat to the dynamically conservative system in which she lives. (1983, p. 332)

Critical theory: an emancipatory or liberatory model

Critical theory sets up a challenge to dominant, usually positivistic epistemologies. It possesses an emancipatory or liberatory quality in that it seeks to detect and to challenge belief systems, ideologies or theoretical constructs that are designed in some way to limit human freedom and democratic practices.

Critical theory has its origins in the German philosophical and sociological movement known as the Frankfurt School, and the work of Habermas (1972) is of recent and central significance within this movement. For Habermas science represents a belief system, despite its attempt to present itself as interested only in a rational, objective and what Weber (1947) would describe as a value-free mode of enquiry. Science depends, like other belief systems, upon ideological assumptions and interests and so-called Enlightenment – reason itself – acts as an instrument of oppression. Therefore, critical theory will encourage an analysis of experience to achieve liberation from psychological, social and political oppression.

The work of Paulo Freire provides a valuable illustration of the way in which critical theory may be creatively employed within the context of post-compulsory teacher education. In *The Pedagogy of the Oppressed* (1972) Freire argues that oppressed people lack a critical understanding of their position in the world. The world is presented to them as 'natural', as an objective reality and one which is therefore unchangeable: in a strictly Cartesian manner, it has become externalized and only observable from a distance, beyond their control. In his involvement in literacy programmes with oppressed people in South America in the 1960s, Freire, through the use of what he called 'culture circles', attempted to bring people into a dialogue, a praxis, with this so-called external world. The 'culture circles' were essentially discussion groups into which Freire would introduce a drawing and invite the participants to identify what was 'natural' and what was 'cultural' in the drawing. Freire used the term 'conscientization' to describe the process whereby the participants gradually began to achieve this process of identification and to see and, therefore, to re-examine their position in the world. This application of critical theory is designed to create a subjectivity and a form of self-awareness, which will encourage reflection upon the world, and the eventual transformation of it. Critical theory proposes a creative approach on the part of the learners because, for the first time, they are encouraged through participation in the 'culture circles' to become actively involved in a praxis which brings together thoughts and actions, subjectivity and objectivity in what is claimed to be a genuinely transformative process.

Boal (1979, 1992), in the setting up of what he called forum theatre, was greatly influenced by the writings of Freire. Boal attempted to involve audiences and to encourage them to become participants in theatre, as a means of motivating them to re-examine and change their own lives. He coined the term 'spect-actors' to describe the way in which people would be encouraged to move from simply and passively observing a particular drama unfold, as spectators, to actively involving themselves in the drama, reinterpreting its themes, taking it into new directions and becoming instrumental in creating change. Boal's methods suggest a creativity of approach that could be actively employed within the context of post-compulsory teacher education. His *Games for Actors and Non-Actors* (1992) is a valuable source of material that can be used within such an approach.

The work of feminists such as bell hooks and Patti Lather have also used critical theory as a means of expressing a radical and creative approach to learning; hooks by attempting to show that theory can be a 'liberatory practice' (1994, p. 59) and Lather by examining 'what it means to do empirical research in an unjust world' (1995, p. 292). Their work also helps to contribute to a much-needed gender balance to the kind of research and practice that is being carried out in the field of post-compulsory teacher education.

A post-structural model

In examining what might contribute to the nourishment of teacher creativity Craft has noted that: 'Our society is transforming. Children, young people and adults are faced with increasing chaos of choice and social identity in all spheres of life. Some of the features of this age are its instability, complexity, transience and lack of conformity' (Craft, 1996, p. 309). Hargreaves (1994) in observing a similar world of 'accelerating change, intense compression of time and space, cultural diversity, technological complexity, national insecurity and scientific uncertainty' sees also an education system that is modernistic and monolithic and which 'continues to pursue deeply anachronistic purposes within opaque and inflexible structures' (p. 3).

A post-structural model of a creative approach to post-compulsory teacher education needs, therefore, to be placed within this essentially post-modern context. The work of Foucault provides an excellent source of material from which to begin an examination of this kind. In his later work Foucault (1988) attempted 'to show that things are not as self-evident as one believed, to see that what is accepted as self-evident will no longer be accepted as such'. It was his view that 'As soon as one can no longer think things as one frequently thought them, transformation becomes both very urgent, very difficult and quite possible' (p. 154).

Evidence suggests that many aspects of post-compulsory teacher education and training have become habitualized and naturalized. For example, in examining the use of the highly influential 'reflective practitioner' model in this context, Ball (1995), Bleakley (1999) and Ecclestone (1996) have suggested that the model can sometimes take on a 'mantric' quality – its often superficial application being seen as *de rigueur* on such programmes. With another specific reference to teacher education and development, Robertson (1992) has argued that masculine values predominate in the construction of learning models and personal identity. A good example of this can be found in Knowles' (1978) highly influential work *The Adult Learner: A Neglected Species*, in which Knowles proposes the concept of andragogy without addressing highly relevant gender issues which inevitably must relate to the study of adult learning. Perhaps when we read writers such as Weiner (1994, p. 5) asserting that: 'the curriculum perspective offered (in the UK) remains mono-cultural, male-centred and technocratic' we should not be surprised.

It is against evidence of this kind that a post-structural model of a creative approach to post-compulsory teacher education needs to be developed. Again the work of Ball (1995) provides a useful starting point when he argues that 'there is a kind of theorising that rests upon complexity, uncertainty and doubt and upon a reflexivity about its own production and its claims to knowledge about the social' (p. 269). The kind of theorizing that Ball refers to here will involve the teacher educator within the post-compulsory sector, who wishes to take a creative approach to practice, in the deconstruction or critical evaluation of the discourses that have been instrumental in the construction of their practices. For Foucault the discourse exists as a 'regime of truth', setting up, through hegemonic processes of normalization and naturalization, the means by which we come to govern ourselves and those around us. The discourse constructs the 'teacher', the 'learner', the 'manager' and the parameters within which they function and perform. It is a system of familiar practices, which might include curriculum development, lesson planning, assessment procedures, equal opportunities and a wide range of policies whose origins might appear to be indistinct. Ball's rhetorical invitation to become an 'intellectual' rather than a 'technician' will require creative teaching practitioners to critically evaluate these familiar practices and to engage in activities which expose the manner in which these practices have been constructed as normal and natural. Not only will such a strategy offer the possibility of new and fresh approaches to teaching and learning practice within post-compulsory teacher education, but also it will begin to unearth the way in which the discourses in question have established truth claims and how they have gone about, through disciplinary procedures such as systems of appraisal and teaching observation, legitimizing them also.

The use of narrative represents a post-structural means of fostering a creative approach to teacher education within the post-compulsory sector. Bruner (1996, p. 39) suggests that thinking takes place in 'two broad ways . . . one seems more specialized for treating of physical "things", the other for treating of people and their plights. These are conventionally known as *logical-scientific* thinking and *narrative thinking*'. Whilst Bruner's use of this binary opposition represents a somewhat questionable methodological approach, his suggestion that the former has been privileged over the latter does help to explain the kind of thinking that traditional curriculum models appear to contain. Bruner further suggests that narrative thinking involves itself in a metaphorical rather than a literal approach, in problem-setting rather than problem-solving, in raising questions rather than answering questions and in openness rather than closure. If we accept the Foucauldian notion of the existence of discursively constructed meanings and identities, the narrative approach that is being presented here offers the potential for new and imaginative teaching and learning strategies to develop. This also supports the view proposed by Woods and Jeffrey (1996, p. 2) that: 'There are biographical, situational, institutional, structural, resource and relational factors that go into the social production of creative thinking.' The kind of 'narrative thinking' that Bruner describes offers a means of releasing these factors within a creative learning context. Encouraging learners to express themselves through the use of stories also provides a means of placing what Foucault has referred to as the 'regime of truth' that the discourse presents, within a relative, evaluative place where the possibility for deconstruction becomes greatly enhanced. The use of narrative, therefore, can provide an approach to post-compulsory teacher education that encourages autonomy, imagination and above all creativity.

A story told by Patrick Slattery (1995) helps to illustrate the need for the creative use of narrative within the context of post-compulsory teacher education and also demonstrates that discourses are not just linguistic, that they can also be material, involving actions, or, as in this case, objects. Slattery, using a vivid expository style, describes his first education course as an undergraduate student: 'thirty students crowded into a traditional classroom with metal desks facing a blackboard. The walls were bare, and fluorescent fixtures filled the room with light. There were no windows. It was as though the outside world had been shut out' (p. 64). Slattery continues by describing the teacher and his methods: 'The students dutifully copied these words in their notebooks. The professor turned to the class and paused for comments. No one dared to say a word'. Slattery continues with his story, adding layers of description to the image created, until he concludes the paragraph in the following manner: 'There was no room for intuition, ambiguity, emotion, intrinsic motivation, complexity and uncertainty in the curriculum of my undergraduate training'.

It is clear from these remarks that Slattery is proposing an approach to the teaching and learning that takes place within post-compulsory teacher education as being both creative and imaginative. A post-structural approach can generally, therefore, be seen to foster the kinds of teacher attitudes and approaches which might help to engender such a creative approach within the field of post-compulsory teacher education.

LOOKING AT POSSIBLE FUTURES

It is possible that the employment of creative, imaginative or innovative strategies within post-compulsory teacher education may help to bring about a reconceptualization of practice that, in turn, might help to facilitate positive change across the post-compulsory sector of education. The approach taken in this chapter, therefore, has been designed to encourage an investigation and application, on the part of practitioners in the field, to engage in innovative teaching practices, risk-taking curriculum strategies and critically reflexive methodologies. The practice design that might emerge from this would help to encourage practitioners to consider an approach to content, method and style which moved them away from their existing and possibly traditional forms of practice. The chapter has been designed to involve practitioners in an examination of new approaches and initiatives. This approach has also been designed to engender a consideration of what may have become habitual or naturalized practices, with a view to encouraging approaches to these practices which might emerge from fresh, different and possibly more original perspectives. So, for example, the teacher who had only considered motivational strategies which were based upon explicit, instrumental and extrinsic goals, within the context of performance and achievement-related curriculum and assessment models, might begin to consider working within different parameters. Such a teacher might be encouraged, for example, to examine outcomes that may well be tacit, hidden and not formally described within the course design and curriculum structure. This approach would be likely to use affective learning strategies; perhaps involving more formative or process based models, based upon the use and trust of intuition and with a focus upon implicit, personal and intrinsic goals. Fryer (quoted in Craft *et al.*, 1997) identifies a number of attitudes, which distinguish teachers most oriented to creativity from those who are not. These include: 'valuing pupil self-expression, and teaching skills which facilitate this', 'aiming for pupils to think creatively', 'wanting pupils to be able to express their feelings' and 'valuing pupils' ideas and questions in assessing creativity' (p. 69). It is clear, therefore, that the teacher in post-compulsory teacher education has also to express and practise a commitment to creativity if such an approach is to influence the practices of others in this field.

So it becomes clear that a creative approach to teacher education within the post-compulsory sector of education has the potential to produce far-reaching effects upon the nature, content and contexts of professional practice. For this to take place, however, any future examination of creative approaches to post-compulsory teacher education must take into consideration the range of possible policies and contexts that might be encountered in its development and application. It must also examine closely the attitudes and dispositions of the teachers who may be involved in such an approach. In conclusion, this chapter has attempted to suggest that by linking a creativity of approach to the kinds of theoretical models outlined here, professional practitioners will be more likely to look at their work in new, fresh and innovative ways. Consequently, it is hoped that through the kind of rigorous critical, evaluative and reflexive approach to post-compulsory teacher education practice being suggested here, they will become immersed in more engaging, meaningful and relevant teaching and learning experiences.

REFERENCES

Ball, S. (1995) 'Intellectuals or technicians? The urgent role of theory in educational studies', *British Journal of Educational Studies,* **43**(3), 255–71.

Bleakley, A. (1999), 'From reflective practice to holistic reflexivity studies', *Higher Education,* **24**(3), 31–30.

Boal, A. (1979) *Theatre of the Oppressed.* London: Pluto Press.

Boal, A. (1992) *Games for Actors and Non-Actors.* London: Routledge.

Bruner, J. (1996) *The Culture of Education.* London: Harvard University Press.

Craft, A. (1996) 'Nourishing educator creativity: a holistic approach to continuing professional development'. *British Journal of In-service Education,* **22**(3), 309–23.

Craft, A. with Dugal, J., Dyer, G., Jeffrey, B. and Lyons, T. (1997) *Can You Teach Creativity?* Nottingham: Education Now.

Ecclestone, K. (1996) 'The reflective practitioner: mantra or a model for emancipation?' *Studies in the Education of Adults,* **28**, 148–60.

Further Education National Training Organization (FENTO) (1999) *Standards for Teaching and Supporting Learning.* London: FENTO.

Foucault, M. (1988) *Michel Foucault: Politics, Philosophy and Culture – Interviews and Other Writings 1977–1984.* New York: Routledge.

Freire, P. (1972) *The Pedagogy of the Oppressed.* Harmondsworth: Penguin.

Ghaye, T. (2000) 'Into the reflective mode: bridging the stagnant moat'. *Reflective Practice,* **1**(1), 5–9.

Goodson, I. (1998) 'Storying the self: life politics and the study of the teacher's life and work'. In W. Pinar (ed.) *Curriculum: Toward New Identities.* New York: Garland.

Habermas, J. (1972) *Knowledge and Human Interests.* Boston: Beacon.

Hargreaves, A. (1994) *Changing Teachers, Changing Times.* London: Cassell.

Heron, J. (1989) *The Facilitators Handbook.* London: Kogan Page.

hooks, b. (1994) *Teaching to Transgress.* London: Routledge.

Knowles, (1978) *The Adult Learner: A Neglected Species.* Houston: Gulf.

Kolb, D. (1984) *Experiential Learning: Experience as the Source of Learning and Development.* Englewood Cliffs: Prentice Hall.

Kuhn, T. (1970) *The Structure of Scientific Revolutions.* Chicago: Chicago University Press.

Lather, P. (1995) 'Feminist perspectives on empowering research methodologies'. In J. Holland, M. Blair and S. Sheldon (eds) *Debates and Issues in Feminist Research and Pedagogy.* Clevedon: Multilingual Matters in association with the Open University.

Maslow, A. (1954) *Motivation and Personality.* New York: Harper.

Robertson, H.-J. (1992) 'Teacher development and gender equity'. In A. Hargreaves and M. Fullan (eds) *Understanding Teacher Development.* London: Cassell.

Rogers, C. (1961) *On Becoming a Person.* London: Constable.

Rogers, C. (1989) *The Carl Rogers Reader.* London: Constable.

Schon, D. (1983) *The Reflective Practitioner.* San Francisco: Jossey-Bass.

Schon, D. (1987) *Educating the Reflective Practitioner.* San Francisco: Jossey-Bass.

Slattery, P. (1995) *Curriculum Development in the Postmodern Era.* New York: Garland.

Usher, R., Bryant, I. and Johnston, R. (1997) *Adult Education and the Postmodern Challenge.* London: Routledge.

Weber, M. (1947) *The Theory of Social and Economic Organization.* New York: Free Press.

Weiner, G. (1994) *Feminisms in Education.* Buckingham: Open University Press.

Woods, D. (1988) *How Children Think and Learn.* Oxford: Blackwell.

Woods, P. and Jeffrey, B. (1996) *Teachable Moments.* Buckingham: Open University Press.

Chapter 8

Creating Danger: The Place of the Arts in Education Policy

Bethan Marshall

Creativity seems to hold an ambiguous place in this country. We appear uncertain as to its value, unable to decide whether it is a good or a bad thing. On the surface there is little doubt that it is a positive force. The reputation of 'cool Britannia' seems in thrall to the so-called creative industries. Diane Coyle's book *The Weightless World* (1998) is clear that music, fashion, the film industry and, more tangentially but equally connected, advertising, small software companies, even tourism, which is so dependent on image creation, have long since outstripped, in economic terms, the manufacturing sector. We British are a nation living on our wits.

Despite the decline of manufacturing, this latter observation echoes the older argument that the success of these industries was also, and still is, dependent on our inventiveness. This, however, has often been countered by the notion that we failed to sufficiently invest in the inventor. But these plucky individuals seem to represent a particularly British take on the 'quirky small guy' against bureaucratic corporates, who represent not so much power as unimaginative philistinism. Such people have entered into the British collective consciousness: Clive Sinclair (who pioneered digital watches, calculators and home computers); Charles Dyson whose vacuum cleaners took on the might of an established technology; the inventor of the clockwork radio, Trevor Bayliss. All echo, to a greater or lesser extent, the struggles of their patron saint played by Alec Guinness in the 1951 film *The Man in the White Suit*.

And yet the title of that 'Ealing comedy' begins to unravel our sense of anxiety about the creative in its gesture towards both the laboratory and the mad house, the scientist and the madman. It is in the arts, however, where the arguments for creativity would seem to be incontrovertible, and that our ambivalence appears the greatest. This is never more clearly seen than in schools. For here, despite the evidence to the contrary of the economic, never mind the personal worth of being creative, creativity has not had a good press for at least twenty years. Part of its decline has arisen from its close association with the so-called progressive education and, in particular, the notion that academic standards have been sacrificed on the altar of the personal growth of the child. Central to this argument, as always in this country, is the curriculum for English. This is no simple reference to a specific form of cultural identity, though in recent years it has certainly meant that it is the much-harder-to-grasp equation of public order and morality with the correct use of language. It was the politician Norman Tebbit who remarked in an interview on the BBC radio *Today* programme, in 1985:

> If you allow standards to slip to the stage where good English is no better than bad English, where people can turn up filthy and nobody takes any notice of them at school – just as well as turning up clean – all those things tend to cause people to have no standards at all, and once you lose your standards then there's no imperative to stay out of crime. (Tebbit, cited in Graddol *et al.*,1991, p. 52)

Such a crudely causal connection between a slip in speech and a life of crime may seem absurd. Yet in the hands of more subtle advocates of this position it appears a more plausible or at least less implausible point of view because it is presented as social commentary. John Rae, the former head of Westminster School, wrote in an *Observer* newspaper article, 'The overthrow of grammar coincided with the acceptance of the equivalent of creative writing in social behaviour' (Rae, cited in Graddol *et al.*,1991, p. 52). More recently the journalist Melanie Phillips, in her diatribe against what she perceives to be the dangers of 'progressive education', writes 'The revolt against teaching the rules of grammar became part of the wider repudiation of external forms of authority' (Phillips, 1996, p. 69).

Such perceptions, widely held and frequently promulgated, though often less explicitly, through UK papers such as *The Daily Mail* or *The Telegraph*, have made any discussion about creativity much harder. The emotive edge that this kind of coverage lends discussion to means that any one who comments on the imaginative qualities of a piece of child's writing, without first mentioning the spelling mistakes and punctuation errors, is guilty of wilful neglect bordering on public disorder.

Melanie Phillips again demonstrates the point well in her book *All Must Have Prizes* where she cites the example of Pat D'Arcy, an English language adviser who in commenting on a 10-year-old's piece of work had the temerity to suggest that despite having made 38 errors had produced a 'highly competent narrative'. D'Arcy even goes on to analyse the type of error which the pupil makes, noting that 21 involved one mistake only. At no point does she suggest that technical accuracy is unimportant, or that she would not encourage the boy to go back and redraft his work, this time looking at the spelling and punctuation. What she does say is that, 'If Paul's teacher had conveyed the message to the children that above all else correctness was of prime importance, stories like this would never have been composed' (D'Arcy, cited in Phillips, 1996, p. 101).

Phillips had first used this example in a *Guardian* newspaper article and received a number of letters defending D'Arcy's position. For Phillips this was further support for her claim that 'These teachers dismissed his mistakes as unimportant and repeated the misapprehension that mastery of the language is a bar to creativity' (1996, p. 101). Yet there is evidence that D'Arcy's approach does make pedagogic sense even if it does not coincide with Phillips' view of an orderly society. A report commissioned in 1998 by the Quality and Curriculum Authority compared the written performance of English and French pupils at Key Stage 2 (11-year-olds) (Osborn and Planel, 1999). It found that primary school pupils in this country not only wrote more confidently than their French counterparts but that they spelled better too, despite the more formal methods of teaching the basics implemented by French schools. Indeed, the report went on to suggest, albeit tentatively, that part of the explanation for the better performance on this side of the Channel may lie in the British pupils' willingness to 'have a go' and not worry about making mistakes.

A similar clash can be seen in a more recent exchange between the children's author and special needs teacher, David Almond, and the Secretary of State for Education, David Blunkett. Almond was awarded the prestigious Carnegie Medal for his book *Skellig*, and he used his acceptance speech to condemn the government's educational policies. The *Independent* newspaper then printed this speech on 15 July 1999. In it he describes a mythical primary teacher, Mrs McKee, an amalgam of the many teachers he has encountered in his career. He goes on to analyse a session where he has been invited into her class to discuss with the pupils his new book. He finds a classroom where the walls are covered in the children's work and he is 'moved by the quality and depth of the children's reading' (Almond, 1999). The ensuing discussion not only covers Almond's own authorial techniques – the way he drafts, organizes chapter lengths, the pace of narrative and so on – but ranges over Blake's poetry (mentioned in the book), the nature of angels and evolution. At the end the pupils are encouraged to write themselves: 'We play writing games that show just how vivid and how quick the imagination is for all of us'.

What possible controversy could such a positive picture provoke, one might reasonably ask. But the sting of his article was, as always, in the tail. Almond writes:

> As I move into the corridor, I realize who Mrs McKee really is. She's the demon. She's the swivel-eyed monster we have read so much about in the past 10 years. Her preferred methods are diabolical. She'd lead children into the dark pit of anarchy and ignorance. She is a progressive teacher. We thought we'd consigned her to the flames, but there she is in our schools: energetic, inspirational, and exemplary. And she gets results.

He goes on to argue that the Mrs McKees of this world should, along with their charges, be allowed to escape the clutches of 'the world of assessment, accreditation, targets, scores, grades, tests and profiles . . . the bureaucratic nightmare' that 'entangles' her for 10 per cent of the year. Almond concludes:

There might be times when nothing is apparently going on, but we will accept your (Mrs McKee's) belief that there is a mysterious zone of the imagination, of intuition, of insight in which the beady gaze of the assessor and the record-keeper would be deadly.

Four days later Mr Almond's thoughts received this reply in the *Daily Mail* from Mr Blunkett. While not referring directly to the article, few doubted to whom it was addressed. Defending the introduction of the literacy hour, something Almond had not directly mentioned, Blunkett writes,

Yet there still remain the doubters to whom these methods remain anathema. I still encounter those in the education world who would prefer the quiet life of the past, where education was 'progressive' and where the failure of half our pupils was taken for granted. There are even those who suggest that learning to read properly threatens creativity. Can they really be taken seriously? Are they actually claiming that to be illiterate helps you to become a better artist? I suspect the real reason why these critics say this stifles creativity is that it ends the ill disciplined 'anything goes' philosophy which did so much damage to a generation. (Blunkett, 1999)

Blunkett made similar accusations on the *Today* programme on the same day, including the parting shot of the *Daily Mail* article that this was 'blatant elitism dressed up as well-intentioned liberalism'.

Of course Almond's article was deliberately provocative, but what is significant is the vehemence of the reply which confirms rather than belies Almond's somewhat gothic description of a monstrous teacher. All he had done was to present a picture of a person that anyone would be glad to have in front of their child. He had compounded that sin by describing a lesson in which the pupils were enthusiastic about books, knowledgeable about how they were constructed and keen to write themselves. Finally, he had had the temerity to suggest that perhaps, for 10 per cent of the time, around one month a year, teachers should be trusted to do more of the same.

In contrast, Blunkett's reply recycles the very false demons of the past to which Almond refers. It is this kind of exchange, or the threat of it, that has made talk of creativity so difficult. If every time someone involved in education, particularly English teaching, mentions the desirability of encouraging the imagination, and is accused of suggesting that 'to be illiterate helps you to become a better artist', there is little hope that any debate will usefully be furthered.

Nor is there is much that is new in this tussle between the creative and the utilitarian. Charles Dickens, the Victorian novelist, uses the classroom to highlight his anxiety about the effects of growing industrialization: it is not simply the putrid air that can choke a child but the education system itself with its emphasis on facts, on mere information, at the expense of imagination. Such concern is found too in the school reports of Matthew Arnold, the Victorian critic and poet, who worked for most of his career as a school inspector. He wanted poetry to enliven the soul. It is there at the turn of the twentieth century in Edmond Holmes, also a school inspector. Profoundly influenced by earlier progressives, he advocated creative writing as way of liberating the child. All these voices find their way into the Newbolt Report of 1921, which established English as the core of any school curriculum. What is interesting to note is the way in which they define their subject, the definition itself acting, in part, as the justification for the centrality of English:

> in its full sense connotes not merely acquaintance with a certain number of terms, or the power of spelling these terms correctly and arranging them without gross mistakes. It connotes the discovery of the world by the first and most direct way open to us, and the discovery of ourselves in our native environment . . . For the writing of English is essentially an art, and the effect of English literature, in education, is the effect of art upon the development of the human character. (DCBE, 1921, ch. 1, para. 14, p. 20)

There is no false dichotomy here. They go on to add that it must be taught as a 'fine art' (para.14, p. 21). These observations, and others like them, led them to the same conclusion as their predecessors, namely that assessing English was highly problematic if the sense of English as an art was to be retained. F. R. Leavis, the influential critic and Cambridge academic, was the heir to this vision and through his own work and that of his disciples like David Holbrook and Frank Whitehead, who worked in education, his influence over the subject lasted almost half a century.

More recently, the debates over Brian Cox's English curriculum expose a similar battle between those who view English as an art and those who do not, and the difference this view makes to their view of education as a whole. His role, first as the editor of the Black papers (a critique of child-centred education practices), and subsequent position as champion of teachers of English, can only be understood in the light of the difference between one view of education which enables and another which is corrective. He claims that his position, that of a 'moderate progressive' (Cox, 1992, p. 146), has not substantially altered in his 30 years debating these issues. Rather, he believes that with the publishing of the Cox report, 'I succeeded in persuading the profession that these were indeed my views' (p. 187). These he states most fully in the conclusion of his autobiography, and it is to Arnold he turns, commending 'the faith of Matthew Arnold in the civilising power of the Humanities', and the way in which 'Great literature helps to keep alive our most subtle and delicate feelings, our capacity for wonder, and our faith in human individuality' (p. 268). It is his advocacy of these virtues that allows him to see himself as the 'moderate progressive' he describes.

In contrast neither Rae nor Tebbit, or even Melanie Phillips, ever speak of 'our capacity for wonder', of 'faith' or 'subtle and delicate feelings' because they do not essentially value the arts in the same way as the Arnolds, Newbolts, Sampsons, Leavises or Coxes, who live and breathe their imaginative power. A Rae, a Tebbit or a Phillips cannot understand how on the one hand you can condemn sloppy practice while at the same time take a complex view of the relationship between creativity and accuracy. For this group, not those who advocate the liberal arts, the two must always be in opposition. That is why Phillips views the Cox curriculum as a 'betrayal' of his former position rather than a fulfilment of it. It is again to creativity that she turns to support the claim.

> As chairman of the Arvon Foundation, which teaches creative writing, Cox was now placing creativity at the centre of the educational project, a view that brought him squarely into line with the basic precepts of child-centred thinking. But no one had told Kenneth Baker (the then Secretary of State for Education) or his junior minister Angela Rumbold, that their gamekeeper seemed to have turned poacher. (Phillips, 1996, p.157)

Yet this potted history does also expose some of the tensions in perceiving English as an art which also need to be acknowledged if the anxiety about creativity in education is to be understood. Much of this revolves around the notion of élitism. There are many on the left, who while not supporting New Labour's education policies in the United Kingdom *per se* would find it hard not to sympathize with Blunkett's suggestion that the liberal arts legacy as represented by Arnold, Newbolt and Leavis is 'blatant elitism dressed up as well-intentioned liberalism'. Both Arnold and the Newbolt committee were arguing for English as a subject to combat the threat of the masses. Arnold was looking across the Channel to France and, when Newbolt reported, the country had just emerged from the ravages of the First World War and Russia had not long ago experienced a revolution. Newbolt's report owes much to the work of George Sampson, a member of the committee. In his influential *English for the English*, published in the same year, he wrote, 'Deny to working class children any common share in the immaterial and presently they will grow into the men who demand with menaces a communism of the material' (Sampson, 1952, p. xv). Leavis too has been questioned because of his attacks on popular culture. As Abbs (1982) comments: 'In new and worsening cultural circumstances, the Cambridge school gave powerful currency to the notion that the teacher, critic and artist had no choice but to oppose the destructive, seemingly inexorable drift of industrial civilization' (p. 12).

Yet it would be a mistake to read any of them in only this light. Underpinning Sampson's work, for example, is a more democratic urge that a superficial take on his comments would belie. For Sampson the main reason for introducing English into schools is to create unity. 'There is no class in the country that does not need a full education in English. Possibly a common basis for education might do much to mitigate the class antagonism' (1952, p. 44). He goes on to add, 'If we want that class antagonism to be mitigated, we must abandon our system of class education and find some sort of education common to all schools of all classes' and concludes, 'The one common basis for a common culture is a common tongue' (p. 45). This was the rationale behind Newbolt.

Both Leavis and his disciples also betray a progressive tendency. At the beginning of his influential book *The Disappearing Dais*, Frank Whitehead quotes Dewey, the modern father of progressive teaching. As we have seen, Brian Cox defined himself as 'a moderate progressive' and began his report with a quotation from the Plowden Report, that famously progressive document of the 1960s on the centrality of the child to the educational process. For some, however, this progressiveness is insufficient. They want to take a more radical stance than they believe traditional liberalism, with its concentration on the amelioration at the level of the individual rather than society, affords them. Instead they look to theories such as critical literacy, which allows them to place any analysis of culture within a socio-political framework. Defined by some of its chief proponents:

> Critical literacy responds to the cultural capital of a specific group or class and looks to ways in which it can be confirmed, and also at the ways in which the dominant society disconfirms students by either ignoring or denigrating the knowledge and experiences that characterize their everyday lives. The unit of analysis is social and the key concern is not individual interests but with the individual and collective empowerment. (Aronowitz and Giroux, cited in Ball *et al.*, 1990, p. 61)

The difficulty with such a position is that while allowing for a more radical critique of society, it too can lead to precisely the same kind of analytical sterility, devoid of creativity, that it seeks to condemn. It has also meant that in all the recent debates about the arts in education the voice of radical English teachers has been curiously missing. While the notion that English had a central role to play as an arts subject is still clearly evident in the Cox curriculum of 1989, it is absent from all subsequent documents including the National Literacy Strategy and the new English curriculum for the millennium, as yet in draft form.

The radical left, then, must also bear some of the responsibility for pushing English to the margins of the debate about arts education. When the lack of arts education is now raised it is almost universally taken to mean music, art, dance and drama. This is not to say that the threat to these subjects should be ignored. Yet the report by the National Advisory Committee on Creative and Cultural Education, *All our Futures: Creativity Culture and Education* (NACCCE, 1999) commissioned by Labour to consider the role of creativity not just in the arts but in all aspects of education, is a good example of the way in which English is no longer considered central to the arts debate. In the appendix, which considers the impact of their proposals, English does not appear anywhere within the list of arts subjects. The contribution of English acknowledged in the body of the document is equally marginal.

Despite this, the report is an excellent document and provides a welcome antidote to the relentless utilitarianism of much of Labour's policy. But the turbulent history of the committee which produced the report betrays the still ambiguous attitude towards the arts and creativity that New Labour shows at every turn.

The final report took almost two years to produce. Professor Ken Robinson of Warwick University headed the committee, set up not long after Labour took office. Originally it did not include Simon Rattle, then conductor of the Birmingham Symphony Orchestra. But just after it was announced, Rattle very publicly criticized Blair's government in the *Observer* for neglecting the arts and he was included at the eleventh hour. In March 1999 the poet Benjamin Zephania, the only writer represented, resigned from the group, complaining bitterly of the constant interference of the Secretary of State, David Blunkett. Zephania's name does not appear in the official acknowledgements on the document.

It is hard to know the truth or otherwise of his claims but it is worth noting that most had expected the publication of the report to occur at least nine months before, in September 1998. There were rumours that it would arrive in late October, then before Christmas, next in the New Year, possibly Easter and finally May 1999 when it finally appeared. Far, however, from giving it the fanfare it deserved, the report was launched on the same day as the Office for Standards in Education's (OFSTED's) annual report and then only on the Internet. Printed versions took at least another month to appear. For a government dedicated to spin it is hard to believe that such things are entirely coincidental.

Ironically the report's strongest argument for the return of creativity to a central place within the school curriculum may well be its most utilitarian one – that of its importance to the economic health of the nation. Such a view was clearly espoused by Alan Greenspan, chairman of the US Federal Reserve Board, at his commencement address to Harvard University in June 1999. To the successful graduates he commented, 'Viewing a great painting or listening to a profoundly moving piano concerto produces a sense of intellectual joy that is satisfying in and of itself. But arguably, it also enhances and reinforces the conceptual processes so essential to innovation' (Greenspan, 1999). He goes on to add,

Specifically, the broadening of one's world view that is acquired through a liberal education almost surely contributes to an understanding of the inter-relationship of different fields of endeavour. Important new knowledge is very often the result of interdisciplinary observation. The broader the context that an inquiring mind brings to a problem, the greater will be the potential for creative insights that, in the end, contribute to a more productive economy. (*ibid.*)

Stephen Ball in the *Cambridge Journal of Education* (Ball, 1999) took a similar tack. He argued that Labour's testing regime may well produce superficial improvements in examination results, but that the flexible workforce of the future would not be produced by those who had simply crammed for tests rather than learn how to learn and exercise their imagination.

Yet such arguments, while satisfyingly hoisting the opposition with their own petard, do little to value the arts and creativity for their own sake. As we have seen, for those who understand the charge of élitism this has always been a problematic rallying call, yet there is another tradition that allows it to be argued for just as vociferously as those who come from the liberal arts – that of radical dissent. This is the tradition which Hitchens also identifies in his essay on Thomas Paine, the eighteenth-century author of the *Rights of Man*.

Paine belongs to that strain of oratory, pamphleteering and prose that runs through Milton, Bunyan, Burns and Blake and which nourished what the common folk like to call the Liberty Tree. This stream as chartered by E. P. Thompson and others often flows underground for long periods. In England it disappeared for a long time. (Hitchens, 1988, p. 16)

It is this tradition that Paulin (1998) reclaims in *The Day Star of Liberty*, his book on Hazlitt, an eighteenth-century writer, but it is a theme which has long dominated his work. In his introduction to the *Faber Book of Political Verse* he writes, 'We have been taught, many of us, to believe, that art and politics are separated by the thickest and most of enduring of partitions' (1986, p. 15). This is not just an attack on Leavis but also on certain forms of critical theory. 'There is an influential school of literary criticism . . . which argues that the political and historical content of literature must be viewed as "extrinsic irrelevance" (p. 15). His central desire has been to wrest criticism from ahistorical, decontextualized disinterestedness.

Paulin's recent portrait of the tradition of radical dissent contends that we have lost Hazlitt's concept of engaged disinterestedness to Arnold's view of impartial criticism. 'This has the effect of removing culture from the world of passions, so that it "returns upon itself"' (1998, p. 69). He continues, 'This idea of free-floating impartiality would have been incomprehensible to . . . Hazlitt', and argues that we should return to the pre-Arnoldian view of disinterestedness, a view that, until recently, has so dominated British literary criticism, 'This would involve recognising that all critical writing is essentially polemical, but at the same time stripping away many of the negative qualities which are so often associated with the term "polemic"' (p. 69).

The recent spate of literary biographies has done much to re-emphasize Paulin's take on the arts as a political act. Motion's biography of Keats the poet demonstrates the significance of Keats' dissenting education. He wrests him from his reputation as the most romantic of the Romantics and politicizes his verse and letters finding, for example, reference to the Peterloo massacre in 'Ode to Autumn'. Once Fintan O'Toole's fascinating biography has been read, Sheridan can no longer be seen as a regency fop writing bawdy farces, only as a radical playwright and politician. Of course it is precisely such a radical edge to creativity that those on the right, and those in power, most dread. And they may have a point. Just because they are paranoid does not mean we are not after them.

REFERENCES

Abbs, P. (1982) *English within the Arts: A Radical Alternative for English and the Arts in the Curriculum.* London: Hodder and Stoughton.

Almond, D. (1999) Carnegie acceptance speech, *Independent*, 15 July.

Ball, S. J. (1999) 'Labour, learning and the economy: a "policy sociology" perspective'. *Cambridge Journal of Education*, **29**(2), 195–206.

Ball, S. J., Kenny, A. and Gardiner, D. (1990) 'Literacy policy and the teaching of English'. In I. Goodson and P. Medway (eds) *Bringing English to Order.* London: Falmer.

Blunkett, D. (1999) 'Commentary: moaners who are cheating your children'. *Daily Mail*, 19 July.

Cox, B. (1992) *The Great Betrayal: Memoirs of a Life in Education.* London: Hodder and Stoughton.

Coyle, D. (1998) *The Weightless World.* Oxford: Capstone Press.

Departmental Committee of the Board of Education (DCBE) (1921) *The Teaching of English in England: Being the Report of the Departmental Committee Appointed by the President of the Board of Education to Inquire into the Position of English in the Educational System of England.* The Newbolt Report. London: HMSO.

Graddol, D., Maybin, J., Mercer, N. and Swann, J. (eds) (1991) *Talk and Learning 5–16: An Inservice Pack on the Oracy for Teachers.* Milton Keynes: Open University Press.

Greenspan, Alan (1999) http://www.bog.frb.fed.us/boarddocs/speeches

Hitchens, C. (1988) *Prepared for the Worst: Selected Essays and Minority Reports.* London: Chatto and Windus.

National Advisory Committee on Cultural Education (1999) *All our Futures: Creativity, Culture and Education.* London: HMSO.

Osborn, M. and Planel, C. (1999) 'Comparing children's learning attitudes and performance in French and English primary schools, in R. Alexander, P. Broadfoot and D. Phillips (eds) *Learning from Comparing*, Vol. 1, London: Symposium Books.

Paulin, T. (ed.) (1986) *The Faber Book of Political Verse.* London: Faber and Faber.

Paulin, T. (1998) *The Day Star of Liberty.* London: Faber and Faber.

Phillips, M. (1996) *All Must Have Prizes.* London: Little, Brown and Co.

Sampson, G. (1952) *English for the English.* Cambridge: Cambridge University Press.

Whitehead, F. *The Disappearing Dais: A Study in the Principles and Practice of English Teaching.* London: Chatto and Windus.

Chapter 9

Poised at the Edge: Spirituality and Creativity in Religious Education

Kevin McCarthy

INTRODUCTION

This chapter begins by exploring some of the common ground of spirituality and creativity to be found in recent writing – mainly government papers – about these dimensions. By examining the work of some highly creative practitioners in religious education, it goes on to suggest that, possibly by virtue of its marginal position in relation to the National Curriculum of England and Wales, the subject has an approach to learning and teaching which offers a way forward for education generally.

> They become things you know, not like facts that you have to remember 'cos you've actually done them. Like if you was to ask me what I done in geography last year, I'd only know if I looked in my books, but there isn't I bet one person in this class who wouldn't be able to tell you about Shabbat, because it's just in there (placing his open hand on his heart). The actual learning becomes a memory, which is part of your life.[1]

This gem comes from a 15-year-old boy in West Sussex in the South of England during the course of a conversation about his experience of learning in his religious studies General Certificate of Education (GCSE) class, the main 16+ public examination. It speaks of a quality of full engagement: spiritual, cognitive, emotional and bodily experiential in the learning process. We will meet him again and hear more later about his remarkable teacher and about many others like her who, in an educational world (at least here in Britain) still held in the grip of the death throes of a mechanistic modernism, are finding new ways of placing meaning-making at the heart of their pedagogy. Religious education is at the edge of the mainstream, a tiny colony on the periphery of the empires of the National Curriculum. This chapter suggests that, if the educational world of the West is evolving and moving, then the best practice in this 'little' subject sits not on the periphery, but at the leading edge.

Spirituality and creativity are notoriously elusive of definition. The attempt to do so can be frustrating. As Derek Webster observes, 'The notion of the spiritual is ultimately impenetrable. This is because it draws attention to what is invisible but not illusory, to what is powerful but not explicable, and to what is non-rational, but not meaningless' (Watson, 1993).

The discussion here in Britain began very well several years ago with some thoughtful and wise thinking from surprising sources. You might well be excused, for instance, for failing to recognize the origin of this: 'education is not only about gaining knowledge and the acquiring of essential skills . . . but also about personal development in its fullest sense'. Or this? 'If spiritual education is to do with seeking answers to life's great questions, then all teachers should be leading pupils towards open-ended enquiry and inviting them to take increasing responsibility for themselves and their work.' Amazingly, they are from an OFSTED document of just six years ago (OFSTED, 1994). The Office for Standards in Education generally represents for teachers the threat of imminent inspection against impossibly prescriptive and deeply mechanistic criteria; hence the surprising thoughtfulness on a big issue. It was preceded by some deeply thoughtful work at the then National Curriculum Council (NCC), a now defunct body superseded by the Qualifications and Curriculum Authority which – notionally – creates and refines the curriculum:

> Without curiosity, without the inclination to question, and without the exercise of imagination, insight and intuition, young people would lack the motivation to learn, and their intellectual development would be impaired. Deprived of self-understanding and, potentially, of the ability to understand others, they may experience difficulty in co-existing with neighbours and colleagues to the detriment of their social development. Were they not moved by feelings of awe and wonder at the beauty of the world we live in, or the power of artists, musicians and writers to manipulate space, sound and language, they would live in an inner spiritual and cultural desert. (NCC, 1993)

Hence, from 1993 onwards:

> (OFSTED's) discussions and observations should indicate whether the school . . . promotes an ethos which values imagination, inspiration, contemplation and a clear understanding of right and wrong . . . opportunities for reflective and aesthetic experience and the discussion of questions about meaning and purpose. (NCC, 1993)

Many welcomed the implicit acknowledgement that education had, in some way, a higher purpose than simply to supply skilled workers to compete in the global marketplace. Baffling too, for some, in a climate totally dominated by testing and assessment, was the clear indication that something in this realm was beyond measurement and assessment: 'Schools are strongly advised not to attempt to assess pupils' spiritual and moral development'.

We will look in more detail towards the end of the chapter at what has happened to the government's own recognition of the all-embracing, universal nature of human spirituality and its own call for:

- a spiritual dimension to be consciously fostered across all the subject, structures and processes of the school community;
- all subjects to engage in some way in open-ended enquiry reflecting on meaning; looking at attitudes, values and beliefs;
- the need to acknowledge the power of feeling, of aesthetic and emotional sensitivity;
- pupils to take responsibility for their own learning;
- the nurturing of qualities such as imagination, inspiration, contemplation, reflection;
- serious thought to be given to the limitations of quantitative assessment (NCC, 1993)

For the moment, it might be worth looking at another, more recent publication, *All our Futures: Creativity, Culture and Education*, the report by Professor Ken Robinson's committee (NACCCE, 1999), easily the most radical report which the Blair/Blunkett government has initiated. There are many echoes. Like the NCC, struggling to cage the wind in its definition of spirituality, Robinson also accepts the essential elusiveness of the term 'creativity'. Acknowledging that it goes beyond the creative arts, he plumps for the inevitable committee-speak of 'Imaginative activity fashioned so as to produce outcomes that are both original and of value.' He, too, insists on its being a quintessentially human universal, not something only granted to an élite: 'All people have creative abilities and we all have them differently.'

There are echoes of the NCC thinking about the ubiquitous nature of spirituality, too, when Professor Ken Robinson suggests that, in educational terms, creativity is a quality and capacity which goes beyond individual subjects permeating 'the methods of teaching, the ethos of the school, including the relationships between teachers and learners'. It is as much about process as outcome. It is also connected with open enquiry and meaning-making, to do with 'making connections, seeing analogies and relationships', a 'way of giving form and meaning to feelings, relying sometimes on "non-directional", intuitive' modes of consciousness. It both gives and requires respect and trust. It, too, nurtures self-knowledge and self-esteem: 'The aim is to enable young people to be more effective in the world; to deepen and broaden awareness of the self as well as of the world; and to encourage openness and reflexivity as creative thinkers.' While rooted in the practical, it has a transcendent, transformative quality: 'Creativity involves a special flexibility in which there may be a conscious attempt to challenge the assumptions and preconceptions of the self.'

It is clear that each of these characterizations describes human potentials which share considerable common ground. Indeed, when Ken Robinson talks of 'a sense of excitement, respect, hope and wonder at the potential for transformative power', we might wonder whether his subject were spirituality or creativity. As Judith Irwin writes, creativity and spirituality are inherent human capacities. 'Creativity is central to what makes us human, what makes our lives fulfilling, and what connects us to ourselves and to others' (Irwin, 1996, p. 140). Again, one senses the interconnectedness, even the interchangeability of the terms.

Clearly, the two are closely related. The literature of each is full of paradox and ambiguity, of gaining and losing the self, of uncertainty and complexity and mystery. Each has a vocabulary of search, a sometimes risky journey into the unknown. Each has its moments of illumination and inspiration as well as its darkness and shadow. And beyond the inspirational 'moment in the rose garden', each has traditions of disciplined apprenticeship, lifetimes of dedication to the patient and steady working out of the 'craft'. Each has its altered states of consciousness, its crossing of the threshold from the daily experience, a liminal quality. Rather like Coleridge's Ancient Mariner, the spiritual or creative traveller may return transformed from the journey bearing some kind of 'message' which will often have an ineffable quality, calling for symbolic or metaphoric expression beyond the limitations of the verbal or the narrowly cognitive. The former is suspicious of both the heart and the body, mistrusting anything that smacks of individualism; the latter, by contrast, accepts the plurality of modes of meaning-making and embraces the individual narrative.

RELIGIOUS EDUCATION AND POST-MODERN PRACTICE

So much for definitions and documents; in real lessons, though, what happens? What kind of teaching and learning can possibly aspire to embrace both spirituality and creativity? Last year, I was fortunate enough, courtesy of a term's secondment by the Farmington Institute of Christian Studies in Oxford, to be able to visit many schools and classrooms, to watch many lessons and to record many conversations with both students and teachers. My 'brief' was the spiritual, moral, social and cultural across the curriculum with special reference to religious education (RE). It was an extraordinary period of grace, the chance to step back after 25 years in the classroom, for which I am deeply grateful. This chapter grows out of that much longer study (http://users.ox.ac.uk/~manc0039/intro.html) which addresses in greater detail what I term the 'pedagogy of relationship' explored below.

For anyone unfamiliar with current thinking in RE in England and Wales or with only dim and distant memories of their own education, it might be as well to mention very briefly some of the curious anomalies of religious education in Britain. First, the subject, though compulsory, still has the right of parental withdrawal. In spite of often heated debate within its professional groups, RE still lies outside the remit of the National Curriculum, with locally agreed syllabuses drawn up by standing committees, SACREs (Standing Advisory Conferences on Religious Education), whose membership is drawn from both education and faith groups. There have been moves towards increased centralization, with the drawing up of model syllabuses, the floating of an eight-point scale and the imminent publication of QCA 'guidelines'.

As far as its pedagogy is concerned, the last half-century has seen a move away from the so-called 'confessional' approach, in which Christian 'truth' was presented for instruction and edification towards a 'phenomenological' World Religions approach. This asked for a sophisticated 'bracketing out' of the student's own beliefs and attitudes in a worthy, but now largely unfashionable attempt to approach the religious traditions with some kind of objectivity. This might be described as RE's modernist phase which has now passed over into an intense and, to an outsider, often vitriolic post-modern debate, set in motion by Michael Grimmitt's (1987) distinction between 'learning about' religion and 'learning from' religion. These terms have become the poles for two diametrically opposed approaches. On the one hand, there are those like Adrian Thatcher (1991) and Andrew Wright (1999) seeking a grounded, critical, cognitive 'spiritual literacy' which 'refuses to ground spiritual understanding in any heightened spiritual experience' and who, like Nick Tate, the head of the government's own curriculum authority, the QCA, see as central to the aims of education, the 'dispassionate study of religion' as a part of 'the transmission from one generation to the next of what previous generations have thought and felt and believed' (Copley, 1997). The other is represented by the likes of David Hay, John Hammond, Jack Priestley, Clive and Jane Erricker.

The Children and World Views Project (http://www.cwvp.chihe.ac.uk/iccs.html) with which the Errickers are closely connected sets out to listen to the narratives of children, allowing them to find their own voice and language, which may or may not reflect that of a religious tradition. Clive Erricker ascribes to 'language' a meaning wider than the coolly cognitive verbal, a meaning that encompasses the metaphorical, the iconic and the pictorial (Starkins, 1993). John Hammond *et al.* (1990) and their colleagues published a seminal book *New Methods in R.E.* which bore the telling and radical subtitle *An Experiential Approach.* It was – and continues to be – eagerly seized upon by teachers seeking to offer their pupils some kind of direct firsthand experience beyond the cognitive understanding of religion, the mere 'learning about' a body of knowledge.

Occasionally eliding the words 'spiritual' and 'religious', Hammond *et al.* argue that huge numbers of people have had some kind of numinous experience or encounter with the sacred and that it is one of the tasks of religious education to 'help pupils to open their personal awareness to those aspects of ordinary human experience which religious people take particularly seriously'. 'There is an extraordinarily rich variety of religious experience to be found within the religious traditions represented in this country. To have a real understanding of those traditions, we need to learn to empathize with that realm of experience' (p. 13).

What Hammond *et al.* gave legitimacy to was the teacher's use of carefully monitored experiences (stilling, guided visualization, meditation) which would provide not simply a cognitive grasp, but a felt connection with religious experience. Arguing that 'a teacher-controlled one-way system of imparting knowledge does not promote understanding and appreciation of inner experience' their recommendation was 'as far as possible, (to) begin with the experiences of the pupils'. 'It is not enough to carry on reading and studying the maps. The lands must be visited – the areas of the spiritual cannot be understood without some degree of engagement' (p. 20). Their critics are few, but powerful. Andrew Wright, for instance, (Best, 1996, p. 141) insists that there is a danger in focusing on the 'affirmation of the isolated self' and is inclined (wrongly, I feel) to detect an implied dualism in talk of 'one's own hidden depths'. In the end, he is tempted to lump this all together as some kind of self-indulgent, neo-Romantic self-absorption, a charge to which I will return.

This debate in religious education circles, then, reflects a deeper movement. Beneath it is the tension between, on the one hand, 'education as cultural trans-mission' of an absolute, universal, unified and total truth and, on the other, a post-modern search for meaning which accepts the relative, local, relational and particular.

CREATIVITY AND SPIRITUALITY IN THE CLASSROOM

My own journey took me to the North-West, the Midlands and to the South-East of England. I had conversations with many teacher educators who were unanimous in their wish to develop their student teachers' own spiritual life, a theme to which we will return. I visited, too, a wide range of schools. From many encounters, I have chosen to concentrate on the work of two teachers whose work manages at once to span the gulf between these two positions, though rooting itself firmly in the latter, and to throw light on the relationship between spirituality and creativity. Both Sue Phillips, who teaches at Bognor Community College, and Anita Haigh in Littlehampton in Sussex, gave me generous access to their classes, extensive time for interviews and the opportunity to gauge their students' responses to their lessons. I am grateful to them both.

Anita Haigh has been Head of RE for two years at Littlehampton School and has taken the opportunity of recent staff changes and new incoming staff completely to revise her course. 'The aim of course is to establish what RE is and what it isn't. We begin in Year Seven with the two Rs of RE: *Re*-spect what others believe and *Re*-flect on what you believe.' The style of the class, her whole way of operating with her pupils, is inseparable from her content. She begins from circle work, strongly influenced, like so many teachers, by the work of Jenny Mosley (Mosley and Tew, 1999). She has a deep regard for 'the rules of the circle, the listening, the respect, the lack of put downs and that the rules apply as much to the teacher as to the pupils'.

As for her aims:

> We're trying to get children to think for themselves and to think about their own values, their own beliefs and the influences that are on them. Our aim is to help them develop into confident, tolerant young people with respect for others, with empathy and insight into others' feelings, an ability to see through attempts to indoctrinate them.

She is realistic about the quality of experience which many of her pupils will have had, with relatively few of them coming from any strength of faith tradition, 'not only are they not religiously connected . . . but there hasn't been a huge amount invested in the spiritual side'. In drawing up her schemes of work, however, she and her new colleagues 'didn't give a second thought to the models', either local or national. On the matter of content, she is unambiguous:

> I have no doubts about what we are doing. We are not just here to say that Christians have altars in their churches . . . Muslims have the Imam who calls them to prayer. If it's just empty facts it trivializes people's religion and belief. You're talking about the most profound parts of a person's being by describing religious ideas and therefore just to do dry content misrepresents that. Knowledge about religion is only a vehicle . . . for us what is more important is the 'learning from'. How can a child in Littlehampton, for example, understand the four noble truths other than cerebrally unless you give them some kind of experience that will help them see the enormity for a Buddhist of what led Siddharta to formulate those truths. The common thread of what is in religion is the spiritual quest . . . How do people answer the big questions, the ultimate questions like, Is there a god? If there is a god, what's god like? Is there another life beyond this one? Is there something special about the created order?

Her course, then, is founded on experience. With the work on Buddhism, for example, she began with a video charting the young life of Siddharta, pausing the tape after his first encounter with the pain and suffering outside the palace.

> Then I divided the class into two, one group which seeks to persuade him that what he has seen outside the palace has nothing to do with him, the other group play some of the people he met. I get one pupil to play the part of Siddharta and the class forms a conscience tunnel where all the people who think he should stay in the palace line up on one side and, as Siddharta passes down the tunnel, each one says his/her reason and then, as he comes back down the line, they all say it together. Then you say: Siddharta, you've got to choose. Drama role-play simulations do a lot to get them to feel what it might be like in a particular situation.

Less physical but just as active is the challenging work she provides on ancient burials in which the pupils become detectives trying to solve the mystery of the baffling tomb findings. More artistic work comes in the unit on Celtic Christianity.

> They [her pupils] tend to carry around such a stereotyped image of what Christianity is . . . from things they have read . . . the heritage of the country . . . parents' previous experience of RE. Whose Christianity are we representing? We try to move away from white, male western Christianity without in any way disparaging that but it has a lot of baggage attached to it.

So after looking at tribal societies she moves to Celtic Christianity: 'it's nature-based, not dualistic. There are prayers for milking and making the bed, some of the ideas are quite animistic'.

She is unequivocal about her aims, 'I make no bones about it, one of the things that I hope they will develop is spirituality: you're crippled as a human being if you don't have a spiritual side' and is equally clear about the importance of both her own and her pupils' creativity both as a response to, and stimulus for, spirituality:

> I write poetry and I like writing songs and sketches, there's that side of me. Because in RE you are dealing with people's deepest held convictions, questions, feelings like anger and frustration, things they don't understand, it would seem like a travesty to reduce [RE] simply to cognitive content because it would completely miss the import of what you're talking about. To my mind because we are talking about spirituality, about aspiration, mystery, things that are difficult to pin down and label, then it seems more natural to me when I'm planning to find creative ways to do it. So with the thing I was doing on incarnation, I just wrote a story, it just came to me, about this duchess someone who's beyond them having or choosing to live like them. I know it might sound twee and the theologians could probably pull it to pieces . . . And I got them to write a poem 'If the Queen were me'. We're meeting on a level of imagination and feeling: how can you get a grasp on these things in any other way?

Clearly, the experiences she offers in the classroom touch and move her students, develop their spirituality, stir them in ways which almost simultaneously evoke some form of creative response, some kind of expression choosing from a wide range of 'languages':

> Without picture or symbol in which to express themselves you'd have many children who'd be forced to silence, you'd end up with a content-led curriculum. Often the kids don't have the language, the vocabulary to put what they feel into words. They might have strong mental images, so we'd let

them do a painting or a collage, because the problem with words is that you end up having to label and to put into a box many things to which you can't give expression. One girl, she drew a maze with gates and this picture of a bird flying out which I thought was incredibly profound. And then in another lesson she talked that through . . . it's to give them other languages to express themselves. On a very practical level, for some of our kids who aren't particularly 'literary' in their approach they nonetheless have very profound ideas and feelings. It's an opportunity for them to express themselves without the fear of failure.

Her classroom is full of such creative responses. Hence, in her work on the Celts already mentioned, Anita Haigh picked out some threads from Celtic Christianity which she linked with Native American spirituality: the interconnectedness of all things, the immanence of god or the great spirit, awe and wonder which nature inspires, especially in 'thin places' of special significance. After looking at the exquisite Celtic artwork of woven knots both in the ancient sites and texts but also in the living work of a local artist, the students' homework over four weeks was to produce their own piece of Celtic artwork which expresses some of the key themes of Celtic Christianity that they felt in tune with. For some, this was two-dimensional painting, exquisite artwork which adorns the room; for others it was three-dimensional, a bird sculpture, jewellery infused with symbolic colours and meaning. Some of the work has verbal explanation, 'because OFSTED was coming'. Both individually and collectively, the work is deeply moving and only one example of many in which creativity and spirituality are interwoven. Why does Anita Haigh think that these pupils put in such effort? And we are talking about the end of Year 9 here, the notoriously challenging 14–15-year-olds:

I think it's because they actually connected with it and it was beyond the cognitive, 'Celtic Christians believe that . . .' They went beyond themselves to articulate some of the things that really matter to them, that they haven't really articulated before or even thought about before . . . even some of the boys! It's a bit therapeutic, too, actually baring your soul . . . like someone who writes songs and shares them with other people.

Sue Phillips is Head of RE at Bognor Community College in West Sussex, a 'genuine comprehensive school' in the words of OFSTED and with more than an average number of pupils with special educational needs. To spend time with her classes is to experience a distinctive teaching style. The tables and desks have been pushed to the walls, leaving an undifferentiated circle of chairs in the middle of which a series of sensory aids of one sort or another is displayed. As Year 11 enter, their chatter quickly gives way to a reverential hush as they listen to the compact disc (CD) playing a rock version of the Lord's prayer. In the centre of the circle is a low table covered in cloth with a number of Christian artefacts: a crucifix, a candle and so on. After a few minutes, Sue Phillips reminds the class of the work they had done on Christianity and, putting on a quiet, atmospheric piece of music, a New Age evocation of the rainforest, invites them to recall and hold in their consciousness 'something that you need as opposed to want, a relationship that needs healing and something to feel grateful for'. Then, using the fingers of one hand, the students recall five people for whom they cared. Gently called back from this meditative, introspective mood, they are then reminded of the structure of the Lord's prayer:

> The exercise is not prayer because it is not directed at any divine being but (it) helps many pupils make that leap of imagination that not only gives religious belief or concept meaning but which also develops their own spirituality. (Phillips, 1999, p. 37).

For Year 9's turn after break, the centrepiece is a huge sheet with several sets of twinkling fairy lights just visible beneath soft muslin drapes. There is a swirling galaxy depicted on the overhead projector (OHP) and pulsating electronic music on the CD. This lesson, the second on the Big Bang, is a mixture of animated exposition and discussion plus some carefully negotiated and differentiated note-taking.

Such bald accounts, however, do little to convey the quality of these lessons. So what else needs saying? First, the mood of these classes was extraordinary: calm, relaxed, warm, quiet and good-humoured. Although no one, least of all the teacher, needed to raise their voice, the discussion was spontaneous and animated with many students, especially on this occasion boys, offering to contribute. Second, Sue consciously identifies herself as an enthusiastic learner, using that very uncertainty as a means of engagement. In the midst of the Big Bang lesson, for instance, she turns to apologize to a deeply troubled boy who's 'hanging from the ceiling in his science lessons' according to his special needs assistant. Now he is insistently poking in his bag for something: attention, basically. Sue's approach is to give him an opportunity to help someone else, 'Sorry, is there something you need? I know it's my problem, not yours but I'm just learning all this amazing stuff and it's really easy for me to get distracted'.

The roots of Sue Phillips' approach go back to her counselling training, to transactional analysis and to much of her earlier work as Head of Personal and Social Education. Despairing of traditional means of teaching a content-heavy syllabus, she has turned increasingly to emotional and experiential learning (Phillips, 2000). Her creativity lies in an extraordinary empathic ability to take the spiritual 'inner bits' (as she deliberately and unthreateningly calls them) and bring this content to her students in ways with which they will connect emotionally, directly from their own experience. It is a dynamic process, not without its moments of inspiration and its invitation to take risks:

If I had to choose a single word to describe the source of my creativity, how I make the inside bits concrete, it would be 'imagination'. I have a strong visual imagination and I'm very aware that not everyone has so that's why it's so important to use the five senses . . . And even in the bath, I'm in the lesson and some of the time I'm just thinking 'Have I got the guts to just go and do this?'

Her students place enormous value on the special circle which she uses to introduce otherwise abstruse concepts. In a study of Judaism, for example, she tackled the meaning of the Torah. 'How, though, do you enable children to empathize with the Torah because it is so special to the Jews that they will die for it?' Her solution was to ask the class to bring to school a precious or special object: the last photograph of their parents together before their divorce, a ring left by a beloved grandparent. Invited, not required, to share the significance of these objects, many pupils were moved to tears. Hearing subsequently about a Holocaust victim going to the gas chamber with the scroll of the Torah wrapped around him took on a new significance and one not lost on the pupils themselves. The lesson has remained with them a year later. 'It brought out a lot of emotions, it helps us understand religions and each other.'

As well as these intensely emotional lessons, Sue Phillips works hard to offer sense experiences, which bring to life the religious traditions she is exploring: 'I began to aim to present all new material through the five senses. At first I created static displays using fabric, flowers, pictures and symbols often together with music and sometimes food' (Phillips, 1999, p. 37). Work on the Greek Orthodox tradition involved building an altar in the middle of the circle with incense, flowers, icons and a recording of the liturgy which gave students the material for their creative empathic visualization of a devout member reverently lighting a candle.

The transition from experience to concept-forming is something Sue Phillips is still developing through a series of differentiated booklets, which link the experience with the faith tradition being studied. Her students are clear about the value of this work in relation to their own learning: 'You can remember the things you've learned more because you've acted them out most of the time.' 'I really liked the set of lessons we did on the Island . . . and its traditions and customs and things . . . It was a good way of explaining how religion is formed and how it develops.' They are similarly unequivocal about the impact on their self-development and their social and cultural awareness:

I used to have such black and white ideas about like marriage and divorce but you like see it from their point of view now . . . it can help you have another point of view . . . I was going round in my own little world . . . it can really help you widen your views . . . it changed me too like the way you are towards your friends as well . . . like if my friends are arguing I think I've really learned to listen and to see both sides . . . I've definitely become more under-standing.

They articulate, too, with clarity and wisdom exactly what I termed at the beginning 'a pedagogy of relationship', which is to say a teaching and learning in which the personal–social dimension is never absent, where what makes learning happen is the dynamics of the meeting, whether that be between teacher and student, between student and student or between the 'out-there' of subject-content and the 'in-here' of the individual's own felt experience: 'Like some lessons you go in and I just don't even know that person's name in the corner, but this lesson . . . well, we really trust each other.' 'It has helped me understand more about myself. It helps me understand about other people and their beliefs and gives me a chance to expand my own. It helps me mature emotionally. You can catch someone's eye across the circle and smile at each other . . . that's how you get relationships going . . . you feel more open, you know you can trust people in here.'

The final part of the conversation with Sue Phillips focused on the extent to which her undeniably charismatic personal 'magic' was teachable to other practitioners. On this she was adamant:

> It's not me, it's the method. I think it is teachable because there are exercises that you can do to create trust so that the power is shared . . . so that you see a group of people coming into the classroom with positive expectations. It just removes the need for all the control, the lining up. There are teachers for whom it's natural and others for whom it's at least something that they aspire to even if at the moment they can't do it because they feel under threat. You can't do it if you don't have the love in your heart. You've got to have a genuine affection and respect for the children because that's what makes it warm and that's what makes it alive . . . and the reason that it has to do with spirituality is because it's about the whole person. An OFSTED inspector once said to me 'It's about going into the classroom and looking into the eyes of the child.'

These two teachers are examples of the interconnectedness of creativity and spirituality. Their work springs from the same deep creative source in the primary imagination and reaches, touches and moves their students in their creative and spiritual journeys, their development as whole persons. We could track in each student's response elements of the infamous 'spiritual, moral, social and cultural'. In practice, however, we are dealing with a much more complex, organic, holistic picture in which these adjectives provide no more than handy hills in what is, in reality, a whole landscape.

These teachers are remarkable, but not unique. Referring to a growing trend in writers and thinkers in religious education, Nicola Slee writes:

> Without denying a rich diversity amongst them . . . for each of them, religious education is far more to do with method then content, it is essentially process rather than programme. It is a process which is characteristically inquisitive

and explorative, rather than instructive and explanatory; experiential and inductive rather than didactic and deductive; open-ended and therefore risky rather than predetermined and safe; personal and relational rather than academic and detached; holistic and integrative rather than abstract and analytical. It is a process that fosters spiritual growth and identity rather than the religious beliefs of any one tradition. (Slee, 1989, p. 131)

The teachers whom I encountered, and especially those on whom I focus here, are first and foremost creatively and spiritually alive. There is no simple line of demarcation between these dimensions of their being. They are warm, confident, generous whole human beings who establish a quality of relationship within their classes, which makes possible a similar quality of learning. As the veteran American Quaker educationist Parker J. Palmer puts it, they are drawn to the body of knowledge of religious education 'because it shed light on (their) identity as well as on (their) world' (Palmer, 1998, p. 25).

In these teachers, too, inseparable from their spiritual/creative ability as human beings is their capacity as teachers to relate their 'content' to where their students are coming from, finding just those points of contact with which their students resonate. 'They are able to weave a complex web of connections among themselves, their subject, and their students so that students can learn to weave a world for themselves' (p. 11) This means touching into their experience, their beliefs and values, their hopes, fears, aspirations and intimations, in short meeting them whole. These teachers are in touch with the deepest sources of their own creativity and spirituality, which is to say that they are aware of having available to them in their own lives, provided other pressures do not 'decentre' them, both the sudden flash, the unsought moment, which in many ways echoes the 'peak experience' of Maslow (1970) or the 'flow' state of Csikszentmihalyi (1992) and a more continuous, perhaps lower level of creativity in the classroom. Although less intense, it seems to downvalue this steadier creative/spiritual stream to call it 'lower'. It lives in the constant checking and monitoring of the mood and reaction of the class, in the intense respect evident in the quality of listening which they both bring to their students and engender in them, in the momentary adjustments, the registering of a glance, the sensitivity to a shift in mood, the acceptance and embracing of spontaneous moments of silence.

So, first, what I will not hesitate to call the 'best' RE teaching *places the student at the heart of the learning process*. Part of this shift means *valuing the direct first-hand sense experience* of the student: from the cultivation of the senses to the visit to the gurdwara, from the playing out of ritual and ceremony to the experience of silence or meditation. It also means *valuing what comes from the heart*. There are so many accounts here which show a level of emotional engagement in pupils, from joy, wonder and mystery to fear, anxiety and grief. This need not cross the boundary between teaching and counselling though there are no fences on this border. But felt experience would remain at the level of self-indulgence were it not for the third characteristic which I am suggesting these educators share: *the ability to nurture empathy*. Far from encouraging any solipsistic self-absorption, these teachers seek, explicitly and implicitly, throughout their teaching to encourage pupils to make the leap of imagination to 'the other'. They manage to make feeling an inherent dimension of understanding.

Critical to all of this of course is reflection. What all this good teaching has is not merely some end-of-course 'How was it for you?' which OFSTED so quaintly commends but a *constant invitation to a raising of consciousness*, interweaving in the very fabric of the learning experience planned opportunities for self-conscious reflection on thought, feeling and action. As David Hay puts it, 'From such a (holistic) perspective, raised awareness itself constitutes spirituality' (Hay and Nye, 1998).

Closely connected with this is the emphasis that these teachers place on *the variety of languages which give expression to this experience*. There is the creative linguistic expression of song, poem or story; the artistic expression through music or drawing; the physical expression of dance and drama. It is an approach which embraces the *interconnectedness of our knowledge*, crossing the artificiality of subjects. Most of all, it is *deeply democratic in its style*. It relinquishes power for solidarity, replaces fear with trust. The circle is its model, the individual and collective story its vehicle with the teacher neither a remote pedagogue, nor a handy technician 'delivering' the curriculum, but alive and fully human shaping and sharing the learning.

MEANWHILE, BACK AT OFSTED

We began by looking at some extraordinarily honest and radical thinking from OFSTED and the then NCC, born out of genuine, clear-sighted, educational vision. When it comes to the current *Framework for the Inspection of Schools* (OFSTED, 1995) and how these dimensions are actually reported, however, we already see a somewhat different picture. Much of the inclusive, holistic quality of the earlier documents is by now completely lost. A fuller account of this descent can be found in my paper, 'Messier than the Models' on the Farmington website (http://users.ox.ac.uk/~manc0039/intro.html). In actual OFSTED reports (www.ofsted.gov.uk) there is clearly a certain amount of flailing and flannelling. For a start, in spite of all that was asserted in them, there is the curious and deeply characteristic disjunction between academic levels of attainment and pupils' personal development. The latter comes in the section concerned with attitudes and behaviour, which although it follows the section on attainment and progress, is not connected with it in any way at all. The spiritual, moral, social and cultural become separate elements, unconnected with one another and subject to superficial and anodyne reporting. Furthermore, when it comes to the spiritual, moral, social and cultural (SMSC) provision, the reports completely separate teaching and learning, so that pupils' response to these dimensions is covered in one section while the school's provision for them comes much later in another. More worryingly, in spite of all that went into the former documents, SMSC provision is still placed in a separate section well away from the really meaty stuff about academic standards, as if all the carefully worked-through rationale were non-existent and as if these dimensions could somehow be sifted out and examined separately. And even though a staggering 49 per cent of schools are currently receiving 'unsatisfactory' reports for their spiritual provision, many seem baffled about what is supposed to be involved beyond some vague provision for opportunities to reflect on meaning and purpose. They are, in any case, far more preoccupied with trying to satisfy what they and everyone else clearly perceive as the 'real' agenda of raising levels of academic achievement.

Basically, it is a mess, as many OFSTED inspectors will readily agree in private. It is a mess essentially because education, as we suggested at the beginning, is currently caught up with the pursuit of the modern (such an old-fashioned word, as a colleague observed recently with wry exasperation). By modernism here, I mean the 'scientism' of objectivity, of readily quantifiable data, whether in the form of league tables, predicted grades based on CATS (cognitive attainment tests), the attempts to link pay with 'performance', the concept of a curriculum as something to be delivered, the loss of sight of anything other than measurable outcomes. Its ultimate source is the Cartesian mistrust of anything beyond the cognitive. Its effects are all-pervasive and, in essence, 'conservative' in just the sense that Tony Blair insists on using the term.

Meanwhile, in the world of developmental psychology, Howard Gardner's theory of multiple intelligences (Gardner, 1984) is finding greater currency, quoted by leading and influential voices (Barber, 1996; Bentley, 1998). Whether his categories are universals or whether they need further modification or amplification, they have broadened our understanding of intelligence and make many current teaching methods seem suddenly inadequate, make contemporary yardsticks look like primitive tools capable of the crudest measures, predicting, for example, GCSE performance across the whole range of subjects from tests which measure at best two intelligences.

But, at the risk of sounding too millenarian, there are deeper currents running. Among the many books on the so-called paradigm shift, Father Diarmuid O'Murchu traces through Einstein's theory of relativity and the subsequent and emerging quantum theory, what he regards as the 'single most important transition taking place today, namely from a mechanistic to a holistic understanding of our world and everything in it' (O'Murchu, 1992, p. 23). Linking his whole thesis to the rediscovery of the feminine, his is a heady picture emphasizing the inevitability of change, the fact of our interdependence and the participatory nature of our relationship with the world, embracing creative complexity, open dialogue and what he terms 'inclusive spirituality'. Life is changing at a dizzy pace. The speed of the information revolution, the extraordinary march of medical technology from crop modification to cell stem technology, the increasing consciousness of issues of sustainability and the already global economy with its impossible imbalances leave us gasping at the sheer complexity of the world for which we are ostensibly preparing our young people.

Many will be familiar with Fritjof Capra whose *The Turning Point* so aptly catches the spirit of this 'new paradigm' thinking when he observes: 'During the process of decline and disintegration the dominant social institutions are still imposing their outdated views but are gradually disintegrating, whole new creative minorities face new challenges with ingenuity and rising confidence' (1982, p. 466). I am not sure about 'creative minorities', which sounds a little precious, but I have constantly pictured the teachers I encountered translated to another 'subject' and given similar freedom to create their own curriculum. What would their science lessons be like? How would their students develop spiritually and creatively in geography? It is not difficult to speculate that each would create a learning community within their classrooms. Simply by virtue of their own inner orientation, they would create that sense of shared journeying and exploration. As science teachers, the learning experiences they provided would explicitly seek to engage at a feeling level, perhaps by using poetry or art to give 'voice' to the intricate beauty of form in the natural world or perhaps grappling through discussion (rather than debate) with the moral complexity of cloning, dam-building, road construction. They would not miss the opportunity to explore at first hand – and not just once, but cyclically and seasonally – the changing face of the natural world in the immediate vicinity of the school. Equally, as geography teachers, they would ensure that their students met local officials, policy-makers or activists and discussed complex, local social or environmental issues. And they would do it in a way that enabled, or at least helped, their students to relate in some way to their own lives, giving them at the same time a sense of responsibility and empowerment. They would seek to grant all students some way in which their understanding and concern could find voice, not necessarily just in the language of the cognitive intelligences of numbers and description. Whatever they taught, there would be opportunities for open discussion, quiet reflection and practical engagement. It is obvious that they would bring with them the same holistic pedagogy, the same quality of relating and relationship to any discipline, stressing always the human element, the feeling for others and the sense of the interconnectedness both of ourselves as humans and of all that we are compelled to study as separate 'subjects'. What would it be like if all students could say, like the lad at the beginning, 'the actual learning becomes a memory which is part of your life'? More importantly, what is going to happen if they cannot?

ENDWORD

There is the old story about the tourists who stop and ask the Irishman (or Belgian or Serb or Swede . . . only my own Irish blood licenses this political incorrectness) the way to Carrickfergus. 'Ah,' he replies mistily, shaking his head, 'Carrickfergus, you say? You can't get there from here.' Some readers may already have been having similar reactions reading this chapter. The fact is that such holistic teaching and learning is already happening and not just in religious education.

As Professor Ken Robinson wryly observes, 'many schools are doing exciting and demanding work . . . in spite, not because of the existing climate' (Robinson, 1999, p. 8). Creativity and spirituality need both clarification and demystification. They are not for the élite; they go beyond the flash of inspiration for the RE or the art teacher. They are universal human qualities, which we are all capable of developing. And that means us, too. We need a climate in which teachers care for their own spiritual and creative well being, a climate in which these dimensions are reflected in the relational patterns across the whole learning community. As David Bohm and David Peat observe, creativity arises out of a spirit of friendship characterized by dialogue rather than debate. It arises from the generative or more specifically the implicate order. This order is primarily concerned not with the outward side of development and evolution in a sequence of successions but with a deeper and more inward order 'out of which the manifest form of things can emerge creatively' (Bohm and Peat, 1987, chap. 6). It is characterized by 'a kind of passionate intensity and vibrant tension'. It becomes sclerotic when confined by 'setting of goals and patterns of behaviour, which are imposed mechanically'. Professor Robinson's committee may yet prove the influential rallying point for this quiet revolution to which our own work at Re:membering Education[2] is also contributing. 'Re-membering ourselves and our power can lead to revolution, but it requires more than recalling a few facts. Re-membering involves putting ourselves back together, recovering identity and integrity, reclaiming the wholeness of our lives' (Palmer, 1998, p. 20).

Finally, as Charles Handy (1994) so eloquently expresses it, 'Change comes from small initiatives which work, initiatives which imitated become the fashion. We cannot wait for great visions from great people for they are in short supply at the end of history' (p. 271). I hope that I have shown that a creative and spiritual pedagogy of relationship is not some distant dream for the élite, but an emerging reality arising in response to the real needs of young people hungry for such fully human engagement.

NOTES

1   All obviously spoken quotations by teachers and students in this chapter are drawn from typescripts of taped conversations in October and November 1999.

2   Re:membering Education is a network of educators widening and deepening educational thinking. We seek, through ongoing contact with government agencies, via our conferences, newsletter and web site and through consultancy and courses to share the practical wisdom of creative and innovative

practitioners. For further details, contact Re:membering Education, 66 Beaconsfield Villas, Brighton, BN1 6HE. Tel/fax: 01273 239311. E-mail remember@mcmail.com. Web site www.remember.mcmail.com.

REFERENCES

Barber, M. (1996) *The Learning Game*. London: Victor Gollancz.

Best, R. (ed.) (1996) *Education, Spirituality and the Whole Child*. London: Routledge.

Bentley, T. (1998) *Learning Beyond the Classroom*. London: Routledge.

Bohm, D. and Peat D. (1987) *Science, Order and Creativity*. London: Routledge.

Capra, F. (1982) *The Turning Point: Science, Society and the Rising Culture*. London: Flamingo.

Copley, T. (1997) *Teaching Religion*. Exeter: University of Exeter Press.

Csikszentmihalyi, M. (1992) *Flow: The Psychology of Happiness*. London: Rider.

Gardner, H. (1984) *Frames of Mind*. London: Paladin.

Grimmitt, M. (1987) *Religious Education and Human Development*. Great Wakering, Essex: McCrimmons.

Hammond, J., Hay, D., Moxon, J., Netto, B., Raban, K., Straugheir, G. and Wllliams, C. (1990) *New Methods in R.E.: An Experiential Approach*. Harlow: Oliver and Boyd.

Handy, C. (1994) *The Empty Raincoat: Making Sense of the Future*. London: Hutchinson.

Hay, D. and Nye, R. (1998) *The Spirit of the Child*. London: Fount.

Irwin, J. W. (1996) *Empowering Ourselves and Transforming our Schools*. New York: SUNY.

Maslow, A. (1970) *Religions, Values and Peak Experiences*. Harmondsworth: Penguin.

Mosley, J. and Tew, M. (1999) *Quality Circle Time in Secondary School*. London: David Fulton.

National Advisory Committee on Creative and Cultural Education (NACCCE) (1999) *All our Futures: Creativity, Culture and Education*. London: DFEE.

National Curriculum Council (NCC) (1993) *Spiritual and Moral Development: A Discussion Paper*. York: NCC.

Office for Standards in Education (OFSTED) (1994) *Spiritual, Moral, Social and Cultural Development*. London: HMSO.

Office for Standards in Education (OFSTED) (1995) *Framework for the Inspection of Schools*. London: The Stationery Office.

O'Murchu, D. (1992) *Our World in Transition*. Lewes: Temple House Books.

Palmer, P. (1998) *The Courage to Teach*. San Francisco: Jossey-Bass.

Phillips, S. (2000) *Can I Teach Your Religion?* London: SHAP.

Robinson, K. (1999) *All our Futures: Creativity, Culture and Education*. London: DFEE/dcms.

Slee, N. (1989) 'Conflict and reconciliation between competing models of religious education'. *British Journal of Religious Education*, **11**(3).

Starkins, D. (1993) *Religion and the Arts in Education: Dimensions of Spirituality*. Sevenoaks: Hodder and Stoughton.

Thatcher, A. (1991) 'A critique of inwardness in religious education'. *British Journal of Religious Education*, **14**(1).

Watson, B. (1993) *The Effective Teaching of Religious Education*. London: Longman.

Wright, A. (1999) *Discerning the Spirit*. Abingdon: Culham College Institute.

Chapter 10

Creative Leadership: Innovative Practices in a Secondary School

Dame Tamsyn Imison

My school (at the time of writing, June 2000, I am the headteacher) is a mixed inner-city comprehensive in Cricklewood, London, with 1,300 students and 120 staff. The school population is wide and varied. We have, traditionally, taken students from over 40 feeder primary schools. The school has a rich ethnic mix with 60 per cent of our roll made up of students from ethnic minorities, 18 per cent of these at an early stage of English language acquisition. Our pupils include those who have relatively recently found refuge through the borough's supportive policy towards asylum seekers (135 pupils are in this category, with nearly a third of these arriving here as unaccompanied minors). Overall there are 78 different languages and dialects spoken by students in the school. Thirty-three per cent of the intake is registered for free school meal entitlement, i.e. are children from very low-income families, and 5 per cent of our roll are students with a statement of special educational needs. A further 15 per cent of our roll is on the special educational needs register at stages 1–4.

In terms of outcomes, over 50 per cent of our pupils attain five or more A*–C grades in GCSE at the age of 16, at the end of Year 11. Well over 90 per cent of our Year 11 students stay on to post-compulsory education. Seventy per cent of these stay on in our own sixth form, and about 25 per cent in other sixth forms and local colleges. (The other 5 per cent are on training courses or we have rarely seen.) From our own sixth form of 250 pupils, we send about 80 students each year from academic courses on to higher education, including Oxford and Cambridge Universities. About 40 additional pupils each year are successful on a range of vocational courses and also progress to higher and further education and training.

THE CHALLENGE OF LEADERSHIP

With such a diverse mix of talents, culture and background as well as social challenge, I am always looking to enlarge the vision and capacity of myself and my colleagues. I aim to develop that 'sparkle in the eye' and tangible excitement that is exhibited by creative practitioners, and which transmits itself like the bees' dances to all in the 'learning hive'.

I am using the NACCCE definition of 'creativity' – a mode of learning which is playful and experimental as well as thoughtful and serious. Creativity is, I believe, a special kind of flexibility and a conscious attempt to challenge existing assumptions and preconceptions – an active attempt to unlearn; a drive to find out, to introduce, construct or reconstruct something new. A key means to achieve these creative objectives is being innovative. It has been a central part of my practice and means using imagination, creativity and strategic action as a leader to solve challenging problems. Being an innovative, creative leader and practitioner at a time when more and more is being prescribed is not for the faint-hearted. However, if education is to meet the rapidly changing needs of children and adults locally and nationally, it is essential that all education leaders are both creative and innovative. The following three case studies exemplify aspects of my innovative and creative leadership in my own school.

CASE STUDY 1: MIRRORING INNOVATIVE PRACTICES

I am convinced that innovative and creative leaders exhibit the same character-istics as creative practitioners in the classroom and I also believe that receptive practitioners often mirror their innovative and creative leaders. In 1995, I gained my Master's degree in Education from the Open University. It represented the culmination of three exciting years for me when, despite long hours reading, studying and researching, I found I was constantly engaged in constructive dialogues with colleagues about learning. In my first year, I had focused on students' perceptions of good teaching and this led to our whole-school re-examination of our teaching and the establishment of an academic code of conduct. In the second year, I examined alternative ways of accrediting and remotivating very low achievers, unlikely to gain even one GCSE grade, by using vocational awards and developing strong links with industry, I was able to create an exciting and meaningful course, which the students valued. In the third year, I focused on the international and future needs arising from the develop-ment of a global economy and reassessed with colleagues the curriculum and the ways in which it should be made accessible for learners. We are now an RSA pilot school, developing a skills-based curriculum at Key Stage 3 (for 11–14-year-olds).

I wanted to make it easy for colleagues to participate in order to get further benefits for our learning organization. By giving financial support and creating an innovative Master's programme, in 1997, we made it easier for those with family and other commitments to take part. The programme was delivered partly in school and with some twilight sessions and weekends. We worked in partner-ship with the London University Institute of Education International School Improvement and Effectiveness Centre.

I was sure that getting significant numbers of colleagues engaged in active discussions with inspirational outstanding academics would have a powerful impact upon the school. It would, I believed, establish a truly creative and actively learning organization. Thus staff from the International School Improvement and Effectiveness Centre at the Institute of Education, London University, were invited to talk with the group. With very little difficulty, we attracted fifteen staff to participate. The outcome of the project is still to be finally determined but already the twelve teachers who remained on this challenging programme have become less satisfied with what they and others were doing. They have become agents for change, considering seriously, thoughtfully, experimentally and playfully, ways in which we might move the school on. They, like me, have been determined to ensure that we are not seen as a 'strolling', 'cruising' or 'sinking' school (Stoll and Fink, 1996).

All have become more flexible and have challenged our existing assumptions and preconceptions. They have shown an active attempt to unlearn a drive to find, introduce, construct or reconstruct something new. They have raised their sights. More specifically:

- Ten have gained significant promotions on the basis of excellent performance – one headteacher, three senior teachers, one acting senior teacher, one head of independent learning, two heads of department, and one acting head of department. One has become a teacher-governor.
- One has raised the profile of staff development, initiated much more lesson observation and prepared the portfolio for our successful Investors in People bid. We are among the first schools who have chosen to apply for the award.
- One has published a very important and professionally acclaimed paper on developing a history web site, which was then improved and refined further by another teacher in another department inspired by her work.
- Several have made important inputs into the development of a new curriculum to broaden and enrich post-16 provision as well as giving more support and extension to pre-16 provision, and emphasizing the skills curriculum. They thought big and came up with a ten-day timetable. This is a very exciting way of ensuring on a two-week cycle that a much wider range of courses and experiences is offered to pupils. One has organized a highly stimulating visit to Paris and Giverny and has introduced a new format for the weekly bulletin. The visit to France started out as an art visit but ended up with both students and staff writing poetry, as well as painting and participating in a truly creative journey of exploration (which can currently be seen at www.Hampsteadschool.org.uk).
- One has been putting together our evidence portfolio for the Excellence Award for links with industry run by the Centre of Excellence for Employability, Work-Related Learning and Business Links offered by our TEC (Training and Enterprise Council). This has involved organizing an

ambitious buddy scheme to link the nearly 60 teaching staff at our school with buddies in industry and commerce.

- One has been developing the assessment and analysis of examination results and has elicited from middle managers the development of active student involvement in the assessment process. This delighted me because I have been strongly promoting student democracy, involving students in a powerful School Council as well as in the selection of staff.
- One has taken a significant role in developing independent learning and the skills-based curriculum. With another colleague, they have taken up the Royal Society of Arts Skills Project, developing a skills-focused Key Stage 3 pilot from September 2000 (Key Stage 3 is a classic time for student disengagement).

I was aware that those colleagues undertaking a Master's programme would be likely to apply for promotions and that many might not stay here to make a contribution for very long, bearing in mind Fullan's warning (1982) that change can be dangerous. But I was sure that 'dangerous' creative changes would drive the school forward. Challenges are essential if any institution is to develop and improve. Even a short contribution from colleagues thinking creatively in the interests of the school is worth more than a long contribution from those whose practice and understanding may be slipping backwards.

CASE STUDY 2: RISKING INNOVATION

In the early 1990s our maths department needed an urgent review due to staff changes and poor examination results. The standard practice in the maths department had been to leave students to work on their own, with very limited interventions and little whole-class teaching. This resulted in very slow progress and under-performance by students.

I suggested three initiatives to the department. The first was to take part in a weekend Socratic Discussion on prime numbers. The opportunity was provided by the vice-chair of governors, who had been using and facilitating such discussions in England and Germany as a way of developing ethical approaches and common understandings to challenging problems. It was one of the most exciting weekends I have ever spent and its use within our school is very powerful. We are currently using the same approach with our School Council to discuss a range of important and relevant ethical issues. The mathematical weekend was both experimental and fun. It consolidated support for and partnerships between the head and deputy head of department and two members of the department. This led on to a useful pilot study on the involvement and support of parents helping their children with maths at Key Stage 3. There were still difficulties in the department and later on in the term I arranged for the post holders to spend a sociable weekend in Suffolk on strategy planning, to encourage the staff to work as a team. Our previous Socratic weekend had been fun and they needed to be away from the department's difficulties to develop their ideas and to strengthen their leadership team.

The second initiative was to enlist us in the Cognitive Accelerated Learning for Mathematics Education (CAME) as part of the pilot project being developed by King's College, University of London. The quality of teaching improved dramatically as students and teachers engaged in exciting conversations about practical and relevant mathematical problems. The Kings College evaluation showed a significant improvement – a 9 per cent rise in GCSE scores for the cohort of students who were involved in the pilot. The deputy head of the department has now become a part-time CAME trainer, bringing further thinking skills into the school. As a result of this success the science department are now involved in the parallel initiative, CASE (Cognitive Accelerated Learning for Science Education).

A third initiative was to encourage the head of the maths department to take up 'financial literacy'. I am on the steering group for the NatWest Bank 'Face to Face with Finance' initiative and I 'volunteered' the head of department to introduce this. He accepted with enthusiasm and having introduced financial literacy successfully at Hampstead School has become an expert and increased his authority both within the department, the school and nationally. It was a risk worth taking to enhance his status.

As a result of my risk-taking the department began to mirror my practice and they put forward their own proposal to run a numeracy summer school in which a significant number of the department's staff undertook training and participated. They all considered it to have been a very positive experience for themselves and the students. Measurable student progress has resulted and many of the strategies were fed into classroom practice at Key Stage 3. A young member of staff has recently been promoted to take on the co-ordination of whole-school numeracy across the curriculum. The HMI inspection of the second summer school was highly complimentary.

Fourth, the school has also become a Kumon Maths Centre with places available free to students who cannot afford to pay. The underlying principles of Kumon are to offer useful strategies which underpin the number rules in maths. Having the Kumon Centre in our school has offered the maths department a way of gaining insights into an interesting and commercial way of increasing student motivation, for the approach actively involves parents and provides instant feedback to students after short, graded tasks. The Kumon strategies are beginning to form part of the maths department's own strategies.

There is now a new head of department and the OFSTED report noted the tangible commitment of senior staff in the department; inspectors were sure that the commitment would lead to significant increases in the achievement and creativity of both staff and students.

CASE STUDY 3: INNOVATORY BARRIER-BUSTING

Developing whole-school cultures

I have always felt intuitively that the creative arts are the lifeblood of any successful school, but it is essential that they are fully integrated into and contribute to, whole-school development. I have taken an active role in establishing *at national level* Plays for Schools, a National Schools Playwright Commissioning Group working in partnership with fifteen other schools across the country. These schools club together to raise the funding to commission both a playwright and a composer to work closely with consortia of these schools on producing good new writing and music tailored for the participating students. We commissioned Adrian Mitchell to write *The Siege*, published by Oberon Books, with Andrew Dickenson composing the music. John McGrath has just finished writing a play about human rights called *On the Road to Mandalay*, with Rick Lloyd of the Flying Pickets composing the music. This is a whole-school project. It raises the status of each school and our new head of drama in fact came to us from a successful participant school in Derbyshire.

In the last two years, the following has happened as a result of the blossoming of the creative arts:

- Examination results have soared at all levels in each department.
- Performances, concerts, exhibitions both in and out of the school have exponentially increased.
- School journeys abroad have become a significant component of the curriculum and have increasingly involved others from many different departments as well as parents and governors.
- Creative arts staff are making important and valuable inputs into whole-school continuing professional development sessions on improving teaching and learning.

Staff in all areas of the curriculum have taken an active part in all of these activities, and regular cross-curricular activity is becoming the norm. Local schools and the community are becoming increasingly involved and we have also had two highly positive inspection reports from Camden local education authority on the creative arts in 1999 and 2000.

Reconstructing selection criteria

The right selection of staff is critical to the success of any organization. Selecting leaders who have a whole-school perspective, requires us to put applicants through a series of activities and to involve a significant number of students, staff and governors including parent governors in the process. Consequently we developed a new procedure and criteria for the 'arts' head of department posts. Applicants were expected to show potential for further promotion and a commitment to working with and supporting other colleagues as well as a commitment to active participation in their own learning and development. We expect all staff to use this experiential learning to improve scaffolding and facilitation of students' learning across the school.

Students evaluated all applicants and their views have proved to be extremely reliable. This is considered by some to be risky but I would argue that it is even more problematic not to involve all stakeholders in this vital process. Leaders, particularly heads of department, must be confident to outreach to all staff, parents and the wider community working with students. In many cases, external inspectors advising us have been surprised that 'age, experience and previous posts' are not of great concern to us in the selection process. They have all agreed however, on each occasion, that the 'risks' they thought we were taking, proved to be outstanding appointments!

SUMMING UP: INNOVATORY TOOLS FOR THE CREATIVE LEADER

My argument is that both innovative and creative leaders and practitioners need a range of tools to carry out their work. This includes being involved in various forms of personal active enquiry and learning. Involvement is most easily achieved if there is a climate of learning within a school, people are willing to take risks and whole-school initiatives are kept to the forefront of our reviews. Finally, access to external specialists is crucial, as is indicated in all three case studies.

It is for these reasons that we have been successful in gaining Investors in People status, have won three successive rounds of Technology College funding and won an excellence award for links with industry and the local communities. All involve and facilitate innovation and creativity.

REFERENCES

Fullan, M. (1982) *The Meaning of Educational Change*. New York: Teachers' College, Columbia University.
Stoll, L. and Fink, D. (1996) *Changing Our Schools*. Buckingham: Open University Press.

Chapter 11

Effective Teaching and Learning: The Role of the Creative Parent–Teacher

Laura Haringman

INTRODUCTION

I am a mother of three boys under the age of 13 (12, 7 and 5). I share parenting with my husband, the children's father, and I generally handle the minutiae of daily childhood life. Long hours at work, coupled with regular overseas travel means even a bedtime story is a rare treat for father and boys, although greatly enjoyed and treasured when they happen.

I am also a teacher who tries to foster creativity among my children and the children I teach. The notion that learning must be enjoyable is the foundation of my creative practice. My disposition (optimistic, outgoing, vivacious and, on occasions, self-deprecating) facilitates and encourages this enjoyment. I also believe that an enthusiastic teacher can assist conceptualization more effectively than a dispassionate practitioner can. Hargreaves (1992, pp. 255–6) points out that the way teachers teach is grounded in the type of people they have become, and I have found that if I am not relaxed and enjoying myself I will be unable to convey information confidently.

Pedagogy during my teacher training in the late 1980s included developing the caring teacher. This reflected the ethos of Plowden (CEAC, 1967), that saw teachers as acting *in loco parentis* (i.e. in place of parents in terms of having a caring, social and emotional responsibility). These teachers recognized the impact the 'real world', in terms of poverty and social deprivation, had on children's learning, and aimed to display patience, understanding, tolerance and sympathy towards the children's own families. My own vision is to be, as a parent–teacher, a dynamic resource of all aspects of a whole person, especially carer and teacher.

However, soon after I qualified, this image of teachers was challenged. Teachers found themselves accused by politicians and then parents of sidelining the science of teaching, with too much 'tea and sympathy'. This perspective was developed among the emerging New Right during the early and mid-1980s, and articulated famously by James Callaghan, a Labour Prime Minister, that primary teaching was an over-caring profession creating illiterate, enumerate and undisciplined members of society. Policy-makers have, since then, in England and Wales, decided that a prescriptive curriculum was essential to rectify what they saw as teacher inadequacy. This approach to teaching and the curriculum has continued into the start of the twenty-first century with, for example, the national literacy and numeracy programmes introduced at the end of the 1990s. This top-down, knowledge-centred approach emphasized the child's knowledge acquisition in subject domains, rather than the 'development of the child as a whole person' (Noddings, 1992; Woods and Jeffrey, 1996) or 'person-making (Brehony, 1992).

My own experience suggests that delivering the curriculum in a prescribed manner does not allow enough time for caring to prevail, although I, like many teachers, struggle to find the time for children also to talk and to share ideas and concerns.

Women, who form the majority of the teaching workforce (many of whom are parents too) are often criticized for being too caring (Woods and Jeffrey, 1996). The foundation for this criticism is embedded in the belief that being a 'caring teacher' is irrelevant to effective teaching. This appears in turn to be based on the New Right assumption that showing care and compassion is incompatible with fostering literacy, numeracy and discipline and that the new teacher is to be the distanced technician, whose function is merely to deliver the curriculum. However, I would argue that we need to integrate the concerns of the parent-figure, the knowledge of the teacher and the humanity of the social being in order to become an effective teacher.

THE PARENT–TEACHER

My teacher work is mediated by my experiences as a parent, and vice versa. As a teacher, I am creatively engaged in assisting both my own little guys and my pupils to blossom during their school years. Reflecting on this dual role I have been concerned to keep formal additional schoolwork within bounds in the home, such as homework and the completion of workbook exercises. There are several reasons for this:

- the value I place on quality time with my children;
- my interest in maintaining a warm atmosphere (relaxed, fun, exciting, encouraging, enthusiastic and supportive);
- prioritization of the need for real-world learning;
- the importance of time for talking (sharing thoughts, extending ideas, exploring possibilities).

I had always assumed that parents could always find time. As a teacher I have said to parents 'It only takes ten minutes, that's all.' Boy! That is one tremendous misunderstanding. In between bouncing around like a 'grasshopper on caffeine', shopping, managing bureaucracy, ferrying a child here, another there and ferociously mopping the fevered brow of relatives, you might find the 'ten minutes', but only if you have remembered to collect the children in the first place.

It is important that my children want to come home and to welcome talking about their school day. This occurs when the child is ready to initiate the conversation. I believe that the children need to detach themselves from the institutionalized culture of the school. In effect they need some space for personal reflection, the internalization of the day's activities and the opportunity for independent problem-solving. Mirroring the prescriptive practices of school at home is, I believe, not creative but constraining, and it stifles the opportunity to experience different tempos and arenas. There are no workbooks or reading schemes at home. I personally cannot see creativity flowing from them. Too many children lose the passion for learning because they perceive achievement only in relation to *completing* a page, book or worksheet. Being able to talk rather than complete curriculum exercises is fundamental to the learning process. Through talking, we are able to share ideas, understand another's perspective, amend our own opinions and develop new possibilities.

DEVELOPING LEARNER EMPATHY

The links that exist between creative teaching and creative parenthood arise out of recognizing creative opportunities for relationship-building in both. The ability to encourage and empathize also stimulates creative solutions. Resourcefulness is a quality that needs to be developed in order to achieve this. I believe that being a good parent assists being a good teacher – that of always trying to understand, caring for children and communicating with them, i.e. to empathize.

Empathizing involves communicating and connecting with the individual, developing respect and trust through an emergent rapport, thus considering an individual's needs and interests. Intrinsic to this is the knowledge of the child within the cultural setting. Incorporating real-life experiences from unique cultural settings into the school culture can provide learning opportunities that meet the needs of the individual. This can be achieved by involving the family/carers and multi-ethnic language support teachers together with the learner.

Empathy is not the sole prerogative of the teacher–pupil relationship. The ability to empathize with the cultural setting of the individual families is important in facilitating achievement. As a student I refrained from being unnecessarily judgemental about a child's family or situation. Once qualified, I was wary about being overly critical of a family without explicit knowledge of the home and wider cultural setting within which they were operating. I subscribed to this perspective because I imagined that I might well exhibit similar behaviours if I was in their position. I often prefaced comments with 'I am not yet a parent so I may not fully understand your situation as a parent; however, as a teacher I would like to suggest that we . . .'

Creative avenues, which I define as wide, aesthetic pathways, should always be sought for communicating with children. Intuitiveness characterizes these situations evolving from knowing the child as a personality, knowing their interests and knowing them as a human being: the intuitiveness is not haphazard.

Both as a teacher and as a parent, I try to achieve this by listening carefully to the language the child uses, focusing both on the choice of vocabulary and expression. Often, I will repeat the child's statement or explanation. This verifies whether I heard correctly and also allows the child a brief opportunity to hear and clarify their opinion. On some occasions they alter their initial view. If this occurs I sometimes freeze the situation and discuss the two perspectives. We then negotiate a new and acceptable standpoint from which to continue.

HAVING A GO

With regard to new situations, I always try to encourage the children to 'have a go'. The fear of failure often limits children's willingness to even make an attempt. This fear appears to me to be endemic in the formal education process – more so during the last decade since the introduction of national assessment Standard Assessment Tasks (SATs) held at ages 7, 11 and 14.

My middle son recently expressed concern that he was facing his SATs. He expressed his teacher's concern that 'all the Year 2 children need to knuckle down and attain the targets'. He seemed anxious to perform and perform well. However, he felt he would not do that well. His elder brother attempted to provide solace by reminding him that the results were only of relevance to the school and government (no mention of us the parents) and this seemed to calm him (until his brother added that he himself had done well in them).

So encouraging children to 'have a go' can be problematic unless new situations are approached with gentle persuasion, coupled with examples that reflect another's personal experiences, so that the child may be reassured that new situations are not insurmountable. Once the child feels more willing to 'have a go' we can then divide the situation into smaller, more user-friendly parts. The mantra of 'I can't do it', and the responses, 'Why not?' ''cos I can't' are familiar to me, both as a parent and a teacher. It is so frustrating watching this scenario and anticipating that it will occur time and again. The answer is to unblock the situation by asking, 'I understand that that's the situation right now, but what exactly would have to happen, for you to be able to do it?'

An example is computer games. My eldest son seemed unwilling to persevere with a computer-gaming strategy and sought the undocumented short cuts built into all good games and known as 'cheats'. This provided me with a dilemma of finding a way to encourage him to solve the game unaided without devaluing his approach and sense of control. At first he was resolute in his belief that using the 'cheats' would heighten his enjoyment. I recognized that this may well have been correct so I had to think carefully. The younger two children are so keen to achieve the same result as their elder brother; they often defer to his expertise to complete the game level.

I explained that my seeing the game as a series of banal procedures removed his sense of individuality 'in my eyes'. I tried to remind him that the game was about finding a pathway through the problem that was unique to him. Eventually, suffice it to say there was a trade-off. He decided that he would use the 'cheats' but would examine the stages in the process. He added that he would then be able to work backwards using the newly acquired knowledge. I hold the view that we learn more effectively if the learning is framed within a 'real-world' context. It is easier to develop understanding if learning is kept embedded in a logical and real experience.

In a school example a child was creating a man from differently sized shapes. When the child had completed the work the teacher's audible comment was 'ooh look, he's got lopsided arms!' The teacher was on the verge of suggesting to the child that the child should correct the 'error', when I, in the role of adviser, interjected. I pointed out that perhaps the child had purposely positioned the limbs asymmetrically. Furthermore, maybe the man was waving. More importantly, I suggested that the child's construction was not in conflict with the task set and the child appeared satisfied with the outcome. Collaborative learning which involves pupil and teacher engagement, including positive encouragement and critique, is 'empathetic challenging' (Bonnett, 1991). In the example given, I would describe my own challenging of the teacher as 'empathetic challenging'.

HANDING OVER CONTROL AND TAKING OWNERSHIP

Although control is basic to the practice of teaching and parenting, it must be discharged with humanity, moral purpose and care for the children. Moreover, control is not always linked with firmness but use of tone. Hansen (1993, p. 397) goes further in describing teaching styles as a set of habits including tone, together with gestures, body movements and facial expressions. All these can be effective in controlling situations. Leaving control with the learner is of paramount importance when assisting them with a task, to gently guide the learner to appreciate another perspective. I consider the attempt to support the learner into adopting another approach to an activity to be the equivalent of initial part-ownership, as gradually the learners come to feel full ownership for themselves.

I recently undertook some English work with Years 3 and 4 children (7- to 9-year-olds), helping them to explore descriptive sentences using adjectives. I used a piece of work they had done previously describing monsters. I listened to the suggestions made by the children and subsequently tried to create the opportunity for alternative choices to flow. I used language that included, 'What does this remind you of?', 'Do you remember?'. They made connections with the previous piece of work with which they were familiar and in addition to the questions, I offered further avenues of exploration, hoping to conjure images from their own experiences. If the child was still struggling, I used prior knowledge of the child's interests and offered suggestions. When the child chose their own example, we discussed why this choice was a good one, i.e. it was closely connected with the child.

Ownership relates to the child feeling that the piece of work belongs to them. I encouraged a Year 6 group to articulate their concerns over some teaching of creative writing. The overwhelming response was that the creativity associated with storywriting was being eroded by a technical approach. The group collectively felt – in my words not theirs – that 'their imagination was being constrained' by the need to ensure that the sections of their story provided the necessary qualities designated within the statutory requirements of the National Curriculum (beginning, middle and conclusion; setting, characters, description, speech, etc). Subsequently, we also discussed writing conventions and questioned the efficacy of removing them. We established that by removing the conventions the children's ideas could flow. They also felt that they might become more prolific writers.

I undertake a period of reflection after most activities with my pupils so there is always the opportunity to talk and share perspectives. We remind ourselves that failures and mistakes are a necessary part of the learning process. I believe that a mistake, when seen positively, encourages the learner to look at unexplored pathways.

BLOCKAGES AND BREAKTHROUGHS

These permeate everyday life and I use them to encourage children to search for possibilities and solutions. Occasionally there are extraordinary breakthroughs, but for most part the learning is a slow, gradual process achieved through creative teaching (Hargreaves, 1983; Woods, 1994). An example of this was a poetry lesson when children felt afraid to interpret a poem in an English session. To alleviate their concerns, we looked at each sentence using my own perceptions of the language as a basis for discussion. When the group seemed more comfortable with the prose, we developed the discussion by extending the possibilities with other perceptions or evidence reinforcing the initial ones.

Another example concerned a maths lesson on 'repeated addition'. I used chocolate Smarties. These are perfect for delineating place value, i.e. representing units, tens, hundreds, and so on, because of their different colours. Moreover their taste is so supremely elevated to gourmet status among these children that it appeared to the children to be worthwhile completing the task. The role of food in fostering creativity and problem-solving cannot be undervalued, although I acknowledge that its role in creating inappropriate behavioural or eating patterns is to be avoided.

I adhere to the viewpoint that an effective teacher is one who has a flexible approach to learning and teaching. For example, I recognize that re-presenting a concept in a different way, is preferable to repeating a specific activity until the learner grasps it. Redesigning the learning experience in an alternative way involves creativity. I revisited the properties of a circle with nursery age children and combined this with the traditional story topic of the 'Three Little Pigs'. In 'circle time' the children helped each other to create a pig painted entirely from circular shapes.

A Kosovan boy had difficulty adjusting to the environment and culture of London schooling. He disliked feeling different, so withdrawal was no option. With knowledge acquired from previous interactions I was able to introduce images of his favourite football team and cartoon characters into the lessons. This was beneficial to him, as he was able to comprehend the language used because of the familiar associations with personal icons.

A family example of a blockage occurred when my middle son announced that he wanted to bake. He is very pedantic and knows exactly what it is he intends to do. In this case, he could describe the type of cake he wanted to make; however, he really wanted to remember the name – and being able to remember the name then became of equal importance to the baking. This obviously created a dilemma. The easy way out would have been to say 'Oh never mind we'll make it another time' or 'When you've remembered what it is called, then we'll make it' or 'Tell you what, when we go shopping we'll get the ingredients then, OK?' All these responses stifle the creative moment. So we rummaged around looking for the necessary ingredients. As we were creating the dish we talked a lot about the ingredients, evoking images of the finished product, until he remembered its name.

STAGING SUCCESS AND ACHIEVEMENT BY PROCEEDING IN STAGES

My role as a parent–teacher is to foster the opportunities for success and achievement. I try to keep abreast of my own and my pupils' development and interests in order to assist them in the pursuit of success. I facilitate this by ensuring that they continuously experience success in small bites. This is 'little c creativity' (Craft, 2000 and Chapter 3, p. 45). Through discussion we try to ascertain any barriers to success, such as the child's area of concern. Once we have established this, we evaluate the small tasks needed to achieve this goal. Then we undertake the original activity, building it stage by stage. An illustration of this was building a model of an aeroplane using a construction toy. A child had an idea and had tried to transfer the idea into practice but had got stuck. He could not find an appropriate piece. Having ascertained that the piece he was looking for was not there we attempted to re-jig the model. He got frustrated as he could see the prototype had failed and that he would have to start from scratch. Instead I suggested he sketch his idea, we sourced similar-looking planes and we ensured that the plane's equipment and fuselage were included before we started. Then we slowly embarked on the activity with the body of the plane first. Too often my children return home from school dismayed and disillusioned because their set tasks were not fully completed. I always try to help them see that they achieved something.

CONCLUSION

My argument is that:

1. Those involved in the formal and informal development of children must demonstrate care and interest together with experience of pedagogic theory and a strong dose of humanity. This is an effective combination for teaching and learning. Sikes (1997) notes with regard to teaching and teacher development that much more is needed than pedagogy, instruction or teaching method alone.
2. Creativity can be seen as the means by which teachers and parents make this combination work.
3. There is no caveat based on being a parent and a teacher. The implication being that using learnings from as many facets (e.g. parent, teacher) of one's own personality as possible, makes learning easier.

REFERENCES

Bonnett, M. (1991) 'Developing children's thinking and the National Curriculum'. *Cambridge Journal of Education*, **21**(3), 277–92.

Brehony, K. (1992) 'What's left of progressive primary education?' In A. Rattani and D. Reeder (eds) *Rethinking Radical Education: Essays in Honour of Brian Simon*. London: Lawrence and Wishart.

Central Advisory Committee on Education (CEAC) (1967) *Children and their Primary Schools, Report of the Central Advisory Council for Education in England* (The Plowden Report). London: HMSO.

Craft, A. (2000) *Creativity Across the Primary Curriculum*. London: Routledge.

Hansen, D.T. (1993) 'The moral importance of the teacher's style'. *Journal of Curriculum Studies*, **25**(5), 397–421.

Hargreaves, A. (1992) 'Curriculum reform and the teacher'. *Curriculum Journal*, **2**(3), 249–58.

Hargreaves, D. H. (1983) 'The teaching of art and the art of teaching: Towards an alternative view of aesthetic learning'. In M. Hammersley and A. Hargreaves (eds) *Curriculum Practice: Some Sociological Case Studies*. Lewes: Falmer Press.

Noddings, N. (1992) *The Challenge to Care in Schools: An Alternative Approach to Education*. New York: Teachers' College Press.

Sikes, P. (1997) *Parents Who Teach*. London: Cassell.

Woods, P. (1994) 'Critical students: breakthroughs in learning'. *International Studies in Sociology of Education*, **4**(2), 123–46.

Woods, P. and Jeffrey, B. (1996) *Teachable Moments*. Buckingham: Open University Press.

Chapter 12

Creating a Climate for Learning at Coombes Infant and Nursery School

Susan Rowe and Susan Humphries

INTRODUCTION

Susan Humphries, the current headteacher, opened the Coombes Infant School in 1971. The school serves a very mixed community: a small rural village, an army base, one of the largest housing developments in the South-East (London commuters and incomers serving the silicon industries of the Thames Valley) and a varying number of traveller children. The nursery unit opened in 1991 and has two daily sessions for 26 children per session. The pupil roll of the school is steadily rising, from a two-form entry, and the school admits children between the ages of 3 years 8 months and 7 years 11 months. There are seven full-time and four part-time teachers, plus a qualified nursery assistant.

The teachers in our school believe that experiences contain the essence of life: they are the pieces of the story about who we are and how the world works. Experiences with a range of people and other living things make us the experts in dealing with our time, place and needs. In our view, opening books, viewing software and watching television can inspire us, but the greatest impact is from firsthand experiences. We believe a curriculum for young children should include planned, connected and multisensory experience as an accompaniment to book learning and formal teaching. We do not want passive learners, even though they might be under expert guidance, because it is very likely that this learning style restricts opportunity for the child. Having a voice and a point of view in your own learning is vital because involved children feel better about themselves and dream bigger dreams of themselves. The inside and outside environments at school are planned so that children react in situations where learners, teachers and parents are working together. The involvement of everyone in the learning process is energizing and full of shared experiences which will create memories to last a lifetime, and which will be the precursors to the setting of adult tastes and preferences.

In describing the ways in which we teach the National Curriculum, we hope our readers will get a glimpse of how the formal DFEE orders are met and expanded at our school, bearing in mind the philosophy outlined above, and as a consequence see how a creative approach to learning is sustained.

We try not to limit our thinking or the children's thinking by following a restricted and restrictive curriculum. Typically we target National Curriculum goals with lots of contrasting activities. They are often physically challenging because we believe that the whole range of developing skills fit together: we do not lock our children into chairs. We build into our daily programme elements of activity and physical engagement to help us model a variety of learning and teaching styles.

A LEARNING COMMUNITY

Choice is crucial; elements of choice should confront the children every day because this gives rise to searching questions. Life itself is a matter of choices. What the children need are the ways to formulate the questions in their heads to bring about the appropriate or right choice. Choice is about information-gathering and evaluation. The young child needs choice built into the curriculum because it is by having to make choice and decisions that he or she builds up the vital life skill of making appropriate decisions. What shape of paper do I want to use? What colour? What implement? We build in exercises on choice-making; we make no value judgements on the outcomes of these exercises: they are an expression of personal taste. For instance, the children might be approached as voters to determine their preference in topping for the pancake they will eat at our pancake parlour on Shrove Tuesday; during investigations into edible plants they will taste and choose their favourite breakfast cereals; around Christmas time, they will vote for a favourite Christmas card from a range brought in by the teacher; they will choose where to sit in the classroom or playground. Presenting the children with opportunities to make personal choices is integral to our teaching style. We see choice as a component of creative thinking: it has impact on lateral thinking and there are no 'wrong answers'. The child has the right to be different: to be the only one who prefers maple syrup, or likes the card with the Dickens scene. On an everyday level there is a choice of meal from the kitchen and with parental help, the children decide what to wear to school.

We make judgements about what we give to the children by regularly consulting them; by listening to what they say and translating their body language to get a view of their responses to our teaching. The pleasure principle is paramount: unless learning is fun and makes us want more we are short-changing the children. The culture in school has to be about enjoyment and pleasure; about the satisfying moment. The outcomes for the children in any school will be the levels of intellectual achievement: at our school we are keen to see that the children also stay in touch with their feelings; that they are socially intelligent; that they are morally and ethically aware; that they are aesthetically tuned; that they are physically stretched; that they are connoisseurs of music and food; that they see themselves as citizens of the world.

The drive to be in the top bracket of performance in schools, as measured by standardized testing, can impose a regime which teaches to the tests in order to enhance results. A huge segment of education (feelings, morals, the intuitive response, and the creative urge) is marginalized. As a staff group we are endeavouring to hold on to all those things that cannot be measured by tests. We recognize our accountability, and do whatever we can to get good test results without sacrificing our professional integrity and knowledge of child development.

The teaching group model conduct for the children: teachers collaborate, share problems and give each other feedback. The importance of giving is at the heart of a creative group; during the act of empathetic listening or of sharing thoughts, we open ourselves to revising and redrafting our ideas. Ideas are improved and kept alive by being spoken and overheard. Help from colleagues in realizing the ideas brings them into common ownership. The process of talking to each other is reinforcing, and we have also learned to use an intuitive mode of thinking where we brainstorm for method, content and delivery. We apply the National Curriculum but, irrespective of this, children at all levels need to enjoy their lessons while being encouraged to make shifts in their thinking from verbal to mathematical, from logical to spatial, from musical to environmental and so on. We wholeheartedly acknowledge that there are many different kinds of intelligence, which make the person, and we set our teaching routines accordingly.

Much of our teaching involves a slight element of risk, and we perceive this to be essential if the creative approach to teaching and learning is to be maintained and taken forward. We are in no sense foolhardy, but we are aware that without risk there is a danger that education could become tailor-made to suit national tests whereas there are many reasons to build it up with dramatic and memorable lessons to increase lateral thinking. Children hunger for more 'involving education' as instanced in the government's 'everyone remembers a good teacher' recruitment films. In one of these short films, the point of the lesson is understood in an experience when the children release flying models, which fill all the air space above their heads. Even the government knows what education should be like, but its current stress on prescribed tasks, mechanical exercises and learning by rote should only be part of the picture. We do not deny the need for structure in the curriculum, particularly in the core subjects, and a considerable percentage of our time is spent on delivering the strategies for literacy and numeracy. We are accountable for the quality of education we offer, and for the children's achievements in the measurable Key Stage 1 and 2 standardized tests and tasks. However, we are concerned to give similar consideration to those immeasurable aspects of education. Not all end results can be reproduced as a set of statistics, but they are equally vital if we are to provide children with the means to become committed lifelong learners. Our fear is that education is not best serving a substantial proportion of pupils and that in years to come there could be an increase in the number of disaffected young people in this country. We are committed to offering a challenging, focused, relevant and broad education, which will contain 'something for everyone' as an engaged learner.

In order to make an authentic curriculum we use the community to set up a range of experiences throughout the year. We draw as much curricular clout as we can from these, and they form the base of our teaching and learning. Parents and grandparents are involved formally as well as casually in the idea, and we also draw on the wider community (craftspeople, authors, illustrators, and specialists in their field, musicians, dancers and the like). Many of these planned experiences are about children seeing creative forces at work. Seeing pottery and pictures produced, meeting musical-instrument makers, exploring calligraphy and meeting performers with original ideas, helps us all to be a part of the creative process. There is often food to eat and a chance to share the occasion with twinned classes from our feeder junior school and our families. By involving a range of people in our work, we encourage them to make creative contributions to a curriculum where learning is visible.

Opportunities to listen to instruments such as the kora, to beat rhythms of African djembe drums and hear singers in an unfamiliar language help us structure teaching about diversity and respect for difference. It is a chance to put the children in a 'world class'. This type of learning is social and co-operative; it puts models in front of the children that are rooted in the real world, and moves us away from simply remembering the right facts at the right time. Education should be so much more than that.

Much of the daily work is sensory: the children record things in the brain through smell and touch as well as through ears and eyes. We believe that the hands are the cutting edge of the mind and that by purposely engaging all our senses, we internalize the learning and start to make sense of it; it is remembered throughout the body. For instance, we tap into the emotions of smell at Epiphany, when we focus on frankincense and myrrh; when we cook chutney and make jam; when we bake bread; when we stand under an apple tree in spring and are showered with blossom; when we work with nosegays of herbs in our history programme; when we light bonfires in the autumn; when we burn incense for Divali. Through the year we work with soaps, shaving foam, wild and cultivated flowers, leaves, fruits, spices and food with a keen scent. Smell can take you to a particular moment in time: circumstances in which it was first experienced are reinvoked and the connective nature of life is recognized.

INTEGRATING THE SCIENCE CURRICULUM

Our school is strong on science: getting the children to be active investigators of their world means giving them lots of time to make discoveries. The children see how much we value their contributions. We stress the importance of being a keen observer of the general and the particular, and we plan and set up for physical participation. The children work individually, in pairs, in small groups and in larger groups, and there is a lot of interaction and discussion. This is non-threatening but challenging learning time when there is a strong emphasis on hypothesizing; all contributions are considered. For instance, it is part of work in the science area to learn about forces; children push and pull one another in different shaped and sized boxes; they experiment with blankets and sheets and pull each other across the hall floor. Ordinary objects like the boxes and blankets give the children lots of fun before the teacher draws them into discussion about the journeys they have made and the inferences of friction, levers and the forces of push and pull. These activities culminate in a transport technology day; the children bring in toys and equipment to transport themselves and each other around the grounds of the school. Additionally this brings in investigations into wheels and gears. The work is further developed in the autumn term, when the children are given the task of bringing in the heavy pumpkins they have grown in the gardens. Some of the pumpkins are huge and would need two adults to shift them; we ask the children to utilize a range of resources to bring the crop in unaided, undamaged and safely. What the children learn from these procedures is transferred to other areas of the curriculum: the pumpkins are not grown specifically for research into forces; they are also illustrations of the seed-to-seed cycle. The 'transport technology day' is written up by the children as a writing exercise and the curriculum is taught in an integrated way.

At some point every year, we do rock and soil studies; clay is gathered from the school grounds and the children become familiar with the characteristics of their local soil. The smell of the topsoil and the smell and feel of the clay reinforce the learning. Earth is one of the most interesting topics to explore scientifically but it also has geographical connotations and figures in our environmental awareness programme. First, the topsoil is examined; we dig up squares of turf and the children pull these to pieces and identify the plants, insects and animals they find. They pull at the fibres to see how the herb layer is meshed together; they examine the strength of this meshing; and they hunt for signs of decomposing matter. They experiment with the soil in water to look at the sediment: they discover that there is air in the soil and they collect the small stones and particles. The clay underneath is compared and contrasted with the topsoil; we then use it for investigations into water tightness and malleability; we look at how the shape of a lump of clay can be changed by applying pressure to it; how its nature changes as we add water to it or dry it out. We make simple pots and a primitive sawdust kiln and alter the state of the clay, returning it to its rock state. The wholeness of experiences such as this, where clay is taken directly from the ground, goes beyond knowing the facts so that you can be tested on them. It goes to true understanding and knowledge. Methods of teaching like this are part of an approach to life where children are making creative contributions to their own learning; the final stage in this unit of work comes when the children take home their fired pot and it becomes a reminder of the work; an icon.

INTEGRATING LITERACY

The onset of the National Literacy Strategy has made the structured teaching of language skills formulaic. Daily routines of prescribed teaching are packaged into timed doses during which the children tend to be passive recipients. Tasks are usually based on children sitting – either on the carpet for whole-group work, or at tables for pencil and paper work. Certain areas of language skills acquisition depend upon structured schemes of work, but we contend that language can never be taught solely in these passive ways: what we are doing to children is 'dumbing them down' rather than raising them to the heights of language arts. Our school follows the prescribed NLS schemata but we add our own flourishes to make the literacy hour active and an exciting part of each day. The emphasis is on co-operation in a range of learning experiences; for instance, phonics teaching is reinforced with singing, dancing, puppetry and eating. The children internalize the 'ee' and 'ea' phonemes by *ea*ting gr*ee*n beans and p*ea*rs or smelling sw*ee*t p*ea*s. We go to our bay trees and take the l*ea*ves from the tree, and put them into our pockets for a fragrant reminder during the day. In ways like these the programme becomes rooted in the real world, rather than being in the abstract or paperbound. The teachers are always searching for imaginative and new ways to engage the children in their learning and to persuade them that it is, or should be, fun.

Knowledge about how the parts of language work and fit together is very necessary, but mastery of this and spelling does not produce good writing. A writer struggles to shape experiences through written expressions, and creating a story or poem about something that has happened in someone else's world will not bring the self-discovery of a personal experience. When a writer uses words to shape and explain experiences to herself and others, she is caught in the process of creative release which depends on her thinking and helps her self-discovery. The Writer's Workshop approach which came from the USA (specifically Graves, 1983) puts writing beyond the awkward targets of punctuation, syllabifying and spelling, and treats all writers as authors. This method teaches the mechanical side of language as the children liberate and respond to their 'inner voice'. When young writers become inhibited they stop exercising this inner voice and fall back on words they can spell and towards the dullest, safest expressions. We believe in the 'children as authors' approach, but via the National Curriculum we are also giving the children a thorough grounding in the mechanics of writing.

It is helpful to our style of teaching to have the shared experiences to talk and write about. It is one way of encouraging a spontaneous natural flow of speech and of obtaining shared observations, which are understood by the class. These experiences also last over time and can be reviewed. Most importantly, the easiest way to write is to write about something you know.

We focus a lot on poetry as a vehicle for raising the children's awareness of the richness of language and how it may be manipulated by them to suit their preferences and imagination. Work on rhyme with the younger children often takes place outside with 'rhyme hunts'. The adults will have hidden rhyming words in the playground or along a pathway or in the woodland areas, and the children work outside to find and link up the rhyming pairs; or teddy bears will be hidden in the trees holding lines of traditional or other well-known verse; the children look for the bear holding the first line, then the second and so on, until they put the whole verse together in sequence, often checking it against a written model they carry. Older children are introduced to the Haiku form and are encouraged to have a go at writing their own, often in our outdoor setting; in our bluebell woods on a warm spring day; by the iced-over ponds in winter; or under falling leaves in autumn. The sunflowers which the children grow every year are a wonderful stimulus for creative writing, and the children's efforts are twinned with the published work of other poets to make a whole package of themed work.

We use more complex poetical forms to whet the children's appetites and give them tasters of what will be available to them as they grow older. Even the very youngest children can appreciate parts of the works of Shakespeare, Frost, Dryden or Plath. Our role as teachers is to offer the best of what is available to the children and to help them appreciate it, as well as to combine this approach with active learning experiences and the more formal prescribed schemes of work.

The teaching of writing, and children's achievements in writing at the end of Key Stages 1 and 2 are national issues which are current, and like all other schools, we are looking for ways in which to improve what we do in order that the children can achieve expected government standards. Children at Key Stage 1 are being put through a huge range of pencil and paper exercises and we think that these basic (and necessary skills) can be conveyed in ways which are age-appropriate. Our children refine their handwriting skills by practising on tabletops with shaving foam, chocolate mousse or talcum powder. They use large chalks on the playground and pathways, or paintbrushes dipped in water on the outside walls. They learn about sentence structure, full stops, capital letters, commas, question marks and speech marks, by becoming 'human sentences': each child will be given a word or component part of the sentence, and they are asked to rearrange themselves into a complete sentence for another group of children to read and check. It is through playing with these writing conventions that children begin to understand them.

A lot of the children's writing will be done as part of a theme, for instance, every year around St Patrick's Day, we act out the story of the Irish potato famines; the children participate in the re-enactment; afterwards they eat boiled potatoes, listen to traditional Irish music and folk tales, and enjoy performances of Irish dancing by professionals. Having been immersed in the culture, the writing task, which follows, will have its roots in the children's prior participation in the range of activities; there will be reasons to write, in whatever genre, about an authentic curriculum.

Our school year is punctuated with these themes (Humphries and Rowe, 1996) which underpin the formal curriculum, and which ensure that our community is constantly being introduced and reintroduced to different aspects of life and tradition. During the autumn term, there is a two-week programme of learning centred on 'fire'. We light bonfires, cook on open fires or barbecues, conduct experiments into combustibility and changes in state, act out the Hilaire Belloc poem of 'Matilda, Who Told Lies' which culminates in setting fire to a small cardboard house that the children have helped to make. Divali, which is a fire festival, usually falls during November and we make a pathway of light with candles and remember the homecoming of Rama and Sita. The finale to our fire studies is the making of a large-scale model of the old City of London. Each child contributes a model house of the period (some quite simple, and others much more crafted and detailed affairs). Most children make their houses alongside parents at home, others will be given time and help in school to make one. We place these models on a large floor map of the city in the seventeenth century, with roads and rivers being identified; the map takes up about half the space in the hall. We keep the model city *in situ* for about a week, and we use it for work across the curriculum: maths, geography, music, history, physical education (PE), language. The children work on and off the model, and have opportunities to get to know it well and use it as a background for seventeenth-century studies. Later on, we shift the map and the models out of doors, and light a fire in the baker's shop in Pudding Lane and watch how the fire spreads and destroys the city.

The children's writing which is associated with this fire theme takes many forms, and each year we trial new ideas; last year, we focused on the writings of Samuel Pepys and the children kept their own diaries, followed by their personal accounts of the fire itself (ours over three hours; the real one which Pepys recorded was written over three days). In other years, the focus has been on writing newspaper reports and publishing a newspaper (incorporating ICT as an aide) which is circulated to the other children and parents. One year, there was a strong emphasis on the poetry of fire and we put together anthologies of our children's work.

INTEGRATING THE MATHS CURRICULUM

In our maths programme, we aim for the work to be based as much as possible in the real world and some lessons are taught out of doors. The National Numeracy Strategy seems to us more child-friendly than the National Literacy Strategy, because it concentrates on concrete examples of mathematics in action, rather than prescribed abstract tasks. Three years ago we carried out a major audit of our maths teaching, and decided to abandon set texts in favour of a scheme based on games, exercises and investigations (Shropshire Advisory Service's 'Calculating Competence'). Within a year of adopting Calculating Competence, the children's measurable achievements in maths at the end of Key Stage 1 had significantly improved, and so had their enjoyment in the subject. Happily for the children, the National Numeracy Strategy relies heavily on tasks similar to those in Calculating Competence.

Maths skills can be comprehensively practised if they can be related to aspects of other work. As well as learning maths in set lessons, we confirm the principles and appeal of maths with ideas on how to create order and communicate mathematically as we cope with the bulk of our work. By ensuring that maths often has a central role in our themes, its value and relevance is maintained.

Sunflower harvest is an annual event, when the children bring in the crop. We plant enough sunflowers for each child to have at least one to pick in the autumn. The children go out to estimate how many sunflowers are in bloom (dealing in fairly big numbers). At picking time, the children have some choice in the sunflower they want to gather, and the plant is picked, root-ball and all. Since many of the sunflowers grow to 2 or 3 metres in height, there are opportunities for comparison of heights between the sunflowers and between the sunflowers and the children. The children take their plants into the playground, and investigate them mathematically, e.g. how many petals/sepals/leaves? What is the circumference of the head? What is the length using non-standard and standard measures? How many seeds are there and what is the best way for counting and recording large numbers? The children make a chalk representation of their plants, and then they take the sunflowers to pieces, sorting and setting the different components. The flowers have cross-curricular purpose as well as mathematical gain; we use them for creative writing, for artwork and exhibitions, as a stimulus for movement, dance and singing and for geographical studies.

In looking at the concept of mass (weight), we get a number of items together which all weigh one kilogram. Boxes of sugar, closed containers of water, bags of tinned goods, baskets of stones are collected in the classroom, and the children pick up different items and get the 'feel' of a kilogram. They walk a measured distance holding a kilogram in each hand and chart and discuss the importance of handles, straps and the shape of containers for ease of carrying. Moving weights is a show of strength; the critical start to measuring mass is the hand/eye/body co-ordination needed to lift things. Until you start lifting, you cannot have a concept of mass – appearance will tell you nothing; our approach means that the children remember in their arms and legs.

Recently, we have had a large crane on site, putting a roof onto a new classroom; the children have been able to observe the crane at work, and to discuss its weight-bearing ability and capacity. They talked with the crane operator, and got a glimpse of how a crane works to lift heavy weights over distance and obstacles: the children perceive the information in a real-world setting and it makes sense to them.

Many mathematical opportunities come from the cooking and sharing of food: apples which are harvested from our fruit trees are weighed and measured in a variety of ways: we do apple fractions by cutting the apples in half, quarters, eighths and then the children are asked to put the apple jigsaw back together again to help in their spatial awareness. We collect a variety of recipes which use apples as a principal ingredient, and the children weigh, measure and cook the raw ingredients – and then eat their learning.

At Christmas time, one of our school traditions is to make Christmas puddings for our Christmas dinner. The children have to follow a complex recipe, and are immersed in all the language of food preparation (cut, chop, squeeze, beat, stir, blend, grate, mix, etc.) as well as in the mathematical complexity of following a recipe and making a finished product from a variety of raw ingredients. They undertake all the preparation and mixing, and the proof of the pudding is always in the eating! As well as being a strongly mathematical focus, these activities are language rich, and also deal with history ('Little Jack Horner') and geography (where do the ingredients come from?). We plot the places of origin on a world map and discuss why different produce comes from different parts of the world. We research different recipes for Christmas puddings and look for similarities and differences. We may go on to undertake studies into the cost of preparing the puddings: every year a group of children is taken to the nearby supermarket to do the shopping and they compare costs of different ingredients. The children have to pay for their purchases with real money, and check that they have the correct change. Upon return to school, they have to divide the ingredients between the six classes and ensure that each class has precisely what it needs to make Christmas puddings.

Throughout the year, there are reliable opportunities for data-handling exercises which are based on real-life experiences for the children; for instance, on Shrove Tuesday we make pancake batter, cook pancakes and choose one of five or six toppings for our own individual pancake. The children record their preferences in the classroom, using conventional bar charts or histograms and also undertake simple statistical analyses using ICT software. After lambing time, the children propose and vote for names for the lambs which have been born; we aim for the feel of a genuine 'general election' complete with voting papers, booths and a Returning Officer; intensely mathematical in nature, this exercise also gives us the opportunity to discuss civics and politics with the children. On some occasions, we ask the children to compare the results of first-past-the-post voting (one person, one vote) and then to trial a proportional voting system (where the children are given a number of points to award as they wish between contenders); so we may set up a voting system for a favourite greetings card, or a favourite breakfast cereal, or a favourite type of bread, or a favourite type of apple from a range of choices; the children vote in the usual manner, and then use proportionality. The results (which are often quite different, despite such a small sample) are discussed and the children try to explain the differences.

INTEGRATING THE FOUNDATION SUBJECTS

The way in which we work in teaching the three core subjects is followed through in our other subject-specific work. The foundation subjects of the National Curriculum have recently taken something of a hammering from central government advisers and their importance in underpinning education has been called into question. We remain convinced that all of the foundation subjects are vital components of our weekly programme, and our approach to them is the same as it is to the core subjects. We try to root them all in the real world and to give the children a wide range of active, participatory learning experiences – an authentic curriculum to which the children respond and with which they interact. Again, the emphasis is on co-operative, collaborative work, which takes place through a carefully planned series of events, traditions and celebrations. There is a strong focus on offering the highest available quality to the children, and so we ensure that in each half-term block, the children will listen to live performances of music of high calibre (the REME Band, the Gurkha Band, internationally renowned harpists, string quartets, African drummers, Indian sitar players, brass ensembles, strolling minstrels, opera singers, instrumentalists, percussionists, etc.); they will experience the work of a range of professional drama groups as well as 'home-spun' drama presented by the adult group; they will work alongside authors and illustrators, artists in residence, weavers, spinners, storytellers, and a huge range of craftspeople.

The work is a mixture of sitting, listening and physical activity: it takes the children into the outside environment and into the community, and in turn it brings the community and the outdoors inside: there is a reciprocity between what is available and used in the classroom and what is available from outside the school building. We call ourselves a 'community school', and for us this means opening the doors to the influence of what is outside and to get parent input. We set out to involve the wider family group of each child (in particular the grandparents), the immediate local community, the national community and the international community in our work. We encourage people to come into school to work with us and to share their talents and expertise, or just their time. The base for our open-door policy is rooted in Jerome Bruner's (1976) belief that education is a dialogue between the more experienced and the less experienced. By putting our children (and ourselves as the teaching group) into direct contact with the 'more experienced', we add value to our work and to the children's learning and make the whole process a hands-on, multi-sensory range of experiences. We also move towards our goal of becoming a learning society.

Over the years, we have undertaken a programme of environmental planting and improvement. Our school grounds, and the diversity of habitats contained within them, are essential components of our work with the children. Each term over the years has seen at least one major project undertaken, and often the stimulus for the project will have come directly from the children's suggestions or from a perceived curricular need. Sometimes, development work will take place because of a previous addition to our gardens and grounds, which leads us on to the next stage. For instance, we have created a series of all-weather pathways that criss-cross the school grounds; as each section is completed, the site of the next needed pathway becomes more apparent. Sometimes, the next phase will be the result of a chance comment from a member of staff, a parent or governor, or a visitor to the school. We make progress in our environmental work by remaining open to new ideas and suggestions, or by evaluating what we have been doing and looking to taking the work onwards. Comments about needing to do something special for the millennium led us to the idea of setting up a geology trail throughout the grounds – at least twelve different types of rock from the British Isles set in different ways. To date, we have seven groups of rock ranging from Cornish granite arranged as a platform seating area, to Purbeck limestone set as 'King Arthur's Chair' on a small artificial hill, to Yorkshire limestone samples set in a formation similar to the central circle of Stonehenge – our very own Coombeshenge. Sometimes, it is the children themselves who come up with the ideas that take us into the next bit of environmental work. Recently they asked for a tree house with a tree growing through the middle, and we are now in the process of building it.

At present, we have a school site which is a major curriculum resource; it provides the backdrop as well as the stimuli to much of our teaching programme, and we are constantly looking for different ways to use it and redefine it. Maps of the gardens are used to teach grid references and the children search within these for the clues to solve riddles or find the source of treasures. Translating the symbols on the maps starts where the child really is, in physical and emotional terms, reading his own setting and recognizing features and plants known to him. The maps are the best worksheets we produce.

When the children plant their different crops in the spring and early summer, they mark their planting areas on maps of the school ground; the site of autumnal planting of spring-flowering bulbs is similarly marked on maps. Cartographers have mapped the grounds for us and the children use these master plans as well as making their own. The very youngest children start out by drawing landscape features, then move on to drawing bird's-eye views before being introduced to the notion of abstract maps and geographical symbols. In early spring of each year, we take the children out to 'Beat the Bounds', our version of the ancient tradition of visiting parish boundaries and instilling a knowledge of it in the children of the parish by beating them at regular intervals! Everyone in school goes out to make a journey around the school perimeter, and using long sticks, which we cut from our gardens, the children beat the boundaries. The grounds also feature strongly in our Epiphany Journey in January, when the children re-enact the journey of the Magi, and follow a planned route visiting different inns, which we have set up in seven different locations. It is by becoming thoroughly acquainted with their immediate landscape that young children start to develop a set of geographical constructs and knowledge of their locality. This is teaching for transfer and we believe that fascination with maps and plans evolves from this type of early experience.

Folk tales, fairy stories and legends are full of lost boys and girls, and there are many examples of this situation/idea. We act out the solution Hansel and Gretel used when they were abandoned in the woods, and we see what happens to breadcrumbs and marked pebbles which usually have a spot of paint on them. We find parallel circumstances in other stories and we look at the predicament of Peter Pan and Rapunzel, Snow White and Goldilocks. This is one of the ways we integrate important stories into the foundation subjects.

The eating of food is also an intensively geographical activity; whenever the opportunity arises, we ensure that the children have the opportunity to help to make and eat foods from around the world. For instance, when we are studying our contrast geographical area of West Africa, the children help to set up a tradi-tional three-stone fire in the grounds, they collect kindling and help to keep the cooking fire alight; we cook simple porridges or vegetable stews with rice and the children then eat communally together out of doors. The celebration of Bastille Day in July is accompanied by a French breakfast of croissants and '*chocolat chaud*' served pavement-café style with accordion music. At Christmas, the children make a traditional Christmas pudding, which includes raw ingredients from around the world; we make sure that we get the most out of the activity as possible in terms of geography as well as language and science.

One-day museums and exhibitions feature regularly in our programme and add zest to our history teaching in particular. We ask the parent/family group of all children in the school, as well as staff, governors and friends, to send in examples of a particular item (e.g. chairs) and to provide some information about their con-tribution. We then set the chairs which come into school into a museum in the school hall; each exhibit is labelled so that the children and adults can access relevant information, and often the older children take on the role of curators for the younger ones. The children visit the museum two or three times during the day and the teacher tries to ensure that the maximum potential of the exhibition is exploited. Other one-day exhibitions have included Victoriana, clocks, laundry equipment, wood and shoes; all have a multiplicity of purpose in terms of curriculum value; for us, the important thing is that the children are engaged as active researchers and interpreters, using the exhibitions as their raw material. History is also taught through drama projects; every year, the older children take part in a week of drama (as well as maths, art, ICT, RE, PSE) set around Guido Fawkes and the Gunpowder Plot. The children are active participants in the drama, either working in a group supporting the King, or in a group of Conspira-tors. When we undertake nativity-based work prior to Christmas, the children have the opportunity to take a variety of roles over four or five re-enactments. The setting is made atmospheric by using candlelight and incense, and each re-enactment is accompanied by the eating of traditional Middle Eastern foods: the historical background is part of the adult narrator's task: she leads the children through the ancient stories and helps them to interpret and translate the traditions. Drama is a powerful teaching tool, and we use it frequently.

Art, craft and design feature in our curriculum, although over the last two or three years they have become increasingly squeezed out of the timetable. However, we still give them time and use them to support much of our work in the core and foundation subjects. We try to remain innovative in our approach and are always keen to trial new ideas; in this regard, the use of the Internet has been a powerful influence; we and the children have instant access to a whole range of information and end-products (although naturally, the children's access to web sites is highly restricted). A lot of our artwork is inspired by artists such as Andy Goldsworthy and Anthony Gormley; the idea of ephemeral art in the environment which can be recorded on digital film for the children is very appealing. We often work outside using the increasingly rich resource of our developing outdoor landscape. At Easter, the children make patterns and pictures using leaves and flowers gathered from the grounds, and they put dyed eggs in them to act as a focal point in the pictures. Flowerheads, leaves in autumn, twigs, stones, willow gathered from our trees are used by the children in their three-dimensional work; often their artistry is set out of doors, but sometimes they bring in their raw materials and set up ephemeral art displays in the classroom or school hall. These are recorded in colour prints, slide images or digital images which are updated on our intranet site.

Revision is literally seeing again; the original experience captured on camera can mean prints or a slide show to give a second sight of the happening to the group who took part. It allows a different sort of evaluation of the happening, which the teacher then defines for the group in order to round off the episode. The vocabulary of the experience is recollected and there are benefits from inter-preting the happening again and of revising the overall feeling. This method of rounding off is a characteristic one for us. Finally, some of the pictures are scanned and entered on our intranet site so that individual children can call them up.

We encourage the children to perceive themselves as artists, and to make bold and large statements in the playground or car park areas. We give the children chalks or charcoal and ask them to put their images on to the tarmac or concrete floors. The next rain will wash away the images, but the act of drawing directly on to the site is very liberating. It takes us back to our distant ancestors who made their marks on the walls of caves and mountains; who set their petro-glyphs into the landscape and whose work in this modern world is perceived as powerful art.

The design technology tasks which we set our children are rooted in the authentic world; we do not ask them to make deductions from models made with small standardized cardboard boxes; the children themselves have an innate understanding of the unsuitability of this material. Instead, we bring in real tools and containers, and ask the children to examine and evaluate their properties. Additional adults guide the activities so that the children reach achievable stages. Whenever building work takes place at school or in the vicinity, we keep the children involved in the changes which are taking place to their environment.

They go outside to talk to the experts and watch them at work; we provide opportunities for them to make their own marks, for instance by writing their names on the foundation bricks or by burying a time capsule of work of the day for future archaeologists. The children see specialized machinery and equipment in action (pneumatic drills, cranes, cement mixers and spirit levels) and, above all, the children can talk to the professionals who are working on site. We may then go on to try some of the techniques in the classroom; we get the children to mix their own mortar and have a go at building a real brick wall; we might ask them to have a go at mixing plaster and plastering a piece of hardboard in the classroom; we give them the opportunity to handle real materials. When the pumpkins ripen, the children are asked to bring them in safely and undamaged in spite of their weight and quantity. We offer a range of equipment (ropes, blankets, boxes, broom handles, etc.) and give them the minimum of adult help to complete the task. In offering challenges like these, the children get to grips with the problems of design and technology, and start to understand their real importance both in the classroom and in the wider world.

Music is an accompaniment to all our work, in all its different moods and with all its richness. We play related music as an integral part of all our thematic work: Irish ballads and the Celtic Harp around St Patrick's Day; male voice choirs around St David's Day; West African djembe drums and the kora in our African studies; handbells around Christmas; the piano accordion for Bastille Day, the lyre for Epiphany. We try to represent the culture of the focal area, and music is strongly evocative. The whole-school family has regular access to quality performance; we invite musicians into school to share their music and instruments; marching bands, string quartets, drummers, harpists, minstrels, steel bands, woodwind groups, buskers, folk musicians, balalaika players and solo instrumentalists. All play for the children, talk about their specialist musical interests and explain the complexities of their instruments. We often play music as a background canvas for children at work; the CD/cassette-player is used frequently in all curriculum areas. Growth experiences can take place simultaneously and music feeds the mind while children do other kinds of work. We are keen on developing the aesthetic right hemisphere of the brain as well as the logical left side, and music is a powerful route into this.

As well as experiencing the essence of concert music, the children are encouraged to be musicians themselves. Our music specialist leads them through a diverse programme with a strong emphasis on rhythm, tonal quality and composition. The initial programme for the youngest children is based on whole-body movement to a range of sounds; the children learn to respond to a variety of sound with their bodies: moving to music is a natural way of exploring it. Rhythmic work using long sticks which have been harvested from the willow, ash and hazel trees in the school grounds is another feature of the programme. The annual coppicing and pollarding cycle gives us sticks, which can be used for rhythm work. The children start their percussion work with claves or short sticks gathered from the environment and progress to the long sticks (often much taller than they are themselves). They learn to work co-operatively to beat out patterns of sound, at first echoing the sound made by the teacher and over a period of time they learn to respond to musical notation alone. In this way, the children progress to fairly complex musical patterns as part of the intended spiral curriculum.

In much the same way, the PE programme is developed to support the children's integrated learning. We start and end each term with a whole-school celebration of dance. Our PE specialist works with small groups of children to interpret an idea in movement, which will tie in with the theme or the ethics shared by us all. At the end of the first week of term, all the children and adult group meets up to dance together. It is an intensely moving experience, which focuses on togetherness, Cupertino and care for each other. Much of our PE programme concentrates on those aspects of movement, gymnastics and games which highlight relationships: we use parachutes, balloons, feathers, scarves to encourage children in individual physical and social skills. Our concern is for self-awareness through whole-body movement and for awareness of one another: it aims to set in us a pride and happiness about ourselves and for each other.

CONCLUSION

We have tried to avoid a rigid timetable as suggested by current government initiatives, and leave ourselves some of the freedoms to use opportunities as they present themselves. We try not to waste a second of our time or the children's time in school; every moment has the potential to be precious. Our philosophy has assumed its present form after many years of growth and change. It is not as desirable as it could be and we try to approach our work with a sound critical attitude, which will bring about further experimentation and change. We grow, but we are always in the state of becoming what we hope to be.

REFERENCES

Bruner, J. (1976) *The Relevance of Education*. Harmondsworth: Penguin.
Graves, D. H. (1983) *Writing: Teachers and Children At Work*. London: Heinemann Educational.
Humphries, S. and Rowe, S. (1996) *Working Together*. London: Forbes Publications.

Chapter 13

A Hundred Possibilities:
Creativity, Community and ICT

Jenny Leach

The child is made of one hundred.

The child has
A hundred languages
A hundred hands
A hundred thoughts
A hundred ways of thinking

. . . The school and the culture
. . . tell the child
to discover the world already there
and of the hundred
they steal the ninety-nine.

They tell the child
That work and play
Reality and fantasy
Science and imagination
Sky and earth
Reason and dream are things
That do not belong together.
And thus they tell the child
That the hundred is not there.

(Loris Malaguzzi, extract from poem translated from the Italian by Lella Gandini)

INTRODUCTION

The poet John Milton travelled from England to Italy in the late 1630s. While there he visited the astronomer and physicist Galileo Galilei, observing the skies above Florence through the telescope from which Galilei was studying the moon and Saturn. When viewed through even the crudest of telescopes, a galaxy is a stunning sight – a nucleus and misty swirl of spiral arms, billions of stars caught in a whirlpool spanning hundreds of thousands of light years. Milton was not to forget this experience, drawing on it in his epic poem 'Paradise Lost' (1667). The poem is suffused with images of the heavens, the stars and planets, the sheer immensity of the universe, most particularly in the description of creation itself. God's pathway to heaven is:

> A broad and ample road, whose dust is gold,
> And pavement
> stars, as stars to thee appear
> Seen in the Galaxy, that Milky Way
> Which nightly as a circling zone thou
> Seest
> Powdered with stars. ('Paradise Lost', Book vii, lines 577–81)

The 'spotty globe', the moon, as seen through Galilei's 'optic glass' is woven into the vision of the hellish, shield-carrying Lucifer. Over a hundred years later Milton's poem was to be highly influential in Joseph Haydn's composition of *The Creation*. A telescope provided the inspiration for this work too. Haydn's diary entry, written in England in 1792, gives an account of his visit to the home of William Herschel, also musician and composer, and his sister Caroline. The Herschels were to become the greatest astronomical observers of the time (Figure 13.1).

Figure 13.1: William and Caroline Herschel.

On 15th June I went from Windsor to (Slough?) to Doctor Herschel where I saw the great telescope. It is 40 feet long and 5 feet in diameter. The machinery is very big, but so ingenious that a single man can put it in motion with the greatest ease. Sometimes he sits for 5 or 6 hours under the open sky in the bitterest cold weather.

This telescopic opening up of the universe made as unforgettable an impression on Haydn as it had on Milton so many years earlier. Biographers have suggested that Haydn stored away at the back of his mind some impression of the vastness of interstellar spaces, which fired his imagination as he later worked on *The Creation*. When it came to the first performance of the Oratorio, not even his chief patron had previewed the section where light is first described. Haydn himself was conducting and, according to reports of the time, his eyes 'flashed with fire' at that point, and the audience was left totally electrified.

VIEWS OF CREATIVITY

This chapter is about the relationship between creativity, community and new technologies. I want to argue that traditional views of creativity have failed to take sufficient account of the social dimension of the creative process. Creativity is an integral aspect of learning and human development, present and ongoing in the daily interactions of any community. And since technological and communicative tools are expressive of the purposes and outcomes of all communities, Information and Communications Technology (ICT) has a significant role in developing and extending the creative process.

It seems appropriate for two reasons, therefore, to begin this chapter with accounts of two of the Western world's most celebrated works about creation, composed in times when new technologies, each in different ways, were causing a sensation. First, the accounts symbolize the development of the concept of creativity itself, facing Janus-like to its origins as well as its future. For although creativity is a twentieth-century word, it has an 'important and significant history' (Williams, 1984), embedded in both the linguistic and semantic origins of the word 'creation'. Consideration of the ways in which 'creation' has unfolded across the centuries provides an insight into contemporary thinking about creativity, as I hope to show. It also helps us understand why the social dimension of creativity has remained largely unacknowledged. Second, these accounts vividly gesture to the creative communities in which individuals such as Caroline Herschel and John Milton participated. In such communities, I suggest, information and communications technology has always played a pivotal role.

Until the sixteenth century, creation (from the same Latin root as 'create') was used solely in the context of divine creation, the beginning of the world. The view that '*creatura non potest creare*' (the creature who has been created, cannot himself create), was integral to the medieval religious belief system. Indeed, the use of 'creation' to denote *present* or *future* human-making was not to emerge in

English until the major transformation of thought that accompanied the birth of humanism during the Renaissance. Long after that period the word continued to be used to invoke a godlike creator; even the first recorded use of 'creative' seems to have been in this older sense – 'this Divine, miraculous, creative power' (Cudworth, 1678). By the time Haydn came to compose *The Creation*, the association of the word 'creative' with *human* art and thought was becoming conscious and powerful. It remained so throughout the nineteenth century – in 1815, for example, the poet Wordsworth wrote to a friend 'High is our calling, friend, Creative Art' (in Williams, 1984, p. 83). Only during the second half of the twentieth century was 'creative' used with increasing frequency across a wide variety of domains. This constant use, notes Raymond Williams in *Keywords* significantly diluted the impact and power of the word; nevertheless, he argues, such changes of connotation are inevitable when 'we realise the necessary magnitude and complexity of the interpretation of human activity which "creative" now so indispensably embodies' (Williams, 1984, p. 83).

Despite this gradual but significant shift across the centuries, establishing creation as an essential element of human meaning-making and development, contemporary views of creativity continue to carry the legacy of the medieval world view. Creativity has come to be understood by many as an innate human faculty. However, unlike the often similarly attributed faculty of language (Pinker, 1995), it is frequently characterized as an elusive, somewhat magical or god-like quality: an attribute to be found only in rare and unusual people. And just as views of language continue to be resonant with echoes of the biblical myth of Babel (Eco, 1997; Leach, 2000a; Steiner, 1975), so folk psychology's spin on creativity is resonant with the notion of an inspirational, unique Creator. This emphasis on the rare, inspired individual has recently been termed the *élite* view of creativity (NACCCE, 1999). It is a view that underpinned the development of psychological studies of creativity throughout the twentieth century, beginning with Binet and Henri's (1896) empirical tests of childhood imagination at the turn of the century, and closely followed by Jung (1977 [1912]) and Bergson's (1944 [1907]) explorations of individual intuition.

A plethora of psychological studies between the 1960s and 1980s further strengthened interest in 'creative' activity, particularly in the areas of literature, music and art. These studies variously identified creativity on the basis of individual achievement, individual personality characteristics or cognitive processes such as hypothesizing or problem-solving (e.g. Amabile, 1983; Torrance, 1963). Domains such as science, business, sports, teaching or parenting were largely disregarded, and thus the concept became firmly associated with the arts. This has been dubbed the sectoral view of creativity (NACCCE, 1999), vividly reflected in the title of Bruner's (1965) seminal study of creativity *On Knowing; Occasional Pieces Done for the Left Hand* [which signifies the 'dreamer, the intuitor, the hunch-follower, the artist'].

From the 1990s onwards, creativity research has looked more closely at the influence of environmental and social factors on creativity (Ryhammar and

Brolin, 1999). However, even in this research, the emphasis on the individual remains. Whilst the opening anecdotes describing the composition of *Paradise Lost* and *The Creation* might at first sight confirm the view of creativity as an essentially individual process, on closer inspection they raise interesting questions, highlighting the enduring difficulties of defining such a concept in these ways. None of the 'artists' in our opening accounts, for example, could have achieved what they did without the collective knowledge and understanding of the intellectual communities in which they participated. It is also unlikely they could have achieved what they did if they had worked within discrete knowledge domains such as music, poetry or physics. Galilei's work was essential to Milton's composition, just as theirs proved to be some centuries later to the work of the Herschels and Haydn. Indeed it is possible to trace an ongoing dialogue between creators across time and domain, far from accidental in its cross-links. *Paradise Lost*, for example, was a significant influence on Mary Shelley, author of the novella *Frankenstein*, as indeed was Haydn's *Creation*, introduced to her by a composer and friend.

Here we can discern communities of thinkers with common preoccupations, shared conversations and acquaintances; a common knowledge which bridged any artificial divide between astronomy, technology, poetry, physics, music, chemistry and art. Such creativity exists not simply in the forging and exchange of new knowledge or innovative products such as poetry, oratorios, optic glasses or novels. It also exists in the collaborative processes of blending and reconfiguring existing ideas, hypothesizing, working with others on common problems from different standpoints, and communicating such 'inter-thinking' (Mercer, 2000) in a way that eloquently speaks to others. From this quite different perspective, creativity – be it in music, science, business, poetry, technology, education, art, industry, the philosophy of ideas or politics – can be viewed as an essentially social process: a process dependent on, and arising out of the participation in particular kinds of communities, rather than from any innate or unusual gift. The democratic view of creativity (NACCCE, 1999) from such a perspective, is far more resonant with this idea of creativity than the élite or sectoral formulations:

> all people are capable of creative achievements in some areas of activity, provided the conditions are right, and they have acquired the relevant knowledge and skills . . . creative *possibilities* are pervasive in the concerns of everyday life, its purposes and problems . . . creative *activity* is also pervasive . . . *creativity* can be expressed in collaborative as well as individual activities, in teamwork, in organisations, in communities and in governments . . . (p. 28)

Recent research on learning (e.g. Bredo, 1994; Lave and Wenger, 1991; Rogoff, 1999) supports this perspective. This work emphasizes that learning is a situated, social process, dependent on interaction and communication.

Processes traditionally associated with creativity are integral to this process. New and innovative thinking is never conducted unassisted, even when it would appear to go on 'in the head' of the individual. The creation of new knowledge is dependent on the interaction of materials, activities and people in particular settings, as well as in the way these interactions are collectively understood. Thus cognition is also distributed: 'stretched over, not divided among – mind, body, activity and culturally organised settings (which include other actors)' (Lave, 1988, p. 1).

From this 'situated' or 'cultural' perspective (Bruner, 1996) knowing and communicating are inseparable. The human mind is viewed, not as a preformed, innate symbol processor, complete with a range of innate attributes including (and only if you are lucky) creativity. Mental life is shaped to be communicated, is lived with others and always unfolds in activity with others. Rogoff (1999) puts it this way:

> an individual's actions and skills cannot be understood out of the context of the immediate practical goals being sought and the enveloping socio cultural goals into which they fit. It is the communities to which they belong that provide the communicative tools for organising and understanding experience and generating new knowledge. (p. 126)

This does not mean of course that there can be no direction or progress in creativity. Communities can collectively and explicitly value and develop creative processes. In the intellectual communities in which Milton and Galilei participated, musical, scientific, literary and philosophical expertise was both valued and shared. But as Sloboda *et al.* (1999) has argued, with illustrations drawn from the field of music, a preoccupation with innate creative talent has inhibited the scientific understanding of the complex phenomenon of creativity, ignoring the importance of a range of other factors, such as technical practice, persistency and motivation. Such factors, he argues, are dependent on participation in a supportive, mutual community – encouragement, early pleasurable [musical] experiences in one's own family or with friends, and the approval of others (be they peers or adults). He cites Messenger's (1958) account of the Anang Ibibo community where in many 'aesthetic' areas, creative achievements are far more widespread than in the West and considered as communal knowledge.

Research carried out by Zuckerman (1997) also indicates the importance of community in relation to achievement hitherto regarded as highly individual – the winning of a Nobel Prize. Zuckerman found that the chance of winning a Nobel Prize increases enormously by virtue of the fact that you have worked in the laboratory of somebody who has already won one. Not solely because of the stimulation, or 'visibility', but because of the shared access to a richer knowledge distribution network. This is in line with Pagano's work (1979) which suggests that creativity develops in association with other creative people. Research also shows that expertise can emerge very quickly in communities, including educational communities, often as a result of deliberate efforts. For instance, in eighteenth-century Venice, the orphanage La Pieta established a cultural ambience in which musical expertise was valued and encouraged. Plentiful opportunities for training were made available, thus creating a community in which a substantial proportion of the orphans became highly accomplished musicians (Howe, 1990).

But if the processes and products commonly associated with creativity in any domain can be seen to be related in a significant way to participation within communities, as well as in the knowledge valued and demanded by that community, they must also be dependent on the technological and communicative tools, the reckoning devices and other artefacts and resources of that community. For communities generally cannot be understood or represented without account being taken of the technologies, as well as related skills and meaning-making activities, intrinsic to them. The specific use made of communications technologies, be they clay tablets or e-mail for example, have changed some communities in often quite momentous ways (Leach, 2000b). Similarly the technological practices in which Galileo and the Herschels participated significantly transformed the knowledge and understanding of the intellectual communities to which they belonged. Technology is integral to the expression and development of communities – their values, their goals and the activities through which we come to know them. It therefore has a critical role to play in contributing to the development of creativity in every field of human endeavour. Creative communities always use technology, as I will demonstrate, to support, nurture, develop and celebrate aspects of the creative process.

CREATING COMMUNITIES

Despite a vast literature on the topic of creativity in educational settings, most recent research indicates that educational institutions do not often promote the creative process. Schools tend to focus on enculturating learners into existing societal knowledge (Sternberg, 1988), driven by a concern for individual learners to acquire past and present knowledge. In researching the nature of pedagogic practice, colleagues at the Centre for Research and Development in Teacher Education at the Open University have articulated six interrelated pedagogic dimensions that characterize any teaching and learning setting. These are: educational goals, learning purposes, knowledge, learning activities, roles and relationships and discourse (Leach and Moon, 1999). If any one of these dimensions is changed, we have argued, it will impact on one or more of the others (Leach and Moon, 2000). Moreover, the nature and practice of these dimensions is always informed by the view of learning held by the participants of any given setting. Initial research suggests that in settings where creativity is an aspect of the knowledge valued, and where creative processes become the subject of learning, teachers and learners collectively share and develop goals, purposes and activities that other commentators (e.g. Gruber, 1985; Koberg and Chusmir, 1987; Perkins, 1981) commonly ascribe to 'creative' individuals. Such communities value past and present knowledge, but they also value knowledge of future possibilities. Such communities also view learning – either implicitly or explicitly – as a social process.

Sources for this research have included learning communities influenced by the work of educationists such as Dewey, Montessori and Freinet. One contemporary and internationally celebrated example is the preschool community of Reggio Emilia in Italy, founded by Loris Malaguzzi. Gardner (1993) has vividly described the kinds of goals, purposes and activities to be found in Reggio preschools, as well as the sorts of knowledge valued:

> Reggio schools are unique, in part by virtue of the type and quality of the activities that the children carry out on a regular basis . . . In each of the classes groups of children spend several months exploring a theme of interest. The themes are ones that offer rich sensory stimulation and raise intriguing puzzles. For example sunlight, rainbows, shadows, the city, a city for ants, the two lions that preside over the central piazza of Reggio, poppy fields, an amusement park for birds built by the youngsters, and the operation of the fax machine . . . The Reggio children are encouraged to approach these objects, themes, and environments from many angles, ponder questions and phenomena that arise in the course of their explorations; create artful objects that capture their interests and their learning: drawings, paintings, cartoons, charts, photographic series, toy models, replicas – indeed, representatives of an ever-expanding, unpredictable series of genres. (pp. 87–8)

Although the children's creations are significant, Gardner argues, they do not represent the heart of the Reggio enterprise. Rather, it is the social dimension of the setting that is paramount:

> In my view, the central endeavor consists of the daily interaction among teachers, students, and sometimes parents and other adults from the community; the equally regular give-and-take among the classroom teachers and their specialized colleagues, the pedagogista and atelierista. And, above all, the astonishing documentation of student work undertaken by the instructional staff during the course of each day. (p. 88)

Reggio Emilia schools, Gardner concludes, are schools that suit the entire community: teachers, parents, the physical setting, the region and, above all, the growing children. Loris Malaguzzi's own account of a project undertaken in one of his preschools (an amusement park for birds) demonstrates the role that technology can play, even within a community of young learners:

Suggestions were made [in class assembly] for houses and nests in the trees, swings for chicks to play on, elevators for the elderly birds. Ferris-wheels and rides with music. And then – everyone laughs – water skiing for the birds, providing them with tiny slats of wood for skis. Then came the fountains, which had to be big and real, and spray the water up really high . . . As part of this project Andrea has drawn an elevator for tired birds. After doing this he goes to the computer corner to build an animated version . . . Andrea is unable to complete the animation by himself; he takes his project home where his elder sister helps him to finish it. The next day Andrea goes to the school workshop area and adds to the animation a picture of a real bird taken with a digital camera, and records birds singing. Once Andrea has completed his work on the computer he shows it to the class . . . Now there is a new project. The children go out to observe actual elevators and take pictures of them. Then they discuss and draw how they think an elevator works. With the help of Giovanni, Andrea and Alice made an elevator using Lego motors and a sensor attached to a 'programmable brick'. The elevator is to be placed in the amusement park for birds. (Malaguzzi, 2000)

New information and communications and technology has a potentially critical role to play in supporting and transforming creative communities at all levels and stages of the educational process. The challenge for educators is to fully research these opportunities, as well as to learn how to successfully sustain the creative process within education. The three case studies that follow explore some of these present and future possibilities.

CASE STUDY 1: A KNOWLEDGE-BUILDING COMMUNITY – THE CSILE KNOWLEDGE FORUM

The first case study (Caswell and Lamon, 1999) shows the way in which computer software is used:

- to make thinking explicit and reflective;
- to support collaborative thinking;
- to enable such thinking to move in new and unpredictable directions.

This setting is a class of 9- and 10-year-olds in Toronto, Canada. The curriculum focus is biology. The classroom has been carefully organized to mirror the way in which the adult scientific research community operates at the University of Toronto's Zoological Department, local to the school. Over a ten-week period the young students are given the opportunity to become immersed in a culture of 'scientific inquiry' by their teacher, Beverley Caswell, who has chosen to make the Madagascan Hissing Roach the focus of research. She has used sustained investigations of this roach, ancient in adaptation and evolution, with previous classes as a way of developing scientific thinking. This experience showed the species to be 'interesting and awe inspiring' for young students.

As the weeks unfold the students take care of and study the roach. Caswell starts with an introductory lesson and the students inspect the live animals, hear some facts about them, as well as taking turns to hold and sketch them. Each child is given a research journal, which Caswell tells them is what scientists at the Zoological Department use for observation questions, research notes and experimental designs. Each student also learns to use the Computer Supported Intentional Learning Environment (CSILE) Knowledge Forum technology as an integral tool for working.[1] This technology is not introduced discretely, but on a need-to-know basis. Initially the students use it as a graphics tool simply to draw the roaches, but gradually they are encouraged to enter questions onto the CSILE database, so that the Knowledge Forum can be used to support and scaffold their scientific thinking. As the work develops, students gradually enter

> one or two pressing questions into the database. Questions ranged from, 'What kind of food do they prefer?' to 'What did cockroaches evolve from?' And because these questions were stored in a database, each child's question could be 'heard' and resources could be gathered to support a child's pursuit of knowledge in a particular interest area. The students also found it very exciting to be adding notes to build up the database. In the course of a week 100 new notes had been entered! (Caswell and Lamon, 1999, p. 143)

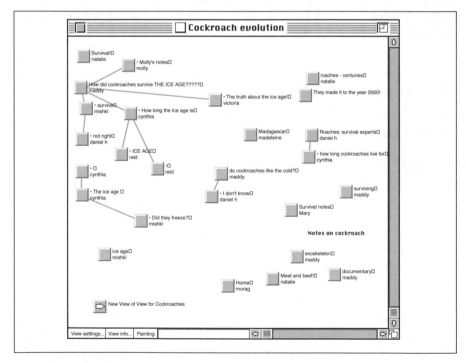

Figure 13.2: Cockroach database

The database shows questions falling into specific categories (see Figure 13.2). These are used to inform the creation of small research groups, variously studying: perception, learning, communication, evolution and anatomy. A variety of other activities is integrated into the classroom setting, such as the collective composition of a cockroach song, the design and carrying out of real experiments, and visits to the Zoological Department to watch a dissection and meet expert zoologists. Finally each group contributes to the making of a cockroach documentary video. The reproduction group asks the Zoo laboratory for a female cockroach so they can film an experiment 'live'; the ecology group film food experiments they have carried out, while the evolution group write a script and dress like scientists to film their section of the documentary.

The detailed student case studies, gathered by researcher Mary Lamon, document the progress and development of students' thinking across the ten-week period. For example, as a result of one student's curiosity after reading a book about the Ice Age, the evolution group decides to investigate '*How did the Madagascan roaches survive in the ice age?*' This problem is entered into the CSILE database and the group plan and carry out a real experiment concluding 'Cockroaches don't like hot areas, they like room temperature.' As a follow-up Caswell invites a graduate student to give a lesson on the Ice Age which is followed up by new entries into the Forum (see Figures 13.3, 13.4, 13.5 and 13.6).

Caswell and her co-researcher are explicit about their intention to create a scientific community which can provide students with a variety of opportunities to reflect on ideas, to hypothesize and which allows for multiple ways of developing understanding. They believe that the understanding of 'deep disciplinary content' knowledge can only grow through a combination of individual as well as group learning activities, as well as through access to a wide range of human and other resources. As the young scientific community develops, both teachers and students become fully engaged and passionate about their new field of study. What is particularly distinctive about this community is the use of 'public forums', such as authentic research reports and the cockroach documentary. These convey to students that a creative process of knowledge building is of value both individually and for the group as a whole. On the visit to the laboratory Caswell observed that the young students were no longer satisfied with superficial answers to questions, they wanted a 'Let's discuss our findings and pursue our interest together' approach, operating as a real scientific community outside, as well as within, the classroom.

Technologies common to scientific laboratories, hands-on investigations, laboratory books, as well as the more complex Knowledge Forum software are integral to the work. The latter is pivotal to the whole project, providing students with a cumulative database, as well as a means of recording information and ideas. It acts as a tool for making thinking explicit, encouraging creative thinking – the making of inspired hypotheses, the articulation of probing questions, the blending of others' findings with one's own, and the intensive

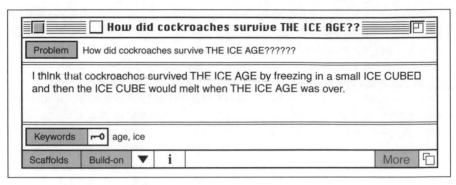

Figure 13.3: How did cockroaches survive the Ice Age?

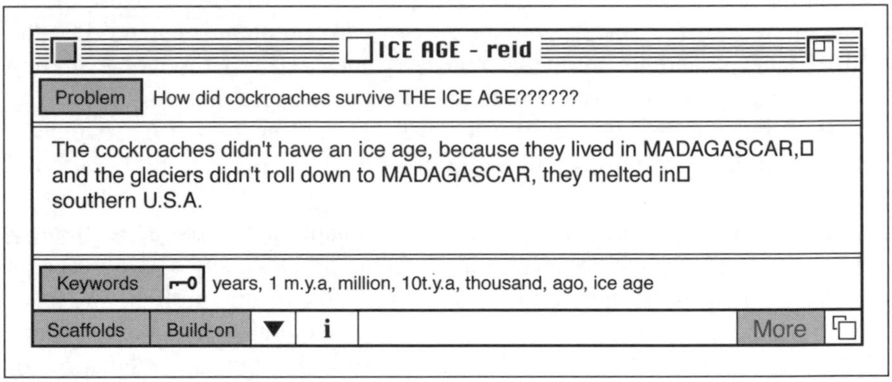

Figure 13.4: Ice Age – Reid

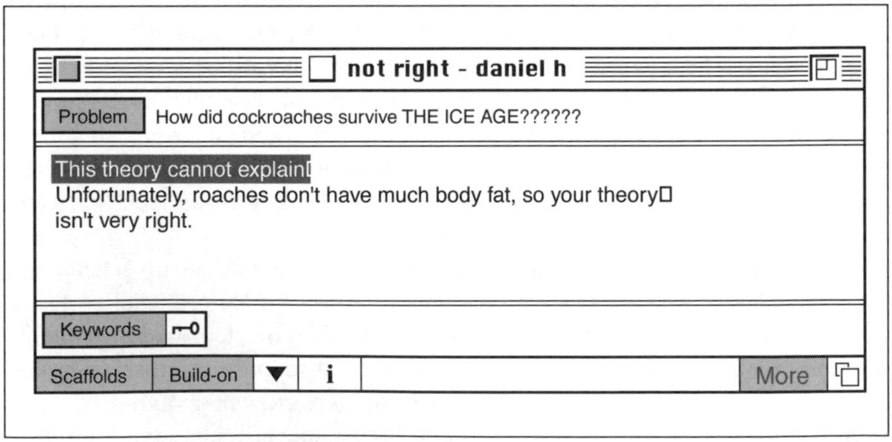

Figure 13.5: Not right – Daniel

attempt to solve authentic problems. 'My theory is that you are right that roaches can learn', Daniel comments after one experiment. 'And I think you have a very good experiment. But how can your experiment proof tha (*sic*) roaches learn?'

```
┌─────────────────────────────────────────────────────────────────────┐
│ ┌───────────────────────────────────────────────────────────────────┐ │
│ │ ≣▢≣═══════════════════ ▢ Learning - daniel h ═══════════════ ▣≣   │ │
│ │ ┌─────────┐                                                        │ │
│ │ │ Problem │  Can roaches learn?                                    │ │
│ │ └─────────┘                                                        │ │
│ │ ┌───────────────────────────────────────────────────────────────┐ │ │
│ │ │ I think that roaches can learn, since our Madagascan giant     │ │ │
│ │ │ roaches have□                                                  │ │ │
│ │ │ learned that if they fall on their backs they can wave their   │ │ │
│ │ │ legs and we will□                                              │ │ │
│ │ │ help them.                                                     │ │ │
│ │ └───────────────────────────────────────────────────────────────┘ │ │
│ │                                                                    │ │
│ │ ┌──────────┐ ┌────┐                                               │ │
│ │ │ Keywords │ │ ┌─0 │                                              │ │
│ │ └──────────┘ └────┘                                               │ │
│ │ ┌──────────┐┌──────────┐ ┌───┐                        ┌──────┐    │ │
│ │ │ Scaffolds ││ Build-on │ │ ▼ │  i                    │ More │ ⌑  │ │
│ │ └──────────┘└──────────┘ └───┘                        └──────┘    │ │
│ └───────────────────────────────────────────────────────────────────┘ │
└─────────────────────────────────────────────────────────────────────┘
```

Figure 13.6: Can cockroaches learn?

This bustling classroom with its whole-group debates, visits to the zoological department and ongoing use of the knowledge forum reflects a 'mutual community' which Bruner suggests:

> Typically . . . models ways of doing and knowing, provides opportunities for emulation, offers running commentary, provides 'scaffolding' for novices, and even provides a good context for teaching deliberately. It even makes possible that form of job-related division of labour one finds in effective work groups . . . the point is for those in the group to help each other get the lay of the land and the hang of the job. (Bruner, 1996, p. 21)

CASE STUDY 2: A DIGITAL ARTS COLLABORATION ON THE INTERNET

New information and communications technology, particularly the Internet, electronic mail and multi-user domains hold the promise of giving access to distributed knowledge and expertise formerly unavailable, providing new means for communicating among teachers and learners. Again, the use of technologies to achieve such ends within learning communities is far from new. *Il Paese Sbaagliato,* written by the educator Mario Lodi in 1970, is a country teacher's diary, peppered with examples of student projects, dialogues, writings and group projects over a five-year period at an elementary school in the village of Vho, in southern Italy. In his school, and that of his colleague Bruno Ciari in the distant village of Certaldo, students were provided with access to the state-of-the-art technology of the 1950s and 1960s. Typewriters and printing machinery enabled them to have direct control over every aspect of the publishing process, writing and editing *il giornalino* or newsletters (*Il Mondo* and *Insieme*) for fellow students, parents and (eventually) subscribers in ten countries (Tonucci, 1981). The process served as a catalyst for students' emerging literacy skills, and 'in effect transformed their classrooms into literacy learning laboratories' (Cummins and Sayers, 1995). Later Lodi and Ciari used audio tape-recorders to encourage students to exchange *les letteres parlate*, or spoken letters (audiotapes) through which they conducted local oral history projects in collaboration with their distant correspondents.

> it was through recordings that students first noticed the marked difference in dialect between the two villages, leading both partner classes to launch a sophisticated linguistic investigation into Italian dialects. They jointly developed a common system for writing their dialects and then tested their new scheme by investigating, recording, and transcribing lullabies from each village's communal traditions. Thus, both partner classes served as catalysts in the creation of new knowledge with their distant correspondents. (Cummins and Sayers, 1995, p. 122)

This work, reflecting an 'immense respect for the intricacies of children's learning' established Lodi and his colleague as two of the most influential European education reformers of recent times. Lodi's work is widely read and available in translation in Spain, France and Germany, although it remains untranslated in English. As one Italian commentator puts it, Lodi and his students were 'surfing on tape' more than 30 years ago as we now wish our students to surf together on the Internet.

Newer technologies provide still greater and more flexible possibilities for creative collaboration. Across schools in Chile for example young students in the Enlaces Project (http://www.enlaces.ufro.cl/) have created the first-ever dictionaries in native dialects by collaborating via e-mail. In the case study that follows, the Internet is used to:

- provide a medium that allows students to move in unpredictable directions;
- extend the range of tools currently available within the discipline;
- enable joint 'products'.

The Virtual Identities Digital Arts Project (Open University, 1999a) involved post-16 art and design students from two Liverpool schools and two Kent schools in the United Kingdom. As in Lodi's work, the project unlocked new ideas and ways of working by encouraging collaboration between students from different geographical areas, cultures, experiences and perceptions. Each student was assigned a partner, with whom they exchanged a digital postcard representing one aspect of their personal identity. Every e-mail image received had to be responded to, modified and interpreted, while retaining 20 per cent of the original in order to provide a sense of sequence.

The stimulus for these images and artistic statements was open-ended, largely chosen by the students themselves. In addition to using images and texts that represented their individual identities, students were encouraged to think about their own values and concerns, collecting newspaper cuttings reflecting local, national or global issues such as ecology or peace studies. One student scanned images of her hand, which she then digitally manipulated and modified. Her teacher comments:

> This was intended to reflect her identity in a subtle way. As with fingerprints, the truth was there, but only if the code could be interpreted. There was a deliberate attempt to be obtuse and enigmatic to see what it would draw from her collaborator. Her image was then altered and posted to the web site. It now contained military elements and reference to the Gulf War, which was threatening to escalate at the time. The hands, which originally appeared to be welcoming, now looked as if they were surrendering or imploring. By restricting the colour of the whole image to tones of red, the fingers resembled flames within a sea of fire. She decided to make the conflict with Iraq more explicit in the work. She used the modified image as a background, overlaying images of war and incorporating the flags of the UN and Iraq. (Open University, 1999a, Exemplar C)

The students' collaborator further developed this notion; the whole sequence of this collaboration can be seen on the Bridge Project web site (www.digital-collaborations.co.uk/thebridge).

As in the Toronto and Vho schools, students clearly became highly focused fellow 'artists', passionate about the project in hand. One teacher commented:

> I was keen to exploit the vast potential of the Internet for art and design. In this sense the collaboration was intentionally creative, indeed this remained the first and key 'possibility' of the project i.e. the possibility of moving in exciting and unpredictable directions.

The use of the Internet enabled students to transform physical objects into digital images. It also provided a medium in which they could explore visual phenomena, experimenting with visual language and extending the range of tools currently used in art, including image manipulation and laycring. As with the cockroach documentary, the resulting images and web site became a visual record of the development of students' ideas, a joint *oevre*, with a potentially international audience that helped to

> . . . produce and sustain group solidarity. They help make a community. Works and works-in-progress create shared and negotiable ways of thinking

in a group . . . externalising, in a word, rescues cognitive activity from implicitness, making it more public, negotiable and solidary. (Bruner, 1996, pp. 22–3)

Again in common with our young scientific community, the Bridge Project clearly drew on a range of expertise both within and outside the schools, including the work of a 'talented and experienced teaching team' and a visiting artist. Technology enabled teachers and students to interact collaboratively, communicating with different audiences at a local, national and international scale. This initiative represented a totally new way of working for both departments and students involved.

CASE STUDY 3: A COMMUNITY OF WRITERS

In the third case study (Open University, 1999b) the focus is a class of 15-year-old students in a Gloucestershire comprehensive school in the United Kingdom in the beginning stages of a two-year GCSE English course. Computer software was used to:

- develop understanding of the subject;
- encourage the creation of a new product;
- enable that product to be publicly shared.

The class teacher (Menon, 1997) was keen to develop a real sense of a writing community early on. In the first few weeks of the term she invited her students to form groups of their own choice, research a poet from a selected list, then plan and carry out a presentation. Students were encouraged to use the Internet as part of this research. She comments:

At such an early stage in the academic year when getting to know a group, the 'freedom' of such lessons is a risk in terms of class management. I very much relinquished any leadership role, but was available to students for reference and suggestions. The time allowed me to get to know the class in terms of group dynamics, student initiative and motivation. Students lead and supported each other in terms of their use of new technologies. Many automatically chose to go to the Internet to find information and several found materials relevant to their work, such as Benjamin Zephaniah's own web site. Once one group had found material on the web, others were keen not to be outdone. A couple of groups floundered in terms of choices of poems, poets or presentation – content as well as method – and I needed to work alongside both individuals and groups. It was interesting to watch the development of students' research skills in the library context. (Open University, 1999b, Exemplar C)

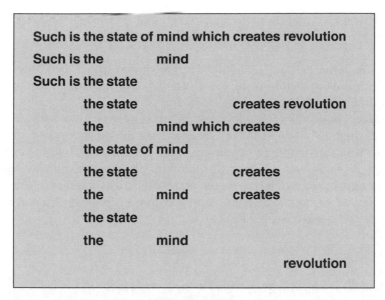

Figure 13.7: Students' own kinetic poetry

In the run-up to the presentation, one student, who had been using PowerPoint software in another subject area, volunteered to put the poems chosen by each group onto an overhead screen for the final presentations. This, he argued, would save the English department a considerable amount of photocopying money! The teacher set up a public document on the school network into which each group typed their chosen poems. One group placed a Caroline Duffy poem, 'Valentine', into the software programme for projection during their presentation. The girls concerned wanted to preface this presentation with a reading of the poem, one of them taking the actual 'voice' of the poem, the other imagining the recipient's response. Not only did the projected text enhance the presentation considerably, the group collaboration on the software during the preparation led to a far deeper understanding of the poem.

This work led directly, but unexectedly, to the students exploring an innovative way of creating their own kinetic poetry (see Figure 13.7):

We started off with a poem by Bruce Naumann . . . we did quite a bit of preparatory work on the poem . . . We were then asked to find a quotation of our own for homework, I used the *Bloomsbury Dictionary of Quotations* and came up with a whole pile which I thought might be suitable. Me and Matt then chose the one we eventually used. After we had the quotation, everything was just plain sailing, we had a great time making all sorts of interesting lines for it. We just kept churning them out and afterwards, took them away and came up with our own version. We decided on the final version together. Then we had the idea, in discussion with our teacher, because we had already been using PowerPoint, of also using PowerPoint to animate the words. (Interview with student)

The final animated product 'Revolution' can be viewed on the Open University's Moving Words research web site (http://www.open.ac.uk/movingwords), demonstrating the potential of the medium to make poetry a multi-sensual experience. The poem exemplifies how multimedia can be used to highlight the kinetic qualities of a text to convey meaning, and the exciting possibilities for students' writing as they draw on music and image or movement to add meaning to text. Texts in this new electronic medium may be non-linear, many layered, combine different media and have an element of duration, thus there are multiple opportunities for young writers to create new forms of writing that extend and challenge traditional conceptions of text.

CONCLUSION

In each of the communities described in these case studies, there is the expectation that participants will share goals, purposes and knowledge, but also that individuals will know different things and speak from different experiences. Creativity is an aspect of knowledge to be valued and is the subject of learning. Participants in each community value collaboration – the social dimension of learning is explicit. Each community I suggest:

- Collectively displays the kind of *goals and purposes* that other commentators have ascribed to 'creative' individuals:
    Fully engaged in and passionate about their subject;
    Strong sense of purpose and ultimate goals;
    A desire to do new things, engaged in change;
    Ambitious and risk-taking.
- Encourages joint participation in *activities* commonly ascribed to 'creative' individuals:
    Initiating projects;
    Considering a range of ideas before settling on one solution;
    Problem-solving, formulating new ideas and hypothesizing;
    Using technologies as integral to work, to make thinking explicit or to create new products.
- Jointly and individually creates the kind of *products* commonly ascribed to creative individuals:
    High quality;
    Explicit about values;
    Innovative;
    Unique.

Margaret Boden (1994) [see Chapter 6, p. 95] has proposed that there are two key aspects of creativity – the historical and the psychological. In this chapter I have argued for the importance of a third – the social dimension. Educators need to pay attention to this dimension of creativity if our young people are to have access to 'one hundred languages, one hundred hands, one hundred thoughts, one hundred ways of thinking' – one hundred possibilities.

NOTE

1 The CSILE Knowledge Forum is a computer software program which provides 'Notes' that represent student ideas and questions, allow these to be built on, and which create new syntheses of collections of related notes. 'Scaffolds' are built in, providing support areas such as theory building and debating. 'Views' provide graphical organizers for notes which can be used to represent different ways of conceptualizing developing knowledge bases, fostering emergent goals and conceptual change.

REFERENCES

Amabile, T. M. (1983) *The Social Psychology of Creativity*. New York: Springer Verlag.

Bergson, H. (1944 [1907]) *Creative Evolution*, translation by Arthur Mitchell. New York: The Modern Library.

Binet, A. and Henri, V. (1896) 'La Psychologie individuelle'. *Annee Psychologie*, **2**, 411–65.

Boden, M. A. (1994) 'The creative mind: myths and mechanisms'. *Behavioural and Brain Sciences* **17**(3), 519–70.

Bredo, E. (1994). 'Reconstructing educational psychology'. In P. Murphy (ed.) *Learners, Learning and Assessment*. London: Paul Chapman.

Bruner, J. (1965) *On Knowing: Essays for the Left Hand*. Cambridge: Harvard University Press.

Bruner, J. (1996) *The Culture of Education*. Cambridge, MA: Harvard University Press.

Computer Supported Intentional Learning Environment (CSILE) http://csile.oise.utoronto.ca/

Caswell, B. and Lamon, M. (1999) 'The development of scientific literacy: the evolution of ideas in a knowledge building classroom'. In J. Leach and R. E. Moon (1999) *Learners and Pedagogy*. London: Paul Chapman.

Cummins, J. and Sayers, D. (1995) *Brave New Schools*. Toronto: OISE Press.

Eco, U. (1997) *The Search for the Perfect Language*. London: Fontana.

Gardner, H. (1993) *The Disciplined Mind*. New York: Basic Books.

Gruber, H. (1985) 'Giftedness and moral responsibility: creative thinking and human survival'. In F. Horowitz and M. O'Brien (eds) *The Gifted and the Talented: Developmental Perspectives*. Washington, DC: American Psychological Association.

Howe, M. J. A. (1990) *The Origins of Exceptional Abilities*. Oxford: Blackwell.

Jung, C. (1977) [1912] 'Psychology of the unconscious', in Fordham, M. and Hull, R. F. (eds) *Collected Works of C. G. Jung*. Princeton: Princeton University Press.

Koberg, C. S. and Chusmir, L. H. (1987) 'Organisational culture relationships with creativity and other job-related variables. *Journal of Business Research*, 155, 397–409.

Lave, J. (1988) *Cognition in Practice*. Cambridge: Cambridge University Press.

Lave, J. and Wenger, E. (1991) *Situated Learning*. Cambridge: Cambridge University Press.

Leach, J. (2000a) 'Mother tongue teaching'. In S. Brown, R. Moon and M. Ben-Peretz (eds) *International Companion to Education*. London: Routledge.

Leach, J. (2000b) 'Breaking the silence: the role of technology and community in leading professional development'. In B. Moon, L. Bird and J. Butcher (eds) *Leading Professional Development*. London: Paul Chapman.

Leach, J. and Moon, R. E. (1999) 'Recreating pedagogy'. In J. Leach and R. E. Moon (eds) *Learners and Pedagogy*. London: Paul Chapman.

Leach, J. and Moon, R. E. (2000) 'Pedagogy, information and communication technologies and teacher professional knowledge'. *Curriculum Journal*, forthcoming.

Lodi, M. (1970) *Il Paese sbagliato*. Turin: Giulio Einaudi.

Malaguzzi, L. (2000) http://www.devon.gov.uk/dcs/a/reggio/poem.htm and http://www.itd.ge.cnr.it/augusto/elevator/html

Menon, E. (1997) 'Not drowning but surfing: navigating the Internet with Year 9'. *English and Media Magazine*, 37.

Mercer, N. (2000) *Words and Minds*. London: Routledge.

Messenger, J. (1958) 'Esthetic talent'. *Basic College Quarterly*, **4**, 20–4.

National Advisory Committee on Creative and Cultural Education (NACCCE) (1999) *All our Futures: Creativity, Culture and Education*. London: DFEE.

Open University (1999a) *CD ROM Art*. Learning Schools Programme, Milton Keynes: Open University and Research Machines.

Open University (1999b) *CD ROM English*. Learning Schools Programme, Milton Keynes: Open University and Research Machines.

Pagano, A. L. (1979) 'Learning and creativity'. *Journal of Creative Behaviour*, **13**(2), 127–38.

Perkins, D. (1981) *The Mind's Best Work*. Cambridge, MA: Harvard University Press.

Pinker, S. (1995) *The Language Instinct*. London: Penguin.

Rogoff, B. (1999) 'Cognitive development through social interaction: Vygostky and Piaget'. In P. Murphy (ed.) *Learners, Learning and Assessment*. London: Paul Chapman.

Ryhammar, L. and Brolin, C. (1999) 'Creativity research'. *Scandinavian Journal of Educational Research*, **43**(3), 259–73.

Sloboda, J., Davidson, J.W. and Howe, M. J. A. (1999) 'Is everyone musical?'. In P. Murphy (ed.) *Learners, Learning and Assessment*. London: Paul Chapman.

Steiner, G. (1975) *After Babel, Aspects of Language and Translation*. London: Oxford University Press.

Sternberg R. (ed.) (1988) *The Nature of Creativity*. New York: Cambridge University Press.

Tonucci, F. (1981) *Viaje alrededor de 'El Mundo': Un diario de clase de Mario Lodi y sus alumnos*. M. Vassallo (trans.). Barcelona: Editorial Laia. (Original work published in 1980 as *Un giornalino di classe* [a classroom newspaper]. Roma Bari: Guis, Laterza and Figli Spa.)

Williams, R. (1984) *Keywords: A Vocabulary of Culture and Society*. London: Fontana.

Zuckerman, H. (1997) *Scientific Elite: Nobel Laureates in the United States*. New York: Free Press.

Name Index

A number in *italics* indicates a figure; **bold** indicates a more significant section within a sequence of pages.

Subject Index

A number in *italics* indicates a figure; **bold** indicates a more significant section within a sequence of pages.